Poverty and Population Control

UNIVERSITY OF WOLVERHAMPTON

Poverty and Population Control

Edited by

Lars Bondestam and Staffan Bergström

1980

ACADEMIC PRESS

A Subsidiary of Harcourt Brace Jovanovich, Publishers

London · New York · Toronto · Sydney · San Francisco

ACADEMIC PRESS INC. (LONDON) LTD.
24/28 Oval Road,
London NW1

United States Edition published by
ACADEMIC PRESS INC.
111 Fifth Avenue
New York, New York 10003

British Library Cataloguing in Publication Data

Poverty and population control.
1. Underdeveloped areas – Population
2. Underdeveloped areas – Ecomonic conditions
I. Bondestam Lars II. Bergström, Staffan
301.32'9'1724   HB884   79–40945

ISBN Hardback 0–12–114250–7
ISBN Paperback 0–12–114252–3

Text set in 11/13 pt VIP Bembo, printed and bound
in Great Britain at The Pitman Press, Bath

Notes on Contributors

Debabar Banerji (Indian), M.D. and cultural anthropologist. He is at present chairman and professor at the Centre of Social Medicine and Community Health, J. Nehru University, New Delhi, and is conducting research on community health practices, including family planning, in India. He is the author of several books and articles and a well-known critic of the past population growth control programme in India. *Present address: Centre of Social Medicine and Community Health, J. Nehru University, New Mehrauli Rd, New Delhi 110057 India.*

Staffan Bergström (Swedish), M.D. He is Associate Professor in obstetrics and gynaecology at the University Hospital, Uppsala, and presently senior physician at the Central Hospital, Eskilstuna. He is conducting research in the field of human reproduction and in obstetrics and gynaecology in the tropics. He has studied health services in Cuba, India, Angola, Tanzania and Kenya and is the author of several articles on family planning and health care in Third World countries. *Present address: Department of Obstetrics and Gynaecology, Central Hospital, S-631 88 Eskilstuna, Sweden.*

Lars Bondestam (Swedish), social scientist. He has worked as a demographer and with disaster preparedness planning in Ethiopia. He is lecturing at Gothenburg University and is conducting research on underdevelopment and international relations. He is the author of books and several articles on Ethiopia. *Present address: Alströmergatan 2A, 411 01 Goteborg, Sweden.*

Göran Djurfeldt (Swedish), Ph.D. in sociology. He has conducted field research in India, and is a university lecturer at the Institute of Sociology in Copenhagen, Denmark. He is at present engaged in a research project on production relations in Indian Agriculture. *Present address: Kullavägen, 3, 230 47 Åkarp, Sweden.*

Bertil Egerö (Swedish), social scientist. He has worked as a sociologist and demographer in Tanzania, and is responsible for the analysis and publication of the results of the 1967 Tanzania Population Census. Since the fall of 1978 he is working with economic planning and statistics in Mozambique. *Present address: Direcçao Nacional de Estatistica, C.P. 493, Maputo, Mozambique.*

v

Madi Gray (South African), born and active in South Africa up to 1972 when she left the country. She was an active member of the "Women's Abortion and Contraception Campaign" in England, and is at present engaged in solidarity work for the South African people. *Present address: C/O Tsalmas, Brännkyrkagatan 41¹¹, 117 22 Stockholm, Sweden.*

Bo Gunnarsson, (Swedish), social scientist. He has for several years studied the political and economic development in Japan and South Asia, and is now working as a correspondent in New Delhi for the Swedish newspaper, "Dagens Nyheter". He is the author of books and several articles particularly on Japan. *Present address: Swedish Embassy, New Delhi, India.*

Erland Hofsten (Swedish), Ph.D. and statistician-demographer. He has been a demographer at the Central Bureau of Statistics, Stockholm, and is assistant professor at the University of Stockholm. He has had several international missions, the latest one as the head of the UN Regional Institute for Population Studies in Ghana. He is the author of several books and articles on demography and population. *Present address: Ursviksvägen 121, 172 46 Sundbyberg, Sweden.*

Staffan Lindberg (Swedish), Ph. D. in sociology. He has conducted field research in India, and is research fellow at the Department of Sociology in Lund. He is at present engaged in a research project on production relations in Indian agriculture. *Present address: Erik Dahlbergsgatan 3A, 222 20 Lund, Sweden.*

Henk Luning (Dutch), agricultural economist and senior lecturer at the University of Agriculture in Wageningen, Holland. He has conducted field research in Nigeria, Surinam, Bangladesh, Tanzania, Kenya, Tunisia and the Philippines. *Present address: Geografisch Inst der Rijksuniv., Heidelberglaan 2, Utrecht, Holland.*

Pierre Pradervand (Swiss), Ph.D. and sociologist. He has worked for many years in the field of population in Africa, and was editor and managing director of "Famille et développement", a popular educational periodical aimed at the development education of the public in French-speaking countries, which is published and printed in Dakar. *Present address: 49, Ch. de Grange-Falquet, 1224 Caene-Bougeries, Geneva, Switzerland.*

Jan Sterkenburg (Dutch), geographer and senior lecturer at the Department of Geography of Developing Countries of the University of Utrecht, Holland. He has conduted field research in Liberia, Tanzania, Ghana and Malawi. *Present address: Geografisch Inst der Rijksuniv., Heidelberglaan, Utrecht, Holland.*

Preface

Blaming the poor for their poverty and for their procreation is still a hallmark of much Western attitudes towards "the population problem". A variety of explanations of the economic stagnation and underdevelopment of the Third World relate poverty to over-population. Population control should, accordingly, be an outstanding remedy against underdevelopment and impoverishment in Third World countries. In this context, "the population problem" constitutes the very basis of poverty, for which the oppressed classes should be reproached. Suggestive concepts like "the demographic explosion" or "the population explosion" add to the prevailing tendency to isolate human reproduction from the environment, in which it occurs: the consumption explosion of the industrialized world is left aside and exponential forecasts of future demographic trends are utilized as disastrous indicators of overpopulation as the root of all evil, the combat of which should be given highest possible priority.

The interpretation and understanding of underdevelopment, exploitation and poverty have been obstructed by a widespread pseudoscientific analysis of "the population problem" as a problem of human reproductive behavior. Until recent years the predominant opinion among Western aid-giving agencies was a neo-Malthusian belief in population growth—as such—as a menace against developmental efforts and social achievements. At the World Population Conference in 1974 in Bukarest a different opinion was launched by several Third World representatives, whereby it was made clear that family planning programmes do not work in isolation and that population policy measures work merely in the context of a simultaneous economic and social development. A gradually widened interest in population issues as important indicators or basic preconditions for family survival has been the result of

vii

the years after the Bukarest conference. An increased attention to migratory movements and to fertility dependence upon mortality trends seems to constitute a step in a less biased direction. However, several attempts to repeat the previously prevailing focussing of resources and efforts upon fertility limitation and population control have been all too obvious to allow for a belief in a real attitudinal change towards the oppressed classes. The well documented coercion exerted in India in vasectomy campaigns is the most malignant sign of compulsory measures undertaken on a wide scale against impoverished people after Bukarest, where the World Plan of Action stated that all countries should respect and ensure "the right of persons to determine, in a free, informed and responsible manner, the number and spacing of their children". As is now well known the coercion did not manage to turn down the Indian birth rate, but in fact the Indian Government.

The contributors to this anthology share the view that there are other factors than population growth that cause economic stagnation and underdevelopment. Some aspects may be discerned in more detail in the chapters. Firstly, the population growth does not in itself explain the prevailing situation in "underdeveloped" countries. Secondly, the population growth in these countries, as in all countries, is the sum of the reproduction of all individuals, which in turn is rational and determined by the social and economic conditions under which people are forced to live. Thirdly, overt or concealed interests in developed countries have nominated issues of overpopulation as priorities (and often preconditions for international aid) in the effort to combat underdevelopment. Fourthly, none of the contributors has anything to object against the self-evident right of an individual to determine her/his own fertility and to be given sufficient support to achieve the family size and child spacing desired by her/his family. In this context, family planning is a fundamental, family-oriented health measure involving both over-fertility and underfertility problems.

The authors are responsible for their individual contributions and the chapters should be regarded as separate articles, though the views expressed tend to coincide in several fundamental respects.

November 1979

Lars Bondestam
and
Staffan Bergström

Contents

The Political Ideology of Population Control

Lars Bondestam

Laws of Population

The first African Population Conference was held in Accra in December 1971. It was inaugurated by the then Prime Minister of Ghana, Kofi Busia. In his address he said:

> The Malthusian theory that population tends to increase at a faster rate than its means of subsistence and that unless it is checked by moral restraints (and we may add, family planning), or by disease, famine or other disasters, widespread poverty and degradation may result, is now being treated with more respect than was accorded to it some years back. In certain parts of the world the squalor and poverty predicted by Malthus is already in evidence.

Many delegates probably did not react or they nodded assent, but others saw these introductory words as a bad omen for the conference. Did Busia really mean that widespread poverty and degradation are the only alternatives to moral restraints, famine and disasters? And who was the prophet Malthus?

Those responsible for the political affairs—Busia was one of them—have to find or construct laws of nature which explain undesirable events and which nobody can manage. When unemployment, poverty, hunger, misery and famine spread and deepen, Malthus's theories offer a rescue. Although they were written down almost two centuries ago, slightly modified, they are still marketable as a pseudo-analysis of underdevelopment and its causes.

These theories can be traced back to Europe in the 18th century. When a death-blow was aimed at the feudal system of France in 1789, the market economy had dominated in Britain for a hundred years. Although British feudalism was dead long ago, the French

Revolution worried the British bourgeoisie, as it reminded them of the possible outcome of their own exploitation of the workers. The industrial revolution, with the introduction of the steam-engine in England towards the end of the 18th century, did not conduce to any immediate economic and social amelioration for the fast growing urban population. The poverty of the masses required an explanation, which did not challenge the interests of the propertied minority, who accumulated the profits from the increase in production. This gave the clergyman and economist Thomas Robert Malthus (1766–1834) an opportunity to present his "Eternal Law of Nature": the poverty of the working class was explained by its overgrowth.

These ideas did not originate from Malthus himself. Already twenty years before he published his well-known "An Essay on the Principle of Population" (1798, revised and expanded five years later), Adam Smith maintained that

> Every species of animals naturally multiplies in proportion to the means of their subsistence, and no species can ever multiply beyond it. But in civilized society it is only among the inferior ranks of people that the scantiness of subsistence can set limits to the further multiplication of the human species; and it can do so in no other way than by destroying a great part of the children with their fruitful marriages produce . . . the demand for men, like that for any other commodity, necessarily regulates the production of men; quickens it when it goes on too slowly, and stops it when it advances too fast. It is this demand which regulates and determines the state of propagation in all the different countries of the world, in North America, in Europe and in China; which renders it rapidly progressive in the first, slow and gradual in the second, and altogether stationary in the last.[1]

The theologian and sociologist Joseph Townsend was another harbinger of Malthus:

> It seems to be a law of nature that the poor should be to a certain degree improvident, that there may always be some to fulfil the most servile, the most sordid, and the most ignoble offices in the community. The stock of human happiness is thereby much increased, whilst the more delicate are not only relieved from drudgery, . . . but are left at liberty without

interruption to pursue those callings which are suited to their various dispositions. The Poor Law[2] tends to destroy the harmony and beauty, the symmetry and order, of that system which God and nature have established in the world.[3]

The ideas and publications of many others likewise provided rich sources for Malthus to draw from. Thus, when discussing Malthusianism one must not only think of the teaching of one particular person but of an opportune ideological tide in England of that time. Malthus, himself allied to the landed bourgeoisie, was just an efficient and well-articulated spokesman of this ideology.

Malthus's writings were also polemics against the Utopian socialists, especially the Frenchman Antoine Nicolas de Condorcet (1743–1794), and the Englishman William Godwin (1756–1836), who interpreted the poverty of the working class as a problem of distribution, which was due to the structure of society, and, therefore, commended the replacement of the old order by a new one, based on equality and utilizing the great potential of man and science.

Many neo-Malthusians still cite Malthus when elucidating the present underdevelopment of the periphery (the third world/the underdeveloped countries/the capitalist dependent countries). Logically, this warrants also the anti-Malthusians in basing their criticism of Malthus's theories upon the experience and knowledge of today. Thus, our critical remarks here are not primarily meant to devalue Malthus as an economist of his time—at least not as much as we question the neo-classical economists of ours—but we want to show that his theory, or rather hypothesis, did not explain the actual causes of poverty of contemporary England, let alone that of the third world today. With the rapid development of capitalism, including the imperialist penetration of the periphery, Malthus deserves no respect at all in today's textbooks on underdevelopment. We shall try to show why.

His fundamental "Law of Nature" said that "The power of population is indefinitely greater than the power in the earth to produce subsistence for man. Population, when unchecked, increases in a geometrical ratio, subsistence increases only in an arithmetical ratio".[4] The check, which he had in view, was in the first place the supply of food. Whenever there is an abundance of food, the rate of population growth is constant. A certain population which grows by, say, 3% annually, will double in every 25-year period. If its size was 10 million in 1800, it would have grown to 20 million in 1825, to 40 million in 1850, etc. Thus, the population increases by geometrical progression, as 1, 2, 4, 8, etc.

This law of constant relative growth, of which Malthus did not provide any acceptable empirical evidence, is questionable. The birth rate of a population (number of live births in one year per thousand people) depends on its age distribution by sex and on the fertility of women of the various age groups (age-specific fertility). Hence, changes in the age or sex distribution, e.g. due to rural–urban migration of certain groups, will cause a change in the birth rate, which may last for decades. It would have been enough for Malthus's purposes to argue that the *additional number* of people increases from year to year, as it indeed does under normal circumstances. This would also have been sufficient for his further reasoning, namely that the yearly absolute growth of food production is constant—the supply increases by arithmetical progression, as 1, 2, 3, 4, etc. However, the combination of the two theses, indicating that the food demand, expressed in numbers of people, always tends to grow faster than the food supply, was coloured by his own states and motivated by the need to prove the inevitability of the existing order. Thereby his deterministic theory becomes rather dry, not least seen from a scientific point of view.

The contradiction between the arithmetic growth of agricultural production and the tendency of population to grow geometrically is solved by means of checks on the population, either "preventive checks", like postponed marriages (among the rich), or "positive checks", like natural disasters, epidemics and high child mortality (among the poor). The asserted impossibility of production to increase faster automatically implies that the size of population, or rather the size of its poorer half, is to be blamed for this drama of conflict. (As we shall see below, exactly this reasoning recurs frequently in the neo-Malthusian arguments of our time, although usually presented in a more opportune and sophisticated form.)

According to Malthus, those in the economic margin, the dispossessed who never were given any chance of taking an active part in production, constituted a surplus population, whose only rôle was to draw from the resources of society without contributing to economic growth. Their existence could hardly be justified. In the first edition of "An Essay" he said: "A labourer who marries without being able to support a family may in some respects be considered as an enemy to all his fellow-labourers'', and in the second edition:

> A man who is born into a world already possessed, if he cannot get subsistence from his parents on whom he has a just demand, and if the society do not want his labour, has no claim of right to the smallest portion of food, and, in fact, has no business to be where he is.

"The right to live" is here made dependent on an unquestioned division of people into wealthy and unwealthy. This outrageous notion of the poorest of the society constituted an important element of the ideology on which he modelled a defence of the private property and of the privileges of his own class.

Malthus's seductive ideas survived as an apology for the exploitation of the working class. The contemporary critics of Malthusianism had obvious difficulties in finding ready listeners in the establishment. Karl Marx gave Malthus a word of acknowledgement for his understanding of the existence of a surplus population as a necessary condition of the modern industry's low cost of production and consequent high rate of investments and high profits, but as to the rest he did not think highly of him. Actually, neither Marx nor Friedrich Engels examined Malthus's writings too deeply. Their critique followed the laws of relations between population and production in the capitalist system which they themselves laid down. Engels denied the reasonableness of an arithmetic growth of food production:

> Where has it been proved that the productivity of the land increases in arithmetical progression? The area of land is limited—that is perfectly true. But the labour power to be employed on this area increases together with the population; and even if we assume that the increase of output associated with this increase of labour is not always proportionate to the latter, there still remains a third element—which the economists, however, never consider as important—namely, science, the progress of which is just as limitless and at least as rapid as that of population.[5]

Engels hints here at what others were to repeat over and over again: with a growing population pressure, the production of food increases in proportion to the demand, unless disturbed by external factors—natural or man-made. If the access to land is limited increased production can be achieved by putting in more labour or by increasing productivity through technical innovations. Higher population density on arable land necessitates a development of the productive forces, and hence, more people do not necessary imply a lower per capita food consumption. Today we have much more data to demonstrate this than both Malthus and Engels ever had at their disposal. Whereas Engels in the quotation above referred to a capitalist economy our thesis of a positive correlation between population growth and production mainly relates to social formations dominated by non-capitalist relations of production. In the latter case, most members of the agricultural society usually have the means of production at their own disposition, but in capitalism the actual producers are alienated from these means. Here, technology has a higher price and is controlled by the capitalist class who possess the means of production. Engels did not deny that it was Utopian to imagine that technology could be used as an instrument to increase production in the interest of the masses. The profitability of the introduction of better technology depends on the size of the market, i.e. the actual demand for food, which defines the limits of capitalist production.

> Too little is produced, that is the cause of the whole thing. But *why* is too little produced? Not because the limits of production—even today and with present-day means—are exhausted. No, but because the limits of production are determined not by the number of hungry bellies but by the number of *purses* able to buy and to pay. Bourgeois society does not and cannot wish to produce any more. The moneyless bellies, the labour which cannot be utilized *for profit* and therefore cannot buy, is left to the death rate.[6]

With optimum utilization of the productive forces, "'Overpopulated' Great Britain . . . could be so developed in the course of ten years as to produce sufficient corn for six times its present population", but "One part of the land is cultivated according to the best methods, while another part—in Great Britain and Ireland thirty million acres of good land—lies waste".[7] If we disregard a possible exaggeration concerning the agricultural potential of the land, which modern ecologists would hardly swallow, the parallels with the conditions in most of the periphery today are striking.

Malthus understood the wages as a function of supply and demand for labour, and he described the periodicity of the economic crises, which caused an imbalance between the two, but he wrongly assumed that fluctuations in unemployment were reflected in a corresponding periodicity in the growth rate of population. He maintained that the uneven relation between the growth of population and the growth of food supplies explained the periodic crises. When population grows faster than the supplies of food the conditions of the poor will deteriorate. If the demand for goods outstrips the supply it will lead to rising prices, and as the number of labourers surpasses the chances of work, wages tend to decline. Higher prices and lower wages result in lower purchasing power, underconsumption, crisis of production, unemployment and widespread poverty, in that order. "During this season of distress, the discouragements to marriage, and the difficulty of rearing a family are so great that population is at stand."[8] At this point the farmers are encouraged by the high prices of food and the low prices of labour to cultivate more land, to develop the agricultural technology, and to employ more people. Production and food supply will again overtake the stagnant population, unemployment will decline, and wages, purchasing power and consumption will go up. "The situation of the labourer being then again tolerably comfortable, the restraints to population are in some degree loosened, and the same retrograde and progressive movements with respect to happiness are repeated."[9]

Malthus here describes a vicious circle which, with some modifications, was to be repeated in the neo-Malthusian literature a century and a half later: population growth–crisis and unemployment–higher mortality and population stagnation–boom period and more employment–population growth, etc. As it was the high living standard of the workers that caused a fast population growth and subsequent crises, these crises could be avoided by lowering the living standard and forcing down the wages also during the good years. Thus, whereas Marx envisaged exploitation and misery as social phenomena which would result in revolts against the establishment, transition to socialism, higher production and a higher living standard of the working class, Malthus, on the other hand, saw misery as a pure economic phenomenon and a necessary condition of higher production.

In his "Principles of Political Economy" (1st edn 1820) Malthus completed this logic with a defence of the affluence at "the other end". His theory of underconsumption (crises of production explained by instable consumption) was a logical consequence of his appraisal of the price of a commodity as the sum of its value (price of labour embodied in the commodity) and the profit. Since the labourers have to be paid less than the price of the commodities which they produce, their purchasing power is insufficient to buy all the commodities that are produced. The surplus, therefore, has to be sold to an unproductive group of consumers—landlords, the state, the church, etc. The constantly increasing demand of this group, as well as the growth of the group itself, was consequently a necessary condition to save the market in order to avoid crises. Malthus here succeeded with his juggle of defending the existence of a growing parasitic upper class and of an underpaid working class: population growth was restrained by forcing down wages, and the surplus of goods, which the labourers could not afford to buy, was consumed by the unproductive bourgeoisie.

Marx showed that unemployment and underpayment can only be understood from an analysis of the surplus value, i.e. the difference between total labour embodied in the commodity and paid labour. The wage is a function of the minimum demands of the labourers, which automatically implies that labour is underpaid—that is how the profits of the capitalist class are made. This overutilization of labour in relation to its price is the basic cause of unemployment, of the relative overpopulation, of the so-called underconsumption and of the crises. We shall illustrate this connection with a simple example.

Assume that the production of a certain commodity demands 90 working-hours per day. The factory owner faces two alternatives —to employ 15 workers who work 6 hours each, or 10 workers who work 9 hours each. As the wage is not directly proportional to the invested labour (the number of working hours), but is rather conditioned by the minimum demands (cost of reproduction) of the labourer, the factory owner prefers the second alternative. If the 15 workers get £5 each per day for their 6 hours and the 10 workers get £6 each for their 9 hours (we are here generous enough to compensate for the longer working-day, but of course not full compensation), the total wages are £75 in the first case and £60 in the second. By preferring fewer workers and longer working-days the capitalist in this example makes an extra profit of £15 per day. Simultaneously he withholds employment for 5 workers. "One part of the working population works 14, 16 hours a day, while another remains unemployed and idle, and dies of hunger."[10]

In the next step, we assume that the factory's 5 old machines are replaced by 3 modern ones with the same total capacity. Only two workers are needed per machine, i.e. the labour force can be decreased from 10 to 6. Four become superfluous and join the other five unemployed, and the profit goes up another £24 per day (minus depreciation of machinery). This surplus of labour, together with all unemployed labour, constitutes a *relative overpopulation*, i.e. they are too many in relation to the constraints of the economic system. This form of relative overpopulation is typical for the capitalist system, according to Marx, because we cannot find it in any other system; it is the population law of capitalism:

> But the conservative interests, whose servitor he (Malthus) was, made it impossible for him to see that an unlimited increase in the length of the working day, combined with an extraordinary development of machinery and with the exploitation of the labour of women and children, could not fail to make a large proportion of the working class "superfluous" . . . Naturally, it was far more convenient to himself, and far more accordant with the interests of the ruling classes (whom Malthus idolised with all the fervour which was fitting in a parson) for him to explain this "over-population" as due to the eternal laws of nature, instead of explaining it as the outcome of nothing more than the natural history of capitalist production . . .
>
> It is the working population which, while effecting the accumulation of capital, also produces the means whereby it is itself rendered relatively superfluous, is turned into a relative surplus population; and it does so to an ever increasing extent. This is a law of population peculiar to the capitalist method of production; and, in fact, every method of production that in the course of history has its own peculiar, historically valid, law of population.[11]

The development of surplus labour corresponds to the development of surplus population, according to Marx. "A surplus working-class population is a necessary product of accumulation, or of the development of wealth upon a capitalist basis", but it is also "a necessary condition of the existence of the capitalist method of production . . .

For its own varying needs in the way of self-expansion, capital creates an ever-ready supply of human material fit for exploitation, and does so independently of the limits of the actual increase in population".[12]

Whereas Malthus related population and population growth to consumption, Engels and Marx related them to production. The former interpreted overpopulation as a surplus of consumers without money, the latter saw it as a surplus of capacity of work, i.e. unproductive labour force. Here, two "laws of population" stood, and still stand, against each other: on the one hand the Malthusian "Law of Nature", which, irrespective of the dominating economic system, defines overpopulation as something absolute and caused by a too fast growing population, and on the other hand the "Law of Capitalism", which defines overpopulation as a relative phenomenon, caused by the mechanisms inherent in the capitalist system. According to the former hypothesis, the problem could only be solved by means of forcing down the wages, which would lead to a natural decrease in the birth rate and/or a natural increase in the death rate. According to the latter, an active, profound and sweeping change of the economic foundation of the society is needed, a destruction of the capitalist system, a social revolution.

The Ideological Motives

With the demographic transition in Europe (a decline in death rates followed by a decline in birth rates and a concomitant slower growth of population) Malthus's thoughts became less and less adequate in their original version. Moreover, even the most ardent Malthusian must have questioned his master during the capitalist crisis of the 1930s. Unemployment then shot up and when food worth billions of dollars was destroyed, millions of Americans were on the verge of starvation. The capitalist system showed its ugliest face: huge amounts of food were thrown into the sea instead of being channelled to those in desperate need of it. But while the depression continued in the west, the economy of the Soviet Union was unaffected. For the ruling class in the market economy, a planned economy under socialism was a threat. At a later date "the yellow peril" contributed to this—China's some 500–600 millions of people on their way to break their old bonds and fetters. More than ever, communism—or rather what was named as communism —became the main enemy of liberal values. Population control was an ingredient in the reactionary counterstrategy. In 1952 John Rockefeller established the Population Council and the same year another neo-Malthusian organization came into being, the International Planned Parenthood Federation (IPPF). Two years earlier a hysterical McCarthyism had secured a foothold in the USA. Just before its instigator disappeared from the scene in December 1954, the concepts *the population bomb* and *the population explosion* were introduced in an American magazine, published by the Hugh Moore Fund.[13] Anti-communism and pro-Americanism as preached in the 1950s and 1960s were definitely not fruits of Malthusian thinking, but they were interlaced—openly or implicitly—with some neo-Malthusian ideological motives to control the population of the periphery, where relative overpopulation had been a reality long since.

Marx once said that capitalism is pregnant with the socialist revolution. This belief in the political reproduction has not yet been manifested in the most advanced capitalist countries. Here the pregnancy has resulted in miscarriage, but in the backward countries the situation is different. Imperialism introduced the first stage of a capitalist mode of production in the periphery, and with it the most malign symptoms of capitalism followed. The consequent "development of underdevelopment", to use the words of Andre Gunder Frank, might be explosive. The masses of underpaid and exploited and the growing number of unemployed and underemployed, particularly in the cities, was and is a menace to the prevailing order. Nobody should deny that the social unrest and the political chaos, which are expected to succeed to the growing gaps of consumption between the rich and the poor countries, as well as within the poor ones, will undermine the worthiness of all those Western values and strategies of development, which have contributed to this process of underdevelopment of the masses. Today, world capitalism faces a greater challenge from the oppressed of the periphery than from the working class of the centre. Obviously, the population growth will strengthen this political pressure—the more potentially exploited and unemployed people that are born, the stronger the subversive forces of society will grow (this does not imply a support of a fast growing population and of misery as a means of achieving revolution, as neo-Malthusians tend to interpret their critics).

Robert McNamara, President of the World Bank, must have sensed this threat as he once warned that "it is only a question of time before a decisive choice must be made between the political costs of reform and the political risks of rebellion". He might have thought of Sri Lanka, an instructive example: in 1965 almost one million people were out of work and a few years later 64% of those in age group 19–25 yr were unemployed. The internal economic policy in combination with the economic dependence on the industrialized countries headed the country towards a chaotic situation and in early 1971 J.V.P., the People's Liberation Front, conducted a desperate attack against the establishment. Thousands of people were killed, many more were imprisoned and foreign interests and the domestic bourgeoisie were deeply shaken. Development planning was now steered in another direction: the military budget, which so far had been modest, shot up, and the birth control programme, which earlier had had low priority, became a focus of immediate interest. In the new five-year-plan, presented half a year after the disturbances, population control got a conspicuous place among the attempts to solve the economic crisis and to subdue the political unrest: "*Under the present circumstances* the importance of family planning cannot be sufficiently stressed".[14]

The wealthy sensed a menace to the unequal consumption of the world's resources and to a continued exploitation of raw products and cheap labour of the periphery. No political, economic or military efforts are spared to protect these interests of the central establishments. In a few countries, like Cuba and Vietnam, they have failed to contain rebellion, but in most cases they have been successful, at least so far, for instance in Indonesia, Iran, Zaire, Brazil, Dominican Republic, Guatemala, Chile, . . . It is not a coincidence that the political operators, whether they are formal citizens of the centre or of the periphery, also are assiduous advocates of controlling the future size of the third world population (the reverse does not necessarily hold: for many organizations working with family planning in the periphery, the pure political incentive is out of the question).

The doomsday prophets, influential in politics when their ideas suit the politicians, see population as a bomb that blows itself—"the population explosion". The qualities of the human being of the periphery are subordinated to her role as a passive figure in the columns of macro-statistics. She is compared to breeding rabbits and to clouds of locusts (this is, for instance, how the new director of IPPF, Carl Wahren, sees population: breeding like the locusts in Egypt).[15] This reminds us of the cover of Paul Ehrlich's book, "The Population Bomb",[16] a small child in a bomb with a burning quick-match. The same bomb served as a prototype of a stamp which IPPF issued in Kenya some years ago, but here the child was replaced by the text THE POPULATION BOMB KEEPS TICK-ING. With the aid of dogmas reality is turned inside out. Mr Ehrlich, one of our modern fanatical Malthuses, gave in his book the following picture of the menace of "the population explosion" to mankind:

> It cannot be overemphasized, however, that no changes in behaviour or technology can save us unless we can achieve control over the size of the human population. The birth rate must be brought into balance with the death rate or mankind will breed itself into oblivion. We can no longer afford merely to treat the symptoms of the cancer of population growth; the cancer itself must be cut out.[17]

Malthus resurrected: the population growth, the reproduction of people, the people themselves are the cause of poverty and the cancer of mankind its symptom! The analysis is blocked.

This preaching of a doomsday philosophy is dangerous, as it diverts the attention from political realities, gives rise to despair, and paves the way for myopic nationalism and racialism. In British newspapers a few years ago one could read big advertisements on "the population explosion" in the Third World and its effects on the global resources. It was a big drive in favour of a global birth control programme, with the affecting name "Countdown Campaign". In a first phase one millions pounds was the intended collection. The campaign, in collaboration with the IPPF and "supported by a team of distinguished and most articulate business men", planned a crusade in the name of Malthus, because, according to the advertisement,

> England is not selfsupporting. In order to feed our 56 million people we *have to* import food. But if the population in those countries, from which we import food, continues to grow at the

present pace we shall have less to manage with, less to export, and all, including the people in the so called wealthy nations, will suffer.

The fear of these campaigners is a delusion. All Africa's total Gross National Product (GNP) is not much higher than the absolute increase in the GNP of Europe in one year. The absolute annual increase in USA's GNP per capita equals that of India's in a hundred years. The population growth in the periphery is a drop in the ocean compared to the increasing wealth per capita in the centre. Half of the world's population today live in those underdeveloped countries which are dependent on the dominating world market economy (i.e. the third world excluding China and a few other countries). Eighteen per cent live in the rich capitalist countries. The former account for 14%, and the latter for 66% of the gross world product. Thus, the inhabitants of the affluent countries are, on average, 13 times richer than those of the poor capitalist countries. This means that a *ninefold* increase in the number of the poorest half of the world's population (with unchanged per capita consumption) would result in the same additional exploitation of the resources of the world as a *doubling* of the living standard of the now living, most affluent one-fifth or one-sixth of the world's population. This shows how the neo-Malthusian focusing on the birth rate in the periphery only serves to mystify and to divert the attention from the ravaging effects of the capitalist over-production in the centre. Valuable, and for the future, indispensable resources of the periphery are exported to the rich countries to satisfy their growing wealth. This has, indeed, nothing to do with the rate of reproduction of the poor.

When the Countdown Campaign stood at its highest it was indeed contrasted with the hundreds of thousands of victims of starvation in Africa. The example of West Africa is illustrative and should teach the campaigners a lesson: political and economic manipulation in parts of the Sahel in western Africa have slowly undermined the means of subsistence of the poor peasants and of the nomads. They normally exist on the edge of hunger and when the rains fail the catastrophe is not far away, with subsequent population decrease. The 1973 famine, which ravaged the people in the Sahel, could have been prevented, but capital was instead invested in large cattle ranches in the region, for production and export of beef to Europe.

An expert on West Africa, Rolf Gustavsson, described this cynical paradox in a Swedish radio programme early 1974:

> The meat consumption in West and East Europe and in Japan is expected to grow rapidly during the coming decades, and the experts are calculating upon a meat crisis. It is difficult to solve it in Europe as the consumption of milk and butter does not increase as fast as that of meat. Hence the butter mountain in the EEC. But the international experts have found a way out of this dilemma: locate the meat production to the underdeveloped countries, for example to the West African savannah. Thereby we avoid the butter mountain and the meat will be cheaper (due to the high labour-intensity of cattle-breeding and the much cheaper manpower in Africa). And all this exercise is facilitated by the drought, because if the nomads succumb to starvation there will be no problems to expropriate huge areas for cattle ranches. It is against this background one can hear so-called experts saying that "the drought and the starvation solve certain problems". But it is only to the benefit of certain interests. For the masses of people, the drought and the starvation are a tragedy and a testimony of their powerlessness.

Thus, partly thanks to a possible decimation of the West African population we can look forward to more and cheaper meat in Europe in the future (note that the 1973 Sahel famine was probably not the last one). National and international organizations in the centre, which had the means to come to the rescue of the people in time, nod in agreement with Malthus and refer to the unavoidable positive check on population.

In October 1972 a number of foreign family planning organizations held a meeting in Dakar, Senegal. The representative of one of them complained that his organization had only been able to utilize 15% of the yearly budget. He emphatically searched for a birth control project where he could spend the remaining 85%. Simultaneously one of the ministers of agriculture of a Sahelian country travelled all over Europe to beg for financial support to prevent expected starvation in his home-country. Twice he returned empty-handed. It was not until half a year later, when the catastrophe was a fact, that food aid started to slowly pour in. There was plenty of money to deter the number of people from growing, but not a single cent to prevent them from dying.

The paradox is not limited to West Africa. In the early 1970s it cost over one million US$ to prevent 8000 births in Kenya. How much would it have cost to eradicate pronounced hunger in the north of the country, or to prevent the starvation in the neighbouring country, Ethiopia, which took well over 100 000 lives? According to "qualified guesses", in the early 1970s over three million births were prevented per year through organized family planning programmes all over the world (excluding China). But many times that number died from under- and malnourishment. It is a cynical rationalism: the one who is never born will never die.

The Malthusian ideology has given birth to various interpretations—divergent on the surface but in reality concurrent. One interpretation is the intuitive fear of the reproduction of the poor, which results in social imbalance. One of the last genuine Malthusians was a German statesman in the 1930s. Like Malthus he reckoned upon "nature" as the adjusting factor:

> Because the inferior are always numerically superior to the better, the former would multiply so much faster—if they have the same possibilities to survive and reproduce—that the better necessarily would be placed in the background. Therefore a correction has to be made to the advantage of the better. The nature offers such a correction by exposing the inferior to difficult living conditions which reduce their number. Concerning the rest, the nature does not allow them to reproduce indiscriminately, but makes a relentless selection according to their strength and health conditions.[18]

The *inferior* and the *better*. Nature will take care of the inferior, the better queue up to get a place in history as the deliverers of civilization. Adolf Hitler was one of them.

Thus, like Malthus, Hitler counted on positive checks on the "inferior" people. But the situation has changed, and one can no longer rely upon nature, as mortality is now declining also among the poor and in the periphery. The neo-Malthusians therefore see birth control on a large scale as the ideological solution to, what they call, the problem. Some even suggest obligatory birth control, like compulsory sterilization, or temporary means of sterilization that could be added to the water or to the basic foods. We here find the main dividing line between the Malthusians and the neo-Malthusians. The former relied on natural checks on population, whereas the latter see no other choice than to favour man-made checks. The preventive checks that Malthus "discovered" among the rich people of Europe are today being artificially introduced by the neo-Malthusians among the poor people and in some under-developed regions of the world.

Dirty and stinking slum quarters, swarming with people, are often used as an illustration of the emerging social imbalance which calls for a check on the poor. For the one who for the first time enters such an area it may be a natural reaction to relate poverty to the crowd of people. That is also how Paul Ehrlich was converted:

> I have understood the population explosion intellectually for a long time. I came to understand it emotionally one stinking hot night in Delhi, a few years ago. My wife and daughter and I were returning to our hotel in an ancient taxi. The seats were hopping with fleas. The only functional gear was third. As we crawled through the city, we entered a crowded slum area. The temperature was well over 100°F. and the air was a haze of dust and smoke. The streets seemed alive with people. People eating, people washing, people sleeping. People visiting, arguing and screaming. People thrusting their hands through the taxi window, begging. People defecating and urinating. People clinging to buses. People herding animals. People, people, people, people. As we moved slowly through the mob, hand horn squawking, the dust, noise, heat, and cooking fires gave the scene a hellish aspect. Would we ever get to our hotel? All three of us were frankly frightened.[19]

Ehrlich cowered in the taxi without understanding what he really saw, and consequently his appreciation of the population growth and of its causes never developed further than to an emotional experience. If he had stepped out of the taxi and stayed to study New Delhi's slum for some time, he might never have written the book on "the population bomb". Then he would have found that the slum people are primarily poor, that poverty is the basis to which they have to adapt. They have to limit their costs of living to a minimum and are forced to live in close quarters—often more than one family in the same house, always many people in the same room. Being poor they do not have the same privileges as the rich who live at the other end of the town. The responsible authorities do not attach importance to drainage, latrines, scavenging and other problems of sanitation of the slum as to the sparsely populated quarters of the rich. The overcrowding, the stench and the dirt are all symptoms of a sick economic system, which favours those already favoured. Neither pills nor sterilization will cure that sickness.

Rather than analysing the causes of poverty one verifies its existence and gets frightened at its growth. Under these circumstances, one is deceived in believing that poverty can be eradicated by artificial reduction of population growth. This also goes for Margaret Sanger, one of the founders of the IPPF, who saw the propagation of the poor in America as a menace to the social balance. She insisted that the American public was too heavily taxed to maintain a "growing stock of morons", who threatened the very foundation of the American civilization. This "hero of the American family planning movement", as Paul Ehrlich later appointed her, had her reasons to be in agony over the reproduction of the uneducated: "It is not surprising to establish that the suffrage of the imbecile is equivalent to that of the genius. The future is not bright".[20]

Puerto Rico, USA—A Case in Point

Margaret Sanger's teaching was successful. In 1937 USA's "associated free state", Puerto Rico, initiated a national programme of birth control as the first country in the world. Another 34 years later, according to Roberto Moran at the University of Puerto Rico:

> In Puerto Rico retarded mothers have an average of five children as compared with an average of two children among mothers with one or more years of university. Assuming that children "inherit" their parents' intelligence, and assuming a constant environment, we should soon observe a most striking and convincing argument for family planning, especially among the mentally retarded. In only two generations the retarded family would have produced 30 potentially retarded children as compared to six children with average or above average intelligence produced by two normal parents. It is obvious that more financial assistance is needed and that more ingenious methods need to be devised if the threat of an overflow of sub-intelligent individuals into the Puerto Rican population is to be avoided.[21]

What is the background to this peculiar statement? Up to the end of the last century Puerto Rico had less than one million inhabitants. Their main economic activities were cattle breeding and small-scale agriculture, including the cultivation of some cash crops. The island was far from overpopulated, mortality was high and the population growth was low. When the USA "took over the responsibility" of the island in 1898 from Spain, two measures were undertaken which were to dramatically affect the subsequent development.

The American army drained the malaria-producing marshes, which led to a rapid drop in mortality. The positive effect of a decreasing incidence of illness was not the only motive, but also to create a more tolerable environment for the white American immigrants, and to encourage the growth of the indigenous labour force.

The other measure was a nationwide deforestation and the bringing of huge inhabited areas under sugar cane and tobacco cultivation. Evicted farmers and cattle-breeders were transformed into wage labourers on their own land. A fast expansion of American plantations and an erection of sugar industries were possible thanks to the great supply of local manpower which had been released. Some decades later, when the American companies had laid their hands upon the best half of the cultivable area, natural limitations set bounds to further expansion. The demand for labour stagnated, but the supply increased—parallel to the rapid growth of population.

The density of labourers on commercially cultivated land had gone down and the poorer soil which was left behind for the original inhabitants could not support them. People moved to the towns but without finding enough jobs. Puerto Rico produced the sugar and the tobacco but the other industry was on the mainland, in the USA. Unemployment grew like a rolling snowball, so did political unrest, and the sugar-labourers carried through a successful strike in 1934. The following year the Nationalist Party demanded the USA to quit the island. The ruling class took this practically as a declaration of war. In 1937 the leader of the party, Albizu Campos, was arrested, and at a demonstration that followed the police massacred many party members and sympathizers. The great capitalist crisis of the 1930s had struck against the economy of Puerto Rico and its political stability. The governor of the island suggested what he thought was the cheapest solution to the problem: population control.

Needless to say, the population programme failed or did not at least solve the economic crisis of the country. As a last resort people had to leave the island. During the 1940s and 1950s 0·7 million Puerto Ricans emigrated to USA, one-third of Puerto Rico's population built up a new slum in New York. In the initial stage the capital from the metropolis had come to the plantation economy, but now the people of the periphery followed the profits back to the centre of capitalism.

Before the First World War some 80 % of the people of the island were working on the land, while today the figure is around 70 000 out of a total population approaching three millions.[22] Industrialization with American "aid" started in Puerto Rico after the Second World War. Industrialists could average 25 % return on investment in labour-intensive factories. In the 1960s some 80 % of the economy of the island was controlled by American capital, most of it ploughed into dirty petrochemical industries. The share of total income earned by the lowest income group has fallen continuously since the early 1950s. Today, half of the families receive only one-sixth of the income produced. "About 30 % of the population is currently considered more or less unemployed."[23] The poverty is manifest and the slum is widely spread. Juan Angel Silén has in his interesting book, "We, the Puerto Rican People", recapitulated the essential problems of the island:

> But there is no "population problem" in Puerto Rico: what we have is a bad division of wealth, a disequilibrium between resources and people, between natural, capital, and human resources. The "population problem" comes from emigration into the cities with its attendant crisis in agriculture; from saturation of the cities, with their areas of decay and poverty; from the investment of foreign capital, causing a flight of savings that is among the world's highest; from foreign debt (including government and individual debt) which amounted to $1·28 billion in 1964–65. These, along with unemployment, health problems (in 1965 diarrhea-enteritis was the fourth highest cause of death), the low average education level, and low wages and incomes, are the sure signs of our resource–population imbalance.[24]

This is the background in brief. Let us now return to Roberto Moran and see how he reached his conclusions above (emphasis added for clarification):

(1) *"Poverty* is intricately related to *high unemployment and low income"*. (p. 91)
(2) There is "evidence of the relationship between *mental retardation and poverty"* (p. 93). The author bases this statement on a most dubious intelligence test (Stanford-Binet) on 4771 Puerto Ricans.

(3) "Poor children are usually the products of poor parents. . . . *Retarded parents* who remain in poverty-stricken areas in Puerto Rico *tend to give birth to high-risk children for any of the physical, social, and psychological disorders and conditions including mental retardation*". (p. 94)

(4) Referring to women, "the lower the *income*, the fewer years of *schooling*, and the larger the *number of children*. . . . For example, mothers of 45 years or more who never attended school (i.e. those who were at school-age when the family planning programme was introduced the first time!—my note) have an average of seven children; mothers with one or more years of university studies have an average of two children". (p. 94)

The variables are identified: unemployment and low income, poverty, mental retardation and many children. The author then formulates a "vicious circle", a common liberal device of describing underdevelopment, in order to keep clear of such crucial, but obviously sensitive, explanatory variables as economic dependency and relations of production:

> The retarded child becomes an educationally disadvantaged adult whose income is inadequate for providing the essential needs of life. He tends to marry young and have large families with more potential high-risk children, and so the process continues *ad infinitum*. (p. 94)

This "vicious circle" includes some unreliable data and asserted connections which are presented in a misleading way in order to underscore something the author desires to prove. Without denying some of the statements, which anyway are of limited interest, it would be of greater value if the author had told us *why* it is so and so. *There is absolutely no causal analysis in the presentation*. The example illustrates the development of the Malthusian logic since the early 19th century. Those who cling to this pseudo-science can only draw one conclusion, the same as drawn by Roberto Moran: "It is obvious that more financial assistance is needed and that more ingenious methods need to be devised if the threat of an overflow of subintelligent individuals into the Puerto Rican population is to be avoided". (p. 96)

After the Second World War the financing of research on preventives increased rapidly. The American medical firm, Syntex, a forerunner in the manufacturing of preventive pills, was looking a field of experiment for its products. The new pills were not admitted to be tested on women in the USA since the side-effects were not yet known. What was more natural than to locate the risky experiments in the colony—Puerto Rico? In 1956, with assistance from IPPF (this, at least superficially, so altruistic an organization, is closely cooperating with the industry), Dr Gregory Pincus and others made research with the newly devised pills on 10 000 women in Humacao in Puerto Rico. "In the late 1950s the clinical testing had gone far enough to ensure that "190-nor steroids" (the pills) would soon be introduced to the public for family planning."[25] By "public" was of course meant the American public, whereas the Puerto Ricans served as guinea-pigs. But to be safe, before the pills were sold publicly they were tested on Mexican lower class women in San Antonio, Texas and in Los Angeles.

The story of the intrauterine device (IUD) was to be a repetition of that of the pill: in 1961 the IUD was first introduced to—needless to say—the women in Humacao in Puerto Rico, three years later to black women in Harlem Hospital in New York and thereafter to black and poor white women in Sunflower County, Mississippi, and in Atlanta, Georgia.

Neither pills nor IUDs could solve the problems in Puerto Rico and consequently an intensive sterilization programme was launched. With massive assistance from IPPF, USAID, Ford Foundation and Population Council, local organizations built up a huge apparatus to operate on and control the population of the island. In 1969 about 30% of the women aged 15–49 were sterilized. The sterilization programme has continued and today this percentage has gone up further. In 1976 the target was to sterilize another 300 000 Puerto Rican women.

Like the pill and the IUD, sterilization has also been introduced among the non-whites in the USA. According to Health Research Group in Washington, which works together with the well-known social critic Ralph Nader, about two million Americans are sterilized every year, primarily black and Spanish-speaking women.

opulation control is used to mean color control"
:sident of the National Council of Negro Women.

all married black women in the US have been
:e times the percentage of white married women,

according to a 1970 National Fertility Study. And a 1973 study showed that sterilization abuse among Spanish speaking women was six times greater than that among white women.
According to a recent government report, 3000 Indian women have been sterilized without being given any consent forms to sign.[26]

What is the next step to control minority groups? Is the same abuse of ruthless population control also found in other parts of the world (apart from India which we know)? Will it reach Europe? The latter being a relevant question bearing in mind the growing tendencies of racism and racialism as one consequence of the present capitalist crisis.

Ideological Explanations of Underdevelopment

We shall first summarize the three ideological motives for population growth control:

—The non-renewable resources of the world are limited. So are the possibilities of a further increase in the production of renewable goods, particularly food. Thus, the high standard of living in the centre is threatened by the increasing demands in the periphery, which are due to its growth of population.

—Population grows faster than job opportunities, causing increasing unemployment. This leads to social unrest not only among the growing body of unemployed but also among the active labourers, whose wages are forced down because of oversupply of manpower. This unrest may easily pass into an open and violent opposition against the established capitalist order of society. There are imminent risks of socialist ideas gaining terrain.

—The poorest and the least intelligent people reproduce faster than the others. When the unintelligent and incapacitated increase and the intelligent constitute a correspondingly smaller and smaller share of the population, society will degenerate.

These three motives coincide to some extent. In all of them, social problems are seen as caused by that part of the population which grows the fastest. But this same part of the population consumes least, totally as well as per capita, and seen both from a national and from an international perspective. Officially, only the problem of limited resources is looked upon as an international concern. But in reality, drastic political changes in favour of the poor masses in the periphery are a headache not only for those in power in the respective countries but for corresponding groups in the centre as well. Thus, the division into three motives, which we made with the purpose of exposing the neo-Malthusian ideology, is blurred when the ideology is put into practice.

With the rapid development of the productive forces during the last century, much of the original Malthusian model of explanation had to be abandoned. The vacuum has been filled with a big dosage of dogmatics and mishandled statistics, despite the better knowledge of demography and of the political and economic role of population that we have today. Neo-Malthusian arguments have grown in quantity but not in quality. We still find the population ghost, combined with simple explanations of development stagnation, such as the vicious circle of population growth, which leads to poverty, which leads to population growth, etc.

The notorious Lester Pearson-report of 1969, "Partners in Development", had a great impact on the World Bank's and other development strategies for the 1970s. Here, not only the absolute poverty of the periphery but also the growing gap between rich and poor countries were explained by the faster population growth in the latter:

> No other phenomenon casts a darker shadow over the prospects for international development than the staggering growth of population. It is evident that it is a major cause of the large discrepancy between rates of economic improvement in rich and poor countries.

These lines reveal a profound ignorance about the economic relations between the two groups of countries. Or is it merely ignorance? We could fill many pages with deceptive statements of this sort, made by organizations and individuals who for various reasons actively participate in or have an active interest in population growth control in the periphery. Several pretentious world models of development have been produced, like the two Club of Rome reports, "The Limits to Growth" (1972) and "Mankind at the Turning Point" (1974), where Malthus is put in a computer.

In these development models a large amount of population data are combined with economic data, on top of which hypotheses are placed on the relations between level of consumption, distribution between investments and consumption, economic growth, productivity, school enrolment, susceptibility of the population to family planning programmes, etc. (the authors of "Mankind at the Turning Point" even presumptuously declare that in their model about 100 000 correlations are stored in the computer). All these data and hypotheses are then computerized and the result shows the degree of development, globally or of the respective country, at a certain point of time, e.g. year 2000. Output depends on input, i.e. on "facts" and subjective hypotheses concerning functional relations between them. A certain combination of input data corresponds to the best result (highest welfare, measured in Western terms). Thanks to the biased assumptions, the models show what they are supposed to show: the earlier the world or the respective country introduces population growth control and the more money that is allocated towards this sector, the more developed the world or the country will be in year 2000. Notwithstanding these models cost millions of dollars and are printed on glossy paper, their reliability is not enhanced. For several reasons they are useless:

—They are usually strictly mathematical and are supposed to be valid in a stereotyped way for all regions of the world or of the periphery without exception. Consequently, they do not, and cannot, take into consideration the political structure and the traditional values of the various countries or of the political and economic heterogeneity of the world.
—They do not take into consideration possible political decisions which may lead to dramatic consequences for development (e.g. land reform).
—They do not take into consideration changes in the world market (e.g. higher oil prices, lower cocoa prices, higher demand of copper).
—They do not, and obviously cannot, take into consideration sudden and unpredictably altered conditions of survival and of economic growth and development. (What happens if the capital city is destroyed by an earthquake, if the grain yield is spoiled by drought or flood, if the peasants revolt?)
—They take for granted that all citizens of the respective countries take part in the money economy on equal conditions and that the distribution of consumption within countries or continents is absolutely fair, which is never the case.

These models, like so many other simplified projections of economy and population, are products of gangs of playful mathematicians, ignorant of the realities of the world. (What does the African peasant care about differential calculus when he decides to buy a new plough?)

The all pervading characteristic of this type of models is the blind acceptance of the prevailing market mechanisms, with the subsequent emphasis on the growth of GNP per capita. When the growth of production is lagging behind the growth of population, everything goes to consumption and nothing is left over for investments. Likewise, a high fertility results in a very broad based age pyramid, i.e. the number of people of working age is small relative to those of dependent age (up to, say, fifteen years). Thus, too many consumers in relation to producers weakens the economic capacity of the population. But if population growth is reduced, GNP per capita will increase faster, the percentage economically active people in the total population will rise, and more can be spent on consumption as well as on investments in higher production, more housing, etc. This is a tempting argument, but a false one.

First, contrary to what is stressed in the neo-Malthusian models, we generally find a positive correlation between population growth and production growth, i.e. the more people the bigger the total labour force and the market and the more is produced. (Kenya, for instance, is "more developed" than Ethiopia but produces less, simply because the population of Kenya is smaller than that of Ethiopia.) Thus, a higher population growth in fact encourages a faster increase in total production. A comparison of 67 underdeveloped countries (each with more than one million inhabitants) shows that, contrary to what the neo-Malthusians claim, during the period 1960–1970 there was no connection between population growth and growth in GNP per capita (all data from "World Bank Atlas", 1972). Actually, the coefficient of correlation was slightly positive, which is in agreement with a statement by Colin Clark who has insisted that countries with a higher population growth also show a faster growth in GNP per capita. Although it casts doubt upon the Malthusian argument, it is not definitely refuted by such ambiguous statistics. With the very heterogeneous economic structures of the underdeveloped countries, cross-national statistical analysis is notoriously deceptive, but it can at least be used to demask simplistic reasoning.

Second, from the asserted general connection between a fast increase in population and a decrease in per capita consumption (a "natural law"), it would, according to the neo-Malthusian models, automatically follow that a smaller size of population results in a higher standard of living. This inconsistently implies that starvation in one area after a while would benefit the whole country (compare the discussion above, concerning the "desirability" to limit the growth of the poor in order to secure the living standard of the rich). This Malthusian paradox was already pointed out by Marx in his study of Ireland: despite the potato famine of the mid-1840s taking almost 800 000 lives and despite the ensuing mass emigration to America, the Irish economy stagnated, unemployment increased and average per capita consumption decreased.

Third, there is no guarantee that a higher average production per capita will automatically change the distribution between consumption and investment in favour of the latter, neither in poor communities where the struggle for immediate survival gets priority, nor among the landed bourgeoisie who often prefer the foreign banks and imported luxury goods to economic growth in the national interest. Moreover, the argument that a higher percentage of people in economically active ages to total population will strengthen the economy and increase the savings is unrealistic so long as a higher production is primarily accomplished through higher labour productivity and unemployment in the periphery often amounts to 20–30%.

Fourth, the rapid decreases in the birth rates, which the modellers predict birth control programmes will lead to, are unrealistic. Tunisia planned to decrease its birth rate from 43/thousand in 1968 to 34/thousand seven years later, Dominican Republic from about 45 to 28/thousand in ten years, Jamaica from 34 to 25/thousand in eight years, India from 40/thousand in 1970 to 32/thousand four years later and to 25/thousand around 1980–82. All these plans should be seen as political manifestations with no hope of being realized. Population growth control programmes in the periphery have so far succeeded in decreasing the birth rate by at most two per mille units. Despite these bitter and costly experiences the unrealistic political targets are translated into mathematical assumptions: an artificial decrease in the birth rate by half in 20–30 years is a common prophecy in these projections. Such playing with figures can, no doubt, only be politically motivated.

Although qualitatively different from the technocratic and mechanistic projections of various optimistic neo-classical economists, another neo-Malthusian approach is the prophecies of future crises, which increased in popularity as a reaction to the political movement of spring 1968. In these pessimistic visions there is no way out of the economic and social degeneration caused by the population growth. One can still scent the ghost of Malthus: man is put in a corner with mouth and stomach but with no hands, as a passive spectator of his own inevitable decay. As a member of the periphery his survival is made dependent upon the goodwill of the centre—the "New World Poor Law". The inherent contradictions of capitalism are not recognized, but the uneven growth of production is steered by undefined and elusive forces. Yearly fluctuations in food supply are made the irony of fate. Hunger and famine become inevitable allies. The well-known prophet of crisis, Georg Borgstrom, insists that the human race has long ago passed the limits of the world's resources. Despite his putting a ceiling of reasonable survival at two billion people, he expects the world population to reach 15 billion around 2025. In another cry of distress, "A Blueprint for Survival" (an appeal by members of *The Ecologist* in England in 1972), the optimum world population is around 3·5 billion but probably less. Paul Ehrlich believes that when we become six billion people on this earth, the death rate will pass the birth rate and the population size will again diminish.

At the antipode we find more of optimism, as exemplified here by J. C. Saigal:

> Keeping in view the real situation, as it exists in the Third World, it can be safely stated contrary to what the neo-Malthusians want us to believe that the combination of much higher productivity and increased planted acreage by bringing the reserves of arable land under cultivation could cater for the food needs of a population many times greater than the present world population. What is required is the basic social and economic change in the countries of the Third World which will bring about rapid increase in agricultural production and productivity. . . .
>
> Although the earth is finite, its potential resources are so large when man's creativity is applied to them that it is meaningless to set arbitrary limits for world's population for an indefinite period in future.[27]

Others are more precise than Saigal. Some believe that the world can cater for a population of one or two hundred billions. A certain Professor Socolow even reckons upon 3800 billions, all with the living standard of the average North American of today. Such unrealistic projections remind one of rather naive expectations of utilizing the moon or the planets as sources of non-renewable raw products, or of removing hundreds of millions of people from densely to sparsely populated areas. All we can say is that the truth is somewhere in between the extremes and nobody can claim to know exactly where. Besides that, an exact figure of the maximum population would be just another academic exercise so long as the political resources do not suffice to keep the present world population away from the fringe of hunger and famine, it is impossible to estimate the upper limit of the potential food production of the world, since the price of a total exploitation of the global resources that has to be paid in the form of a degenerated environment, can hardly be valued. Instead of mere guesswork of alternative futures the possibilities for the future are better understood through an analysis of present-day underdevelopment. We shall here limit this analysis to the causes of rural exodus and urban poverty. Such an analysis implicitly refutes any neo-Malthusian explanation.

When Marx analysed relative overpopulation he referred to the victims of capital accumulation in Europe during the early phase of the industrial revolution. However, in order to better understand the economic conditions of the broad masses of the periphery the concept demands a widened definition. A majority of the population are small subsistence peasants, who are too weak to withstand external economic pressures.[28] Because of the very biased ownership and control over land in many countries, most of the farming population have to depend on small plots of land which hardly sustain a minimum of subsistence. Simultaneously, a minority of big farmers enjoy extensive areas of fertile land. In these countries the relative overpopulation is striking, not measured in the average population density but in the small peasants' access to land. The rural economic structure in Central America of the mid-1960s may serve as an illustration. Here the landownership was (and still is) concentrated to a small group: whereas 90% of the holdings constituted less than 20% of the land, 1·4% of the holdings grasped 52% of the total areas.[29] This means that over half of the total cultivated area was on farms which were, on average, 170 times as large as the plots of the poor peasants. While a few powerful landowners and foreign companies produce a surplus for export, lack of land and food is a reality for a major part of the peasant population. The latter belong to the relative overpopulation of the rural areas.

During the early industrialization in Europe people were to some extent "pulled" from the countryside to the towns. A growing industry swallowed some of the manpower that was released from the agriculture through rationalizations and the introduction of more efficient techniques of farming. In the periphery of today the situation is somewhat different: people are evicted from agriculture and "pushed" to towns, often against their own will and usually without finding new jobs. Land was expropriated by the colonial powers, or concentrated on big estates, and large areas were transferred from food to cash crops. These are processes which were started in the eighteenth and nineteenth century. They were the foundation of the biased agricultural structure which has developed in several countries during this century. The last decades have been characterized by rural economic growth and more poverty, side by side.

The so called green revolution gave new hope for the 1960s. In several countries wheat and paddy production increased, thanks to the application of high-yielding-varieties (HYV) and of fertilizers. But technical backlashes turned optimism into another era of pessimism in the early 1970s. Moreover, those who could take the main advantage of the higher production were the middle-peasants and above, i.e. those who could afford the high costs of modern inputs. Poor peasants, who could not get access to the new technology, not even on credit, fell out of the picture in this "revolutionary process". In several countries this led to a further concentration of land ownership and a strengthening of the capitalist mode of production.

Mexico was the first victim of the "green revolution", introduced by the Rockefeller Foundation and Norman Borlaug (which later rendered him a Nobel Prize in Peace). The wheat yield reached unprecedented levels but not for the benefit of the active farming population. In 1960 over half of the agricultural labourers were landless. In the countryside 28 million people lead a life as wretched as before the Mexican revolution. Twenty per cent of all arable land and 60% of all irrigated land are still in the hands of a few big landowners, who produce 90% of all marketed foods. A few own

much land, many own little, and more still own nothing. Consequently, Mexico City has grown from 1·5 to 10 million inhabitants
from 1940 to 1970 and is now the second biggest city in the Third
World. The parallels with Puerto Rico, as discussed above, are
striking: the economic system of Mexico cannot any longer accommodate its own people, and seven million Mexicans are permanent
or seasonal labourers in USA, working for wages close to minimum
of subsistence. Mexico not only exports its surplus population but
also its surplus food: every day vegetables and truckloads of live
cattle find their way to the rich market in the north. That is how the
average American is able to gobble up some two kilos of meat every
week, while his southern neighbour goes hungry.

The example of Mexico refers to changes within peasant agriculture and to capitalization of the agriculture, but the relative overpopulation is also found within large-scale commercial farming.
After comprehensive studies of the plantation economy, the West
Indian economist, George Beckford, has found that

> Plantation owners have a vested interest in securing as much
> available land as possible, not so much to use it, as neo-classical
> economics suggest, but rather to withhold it from use, thereby
> ensuring their perpetuation as a class and the plantation system
> as a whole. The association between underutilization of land and
> labor is evident everywhere in the plantation world. . . .
> The important conclusion we wish to draw is that unemploy-
> ment and underutilization of land in plantation economies are
> structural phenomena that inhere in the system itself. This has
> hardly been recognized anywhere in the abundant literature on
> unemployment and underemployment in underdeveloped coun-
> tries. Yet it is as important as most of the currently accepted
> causes of unemployment in these countries.[30]

Agriculture still constitutes the main economic sector in the
periphery but the uneven distribution of the fruits of production
does not allow a major part of the population a reasonable nourish-
ment. The lack of food for domestic consumption should further be
confronted with the large areas of un- and underutilized land, the
relative rural overpopulation, the rural exodus of manpower, and, in
some cases, the export of food and cash crops to the rich countries.
The effect of this sad paradox is seen in the growth of an unproductive and undernourished proletariate in the towns. The severity of
the problem varies from continent to continent, from country to

country, and even within countries. The rate of growth of urban areas is a function of political realities and consequent rural conditions of the respective countries. Thus, contrary to the neo-Malthusian assertion, the rate of urban agglomerations is not related to the rural population density. A study of 31 randomly selected African countries, based on data collected by the Economic Commission for Africa (ECA) around 1970, actually shows a slightly negative correlation between the percentage of population living in towns with more than 20 000 inhabitants and the rural population density, measured in number of people per square kilometre of arable land. To make it clear: the study of those countries does not indicate that the rural population density has anything to do with the number of people who move from rural to urban areas. As we have seen, the reasons for the rate of rural exodus are of a political nature.

The rural depopulation can be slow but still have noticeable effects on the growth of urban areas. In Africa about 20% live in towns and 80% in the countryside. Every year about 1% of the rural population—far below the natural increase (births minus deaths) migrate to towns. This means a contribution to the urban growth of as much as 4% per year. To this should be added the urban natural increase of about 2·5% yearly, and the resultant total urban growth is 6–7% yearly. But since most of the urban immigrants are young people, the labour force grows even faster, maybe by 8–10%. This figure should be compared with the yearly increase in employment opportunities in productive work, which is rarely above 3–4%. Had there not been opportunities of unproductive employment in the public and private service sectors, the rate of unemployment would have gone up by some 5% yearly. Thus, the visible urban relative overpopulation is partly alleviated by a growing public sector, with all its implications of bureaucracy, corruption, and allocation of potential development resources towards unproductive activities, and by a growing army of cheap private service personnel who attend on the well-to-do and further articulates the imbalance between demand and supply, i.e. the contradictions between rich and poor.

Capital intensive investments in industry usually tie a certain portion of the domestic capital (joint ventures between foreign and domestic public capital are an effective means for the transnational companies to eliminate competition and to avoid labour disputes, in both cases with assistance from the host state); this leaves less capital for local investments in the labour-intensive sectors, which further accelerates the rate of unemployment. Since they are too poor, a majority of the population are locked out from the consumption of locally manufactured goods above their basic needs. Only a minority of the employees have incomes sufficiently high to allow for the purchase of goods beyond these needs. With the exception of light industries, like breweries, food and textiles, we can without exaggeration assert that when the needs of the upper and middle classes are satisfied, the market is more or less exhausted. New investments become less and less profitable, unless directed towards the export market (cf. USA's investments in Latin America, and Japan's in South East Asia), and the growth of those industries which produce for the local market is hampered. Capitalism places a pitfall in the way of development, unemployment persists and the circle is closed.

Ethiopia can illustrate this argument. Prior to 1975 the exploitation of the peasantry and the poverty in towns meant that the circulation of money was mainly limited to the small upper and middle classes. With almost non-existent purchasing power in the rural areas and the low purchasing power in the towns, the market for manufactured goods was limited. This was the main bottleneck to an expanding industry in Ethiopia. Industry production increased by 15% yearly during the second half of the 1960s—a fast relative growth but slow in absolute terms, due to the low starting point. These 15% can be broken down into an increase in labour productivity of 11·3% and a growth of employment of 3·3% yearly. That is, the increase in production was to three-fourths due to imported new machinery in a progressively more capital-intensive industry, mainly controlled by foreign interests. In 1970 only some 100 000 people worked in the industry sector (industries with more than five employees), corresponding to much less than 10% of the potentially economically active urban population (all able-bodied non-students aged 15–60). The employment growth rate of 3·3% should be compared with the population growth of the bigger industry areas which was 7–8%. Accordingly, unemployment rose in the bigger towns, in absolute as well as in relative figures. Those with a job often had a working-day of ten hours or more. The labour exchange offices of the three biggest towns—Addis Ababa, Asmara and Dire Dawa—were able to find jobs for 22% of those who were in search work in 1968 but only for 9% three years later. The profit motive, not the necessity of more employment, governed the model of economic growth. A too high degree of capital-intensity in production and long working-days preserved a high rate of unemployment and a ruthless competition for work, whereby wages could be forced down to levels even below the poverty-line. Those in Ethiopia who could not find productive work or employment in the state sector either had to live as parasites on relatives or to join the already overpopulated private service sector, as domestic servants, street vendors, shoe-shiners, bar-girls, etc. (the situation has not really changed today, half a decade after the overthrow of the old feudal system).

In Asia (except Japan and China) production within the import-substituting light industry and the export industry increased by 125% between 1955 and 1966, according to UN-statistics. Imported technology accounted for almost half of this growth. In India, where some £200 in investments would suffice to employ two persons in useful production, in the early 1970s every new job in modern industry costed almost £70 000, on average. Under these circumstances not even an entirely effective population growth control programme could hinder the swarms of unemployed to grow. Despite this the Indian government spent some £50 million on such programmes in 1972 (a sum which would have been enough to create half a million new jobs), to which should be added contributions to these programmes from at least 23 various bilateral and multilateral organizations. This is how Pierre Pradervand looks at it:

> Certain countries like India, feeling themselves "up against it", multiply by five the reward given to men for having themselves sterilised, and sterilise from 70 000 to 200 000 persons in a few weeks in family planning "festivals", which the foreign experts describe as "a tremendous success". Success? Or a sign of failure of a system which offers the surgeon's lancet as an alternative to unemployment?[31]

We shall stay in Asia and end this chapter with a brief comparison of India and China. Towards the end of the 1940s these two big countries had about the same preconditions of development (here, religious and other cultural variables are admittedly left out of the comparison), and about the same population growth rate. Today, economic self-sufficiency, a high rate of investment, lack of unemployment, and absence of inflation in China stand in sharp contrast to the development stagnation of India. In India, land reforms have been planned, in China they have been implemented; in India much of the surplus production is spent on luxury consumption, in China it is invested; as we have seen, in India investments primarily go towards capital-intensive industrialization (some with capital from abroad, though the national bourgeoisie is strong compared to the situation in most other underdeveloped countries), in China investments are balanced between the growth-generating and the mass-production sectors of the economy (since the withdrawal of Soviet aid in 1960, entirely independent of foreign aid); in India development is measured in the growth of GNP, but in China in employment and consumption for everyone—and yet the average annual GNP growth rate over the period 1952–1972 was higher for China than for India. More than two decades ago, India attempted to develop with the help of population growth control, so far with few noticeable results, but in China family planning activities with active popular involvement did not start until the mid-1960s (during the Cultural Revolution) when people were economically more motivated to limit their number of children. According to its own statistics, China's population growth rate dropped in ten years from some 2% to 1·2% annually in 1975.

Needless to say, the western and westernized neo-Malthusians do not consider those factors which so far have steered China's development. But they gladly refer to China's national family planning programme in order to justify similar programmes in India or in other countries. Bearing in mind the qualitative differences between Indian capitalism and the Chinese model of socialism, this is an opportunistic argument, as a last resort, the ultimate purpose of which can only be to disguise the inequalities and the deep economic contradictions within the Indian society.

It is too often stressed that the reproduction of population in the Third World is the result of unplanned and irrational behaviour and, therefore, a pure biological concern. This biological phenomenon is portrayed as the main obstacle to socio-economic development, and it is suggested that an artificial reduction of fertility would contribute to the eradication of the most serious manifestations of underdevelopment. This is the view held by many "scientists" who have not attempted a definition of "underdevelopment" or an investigation of

trends in births and deaths and their interrelations with the economic causes of misery, hunger and famine. These "scientists" deny
that the causal connection is the reverse, namely that high birth and
death rates and rapid population growth subsist as consequences of
the socio-economic conditions. A reduction in fertility and in the
rate of population growth can therefore only be achieved through
means which concentrate on the very causes of this high growth
rate, i.e. the unfavourable socio-economic conditions of the masses.
In the light of the present situation in most parts of the periphery,
there is therefore no rationale for a policy which aims at decreasing
the growth of its main asset in the development process—its
people.

To tackle population without recognizing its political and economic environment ultimately leads to results unaimed at or even to
failures. The individual's economic situation, which is partly decisive of her social behaviour and general welfare, is a reflection of
the economic system of the society to which she belongs. But as the
Third World looks today, this system depends to a large extent on
external economic relations which prevent self-reliance. These relations are well-known: the connection between the Sahel famine and
European colonialism and neo-colonialism, between the starvation
wages of the Chilean labourer and the CIA and ITT of USA,
between the underdeveloped agriculture of Colombia or Pakistan
and the American Public Law 480 (dealing with US grain "aid"),
between the undernourished child in Brazil or South Asia and the
Rockefeller Center in New York.

To control the reproduction of the poor people is a piece of
cynicism unless they have themselves asked for it and unless they
are allowed to take active part in the planning of such a programme. To facilitate for people to plan their families according to
their own wishes is a matter of course. If a woman finds it
essential to limit her number of children, she should be given the
opportunity to do so, but she should also be given the right to
education, a productive job, a stable economy, a meaningful social
standard and other fruits of a well-planned development. Population control means that people are controlled by others, family
planning means that people control themselves. The two concepts
are irreconcilable.

Notes

1. Smith, A. (1973). "The Wealth of Nations", 182–3. Penguin.
2. Townsend here refers to the English *Poor Law* of 1601, which decreed the duty of the propertied class to take care for the livelihood of the poor. The law was replaced in 1834 by *The New Poor Law*. Its new approach was in line with Malthus's ideas.
3. Townsend, J., "A Dissertation on the Poor Laws, by a Wellwisher of Mankind", London, 1786; quoted by Karl Marx, *in* "Capital" (Everyman's Library, London, 1968, p. 715).
4. Malthus, T. R. (1970). "An Essay on the Principle of Population" (1st edn London, Macmillan and Company, 1926, p. 13), p. 71. Penguin.
5. Engels, F., Outlines of a critique of political economy. *In* "Deutsch-Französische Jahrbucher", 1844; quoted by Ronald L. Meek, *in* "Marx and Engels on the Population Bomb", The Ramparts Press, Berkeley, 1971, p. 63.
6. Engel's letter to Lange of 29 March 1865, quoted in Meek, op. cit., p. 87.
7. Engels, "Outlines of a Critique of Political Economy", op. cit., in Meek, op. cit., p. 57.
8. "An Essay on the Principle of Population", op. cit., p. 77.
9. Ibid.
10. Engels, "Outlines of a Critique of Political Economy", op. cit.
It might be of interest to note that the length of the working-day was a more important issue than that of wages during the end of the nineteenth century. Higher wages are in the interest of the active labourers whereas fewer working-hours are in the interest of the whole working class, as more pebple are given the opportunity to find jobs. So, for instance, the International Metalworkers' Federation was established in 1893, when metalworkers in several European countries decided to join their efforts in the fight for an eight-hour day.
11. "Capital", p. 574n and pp. 697–8.
12. "Capital", p. 698.
13. Hugh Moore was a big capitalist—started Dixie Cup Company—and has spent almost one million US dollars on campaigns for population control. He was president, auditor and director of his own organization, the Hugh Moore Fund. He was also one of the founders and then vice chairman of Population Crisis Committee, vice president of the IPPF, chairman of Population Reference Bureau and director of Campaign to Check the Population Explosion, a campaign that during the late 1960s preached that "a world with mass starvation in the underdeveloped countries will become a world of chaos, riots and wars. And a perfect ground for communism to breed. We cannot afford another half a dozen Vietnam or even one more. . . . In our own interest we have to go out and help the underdeveloped countries to control their populations".
14. See, for instance, The armed uprising in Ceylon. *In* "Monthly Review", January, 1972; and Gough, K. and Sharma, H. P. (1973).

(Eds). *In* "Imperialism and Revolution in South Asia", MR, New York (especially the chapter by J. Obeysekara, "Revolutionary Movements in Ceylon", pp. 368–395).

15. Carl Wahren in an article in the Swedish magazine, "Ekonomisk Orientering", No. 4/1971, p. 21. Wahren was by that time the head of the Population Department of the Swedish International Development Authority (SIDA).

16. This book was written to induce the 1968 candidates for president to take up a position towards "the population problem" in their speeches. During Nixon's first period, 1969–1972, the USAID increased its yearly assistance to population growth control in the periphery from $35 million to $123 million.

17. Ehrlich, P. (1971). "The Population Bomb", p. xii. Pan/Ballantine, London. (First published in the USA in 1968).

18. Hitler, A. (1934). "Mein Kampf", p. 313. Münich (translated from the Swedish edition).

19. Ehrlich, op. cit., p. 1.

20. Sanger, M. (Ed.) (1925). *In* "International Aspects of Birth Control", p. 5. 6th International Neo-Malthusian and Birth Control Conference, New York (Introduction by Sanger).

21. Moran. R. (1971). (College of Education, University of Puerto Rico), Mental retardation and family planning in Puerto Rico. *In* "Proceedings of the Conference on Psychology and Family Planning", (Ed. by David, H.), p. 96. Nairobi (Kenya).

22. "Financial Times", 19th October 1974.

23. Ibid. The official figure for 1977 was close to 19%, but official unemployment figures are always underestimates, all over the world.

24. Silén, J. A. (1971). "We, the Puerto Rican People", pp. 92–3. Modern Reader, New York. See also Lewis, G. (1963). "Puerto Rico, Freedom and Power in the Caribbean". MR Press, New York.

25. "A Corporation and a Molecule—The Story of Research at Syntex" (1966). p. 51. Syntex Laboratories, Incorporated, Palo Alto, California.

26. Brody, J. and Lewis, J. (1978). The rising abuse of sterilization. *In* "Weekly Guardian", Jan. 4, p. 8.

27. Saigal, J. C. (1971). " 'Population Problem' and Economic Development", pp. 6–7. I.D.E.P./ET/2521, Dakar, April.

28. Chayanov, A. V. (1966). In his "The Theory of Peasant Economy" (Homewood, Illinois), he referred to the pre-revolution Russian peasantry, but that situation has little—if any—relevance to the periphery of today.

29. Marroquin, A. (1965). Cambios en la agricultura y sus repercusiones sociales. *In* "America Latina", VIII, 3.

30. Beckford, G. L. (1972). "Persistent Poverty—Underdevelopment in Plantation Economies of The Third World", p. 178. New York, Oxford University Press.

31. Pradervand, P. (1973). The best pill is development. *In* "CERES", p. 8. November–December.

Fertility and Subfertility as Health Problems—Population Control Versus Family Planning by the Family

Staffan Bergström

Procreation in a population is historically an allegedly rational phenomenon, a balanced reproduction for survival. Since the reproductive ability is related to the basic health level in the population, and thereby to the degree of poverty and misery, the pattern of procreation in a society must be considered an entity highly dependent on prevailing economic realities.

Control of procreation, fertility limitation or "family planning" has long been a controversial concept, mostly due to a widespread reluctance—religious and moral—against artificial interference with human reproduction. For more than two decades family planning has increasingly been a recurring ingredient in the supply of material assistance from Western countries to countries in the Third World. From the beginning opponents to this aid policy appeared to exist particularly among Catholics and among orthodox Marxists. The notion of "an unholy alliance" between Catholic and Marxist ideology was created.

The early controversy regarding the role of family planning in the development aid to poor countries was often due to an absence of a precise definition of "family planning" and its implications. Astonishingly seldom the question was raised: *who is planning what for whom and why?*

The concept of "family planning" evidently focuses on something of fundamental importance for the family. In everyday language the concept of "planning" usually implicates the determination of a certain need, which the planning is aimed to meet (urban planning, traffic planning, hospital planning, etc.). If, for a while, we consider these examples it seems obvious that the meaning (purpose) hardly is (or should be) to plan for the sake of the town, for the traffic or for the hospital, but rather for those people who are affected by the urban environment, by the traffic or by the health services in the hospital. No politician would dare to admit something other than this—at least not officially. With the same reasoning we should look at the concept of "family planning" and recognize—in analogy with the above examples—that family planning should mean a planning to be implemented according to the needs of the people primarily involved, i.e. the family.

This may seem self-evident to most people; as we shall see later, however, there is an opinion that has questioned this and is opposed to "family planning by the family".

In the Third World "family planning" is often met with sceptic attitudes. Obviously, much impoverished people reached by family planning propaganda do not recognize that there exists an absolute and exclusive priority for family planning offered to them as aid from developed countries. Traditionally the family in these Third World countries has always been planned—a fact often disregarded in the current debate. Already here, in the confrontation between today's essentially Western ideas of family size limitation and traditional concepts of family survival, the modern and technically advanced alternative is controversial by its isolating human reproductive behavior from the constant menace of extreme poverty in which this behavior takes place.

One of the invariable stigmata of poor families is an exceedingly high infant mortality. Since many basic economic and social conditions for a Third World family are reflected in terms of illiteracy, deficient latrine and water hygiene, communicable diseases, bad housing, malnutrition, etc.—all of which substantially contribute to an elevated infant mortality—child loss is a perpetual threat. This threat must be understood as a fundamental insecurity, strongly promoting reluctance to family limitation among impoverished families. Both subfertility and elevated infant mortality contribute to childlessness and to the problem of too small families. As a family health problem threatening family survival, childlessness is a neglected family planning ingredient.

Childlessness as a Global Health Problem

It is quite obvious that childlessness is a huge but badly recognized problem in many countries in the Third World.[1] For the woman in these countries subfertility or infertility means social victimization and persisting barrenness means destitution. The tragedies of barren women in the Third World are well known and unmercifully reflect the huge problem of infertility.[2]

Many epidemiological investigations demonstrate that infectious pelvic diseases and their sequelae constitute the principal cause of subfertility or infertility in the populations of Third World countries. Persisting tubal occlusion with poor prognosis means a lifelong punishment. These pelvic inflammations often display a more severe course than in rich countries.[3] This is due to malnutrition and other wide-spread infectious diseases prevailing in the poor countries. The fertility chances for Third World women suffering from an inflammatory pelvic disease is exceedingly bad and a cure conveying restored fertility is very seldom possible.[4]

Recent surveys indicate that roughly 10% of all women consultations to doctors (all categories) in the Third World touch upon infertility problems and that 25–50% of all gynaecological consultations concern subfertility or infertility.[5] These figures are particularly valid for African conditions but presumably hold true for vast rural regions in other Third World countries. A high prevalence of infertility has been reported by health personnel and scientists who have been working in these countries. It has been estimated that from the view-point of individuals the problems of infertility are five to seven times as frequent as problems of overfertility.[6] Still, an overwhelming feature of the family planning discussion in Western countries is the focusing on overfertility instead of paying a balanced and due attention to the problem of childlessness.

The community reaction to the barren woman in traditional societies is often harder than in "modern" societies. Obviously it is important to understand this reaction properly. Among materially poor people a large family is an asset and an expression of wealth and social status: each new child is not only one more mouth to feed but soon also has two hands, useful for the subsistence of the family. This is particularly valid in societies where social security is hardly available, not even for minimum material standards. In some regions in Tanzania this severity of barrenness as a social stigma is illustrated by the predominant opinion that the deceased barren woman should not be buried but left to decay in the woods.[7]

In order to understand the community reaction to childlessness it is of importance to distinguish different meanings of this concept. Three categories are usually recognized:[8]
(1) infertility
(2) pregnancy wastage
(3) child loss.

The extent of childlessness can be measured in various ways; common to most of these is the problem of underestimating the prevalence of miscarriage and intrauterine foetal death. These events are often associated with negatively charged taboo concepts and accordingly concealed on direct questioning. Furthermore, infant mortality is often regarded as shameful and as a sign of maternal neglect; thus there is a tendency that the prevalence of both pregnancy wastage and child loss is underestimated. This tendency is further aggravated by the fact that interviews regarding childlessness are often undertaken when the respondents have passed the fertile age, which means that most of the reproductive performance occurred 20–30 years back and is accordingly inexact.

The social implications of *infertility* can be illustrated by figures from several Third World countries. In Kenya up to 20% of all marriages are reported to have problems with low rates of fertility or infertility. A Kenyan physician has approximated that about 300 000 women in the country (of a total population of about 13 million) are suffering from involuntary infertility.[9] In countries like Cameroun, Mali and Upper Volta the infertility problem is equally severe.[10] In Gabon the low crude population growth rate of about 1% per year is considered to be due to the widespread infertility in the population.[11] In some parts of Zaire more than 50% of all women are affected by infertility.[12] Similar levels have been reported from Sudan and from other African countries.[13]

The main ethiology of *pregnancy wastage* is seemingly sequelae of earlier complicated pregnancies and deliveries, particularly soft tissue injuries in the genital tract. Among other causes, syphilis and various non-venereal communicable diseases play an important role. In endemic regions malaria is a major factor in pregnancy wastage as an additional anaemic component in the widespread generally prevailing anaemia among pregnant Third World women.

Child loss is perhaps the most important and most often neglected ingredient in the total picture of childlessness. Both gynaecologic and paediatric "causes" of childlessness are obviously in themselves only symptoms of a more fundamental impoverishment due to maldistribution of wealth and security. A high infant mortality rate has been shown to be related to a wide variety of poverty symptoms and in fact directly to economic downturns in a society.[14] Childlessness is thereby rendered its appropriate place in the family planning context: as a phenomenon directly related to the impoverished reality where procreation takes place. This perspective allows us to consider childlessness in a more accurate manner. There is one "input" factor (subfertility, infertility and pregnancy wastage) leading to a reduced procreation in relation to the need of the individual family and one "output" factor (elevated infant mortality and loss of children after the first year). Both these factors contribute to the perpetual threat against family security and survival and hence to the reluctance against isolated birth control campaigns.

For most people in Western countries it is certainly strange to think of helping Third World women to achieve the survival of *more* children. Would that help not be totally wrong and completely misdirected? Probably not. The bad reputation of much family planning assistance from rich to poor countries is readily explained by the conspicuously biased propaganda carried out in terms of overt population growth control. This mistake has made the United Nations Fund for Population Activities (UNFPA) pay attention to the problem of subfertility; UNFPA has declared that it is "prepared where it is possible, to support activities aiming at a solution of problems of underpopulation and too low fertility".

If this declaration is seriously intended and written with the purpose to be practised, family planning thereby has got its only reasonable place: as *one* integrated part of mother and child health care.

In traditional societies overfertility has been met in various ways.[15] The motives were—and are—to give the family a certain protection against too frequent deliveries. The spreading out of pregnancies (child spacing) is achieved mainly by different taboo concepts, for instance coitus prohibition during lactation. The milk production during lactation is often negatively influenced by starting a new pregnancy in the lactating mother. The consequence is that the breast-fed child gets less milk from the mother. If the waning breast milk must be replaced by (often infected) bottle milk, the risk of diarrhoeal diseases increases with ensuing mortality risk of the child. In these societies a relationship between sexual intercourse during lactation and decreasing amounts of breast milk has long been empirically clear to the puerperal woman and her husband. A consequence of this experience is the belief in a poisonous effect of the male semen on the breast milk. Lactation periods of several years are usual in the traditional communities and long periods between deliveries are therefore natural in these communities.

Migration and urbanization often lead to partial disappearance of customs, habits and taboo concepts of the original environment. Also customs and habits relevant to the reproductive pattern may vanish and be determined by the social and economic realities in the new environment. In an urban environment, for instance, an earlier habit of polygamy may disappear. This contributes to the different position of the woman as a sexual object in the towns. Venereal diseases may be more frequent with ensuing risk of infertility. The pregnancy risk may be greater and the woman must therefore look for different contraceptive possibilities to achieve a desired child spacing. In this situation, as we shall see later, illegal abortions represent the most probable but also most dangerous alternative to continued pregnancy.

Family Planning Versus Family Limitation

Family planning is often regarded identical to *birth control*. The meaning of the latter concept is seldom clear and at least two usual meanings can be distinguished, here tentatively called "individual" and "national" birth control. The first one is usually signifying prophylaxis or simply deliberate separation of sex and reproduction by use of contraceptives. The second one can either be expressed as "child spacing", like in Tanzania (where President Nyerere has expressed his concern about the risks of too frequent deliveries and about illegal abortions[16]): this concern has resulted in a positive attitude towards woman-oriented child spacing as a national objective in line with the Ujamaa ideology) or be expressed as a concern regarding national population growth in relation to national development efforts such as construction of schools, hospitals etc. This significance of "birth control" can be found in five-year plans in some countries in the Third World. The most known example is perhaps China, from which a great number of studies have been published.[17]

The "national birth control" may appear identical to another meaning of the family planning concept, viz. *"population control"*, or more correctly, population growth control. However, it seems clear that there is a distinction in the use of these two concepts. As we can see from the examples of Tanzania and China, birth control as a national goal remains distinct from what is generally recognized by the term "population control". In Tanzania and China family limitation is never regarded as a major prerequisite for social and economic development. In contrast, advocates of population control as a high priority measure generally regard family limitation as such a prerequisite in the efforts to combat underdevelopment. These divergent views clearly reflect the distinction between Malthusian and non–Malthusian ideology.

A common standpoint in the family planning debate is that the smaller the family, the greater share will be given to each of the family members. In Latin America posters are often announcing this message. In a trivial sense the message of the posters is naturally correct if one (wrongly) supposes that additional children constitute merely a heavy burden of subsistence and no contribution to the production within the family economy. This assumption is based on the fact that with a constant size of the total cake a bigger share will be given to each member if the family is smaller. But the posters want to tell us more than this: they want to demonstrate that the small family *in itself* is an asset since the family size as such is said to be decisive for the bad wealth of the family. This conclusion is consistent with the impression of the posters, e.g. the one from Colombia (Fig. 1); in this example nothing but the family size is differing in the two cases. The idea is clearly that by controlling the family size (by distribution of contraceptives) all families will have a better share of the existing wealth. It is obvious that this simplified reasoning must meet with antipathy and that campaigns of this kind have failed. Consequently, the establishment supporting this idea of population control has abandoned the overt propaganda favouring family limitation. Advocating such a limitation must be offending in communities, where children constitute a future precondition of survival for the parents.[18] In the absence of any economic support from society to old people in poor countries, ageing without support from children simply means starvation and probably death.[19] In this context the message of posters advocating family limitation evidently tends to focus our attention on the family size—leaving out of the discussion any aspects of economic injustice in the community—and is thereby a plea for a political status quo and for a maintenance of the prevailing economic order.

FIG. 1.

This figure represents a typically simplified message to overcome poverty merely by reducing family size. The message that "the best pill is the pill" is far from the better founded "the best pill is development".

Family limitation in Latin America often rests upon the idea of diminishing the huge underemployment on this continent.[20] In a study by the Latin American Institute of Economic and Social Planning (ILPES) and Latin American Demographic Center (CELADE) it was estimated that around 1960 between 40 and 45% of the economically active population was underemployed.[21] From this data an unemployment of a little less than 30% can be calculated, a figure that was valid at least as late as around 1970. It is often said that the pressure on national budgets in Latin America in terms of education and public health expenditures constitute an important argument in favour of family size limitation. It can be clearly demonstrated that alleged savings on education and public health are bound to be minimal because these sectors consume very little of the national product with the present distribution pattern of resources in Latin America.[22] The strategy of birth control will therefore be a failure, particularly since overpopulation is directly linked with the capital accumulation. As can be shown, the control of capital is limited to the high income sector of the population, which results in a highly distorted distribution of income in most Latin American countries. The ensuing underutilization of capital will lead to under-utilization of the labour force and thereby aggravating the underemployment situation in Latin America. Thus, family size limitation is no solution to "the problem of overpopulation" (=underemployment). The solutions are rather to be found in the interruption of the prevailing impoverishment by redistribution of wealth and security.

It is illustrative to consider the reaction against the idea of family limitation as a measure against poverty. In the USA black people have reacted violently against the disinclination of the Congress to organize "rat control" campaigns in the slum Ghettos, while the Congress is in favour of "population control"; the experience of the blacks is that

> in the communities where they live there is also a disproportion-ate amount of bad housing, a disproportionate amount of bad health and welfare facilities in general, or the non-existence of health and welfare facilities, a disproportionate amount of unemployment, and all that appears to them to be shiny and bright is our birth control services. In most instances, you people say family planning and use the word planned parent-hood, which denotes family to us, which means unit to us (one or more), and parenthood, which means production of children, and yet we hear very little concern expressed by you people about children already born. This lack of expressed concern and action causes us to be suspicious of your motives, produces our fear of your programs and raises questions in our minds about genocide.[23]

Why Have Family Planning Programmes Failed?

Controlling population growth in reality means control of the birth rate if we assume that the death rate is largely impossible to increase with politically acceptable measures (decreasing the expenses of health care facilities, hospitals etc.). What is then the experience today in Third World countries of the effects of implemented campaigns in favour of family limitation? It is a well known fact that family planning campaigns up to now have had small influence on the birth rate in the world. Although the numbers are uncertain it was estimated that during 1970 around three million births were averted as a consequence of organized family planning activities. These three millions correspond to a little less than 4% of the total world population growth during one year. Until recently it was not even disputed that family planning activities play an important role in the declining birth rates in some Third World countries. Demographic analyses have displayed that birth rates have not declined significantly in several countries with family planning programmes unless there have been spontaneous declines in the birth rates before the family planning activities were started. It is, for example, a common misconception that Japan constitutes a good example of the effects of a very intensely implemented family planning. As a matter of fact a long time before the national family planning activities were started a decrease in the birth rate was noted—from 34·8 to 16·8 per thousand during a period of about 35 years (1925–1961). It is reasonable to assume that the access to contraceptives in a society where economic development results in decreased birth rate—as in Japan—results in a demand of such contraceptives and an acceleration in the birth rate decline.

In the Third World there are a few, rather limited regions where family planning activities have been an alleged success. For the advocates of population growth control it must be discouraging that in spite of immense propaganda efforts and important investments, an essential reduction in the birth rate have not been attained but in small areas. Before the World Population Conference in Bucharest in 1974 a conference pamphlet announced the successful "island approach" as an encouraging fact.[25] This approach demonstrated the positive effects in Singapore, Hong Kong, Trinidad and Tobago, Mauritius, Jamaica and Sri Lanka. These regions are geographically isolated and are also in other ways different from the typical pattern of a poor Third World country. Moreover, they have a comparably low infant mortality which makes them different to other underdeveloped regions. Also advocates of family planning programmes (as a prerequisite for development) have admitted the failures of several such programmes in the Third World. The fact that formulated objectives in the family planning campaigns have not been attained has been recognized by demographers for many years. There exists even today a widespread and misconducted view that the priority in our time is more intense support still of population growth control activities in underdeveloped countries in order to make development at all possible.

In a recent survey Malcolm Potts of IPPF stated the failures of family planning programmes in the following way:

> In the giant populous countries of the world such as India and Indonesia, there is to date no evidence of any demographic impact from the effort that has been expended in the field of family planning. When India began its national family planning program the growth in population of the country was approximately 5 mill a year: now, after two decades of considerable effort (in relation to the limited resources of the country) the rate of population growth is approximately 13 mill/annum.[26]

To get an answer why the vast majority of family planning programmes have been failures it is of interest to study demographic characteristics of those countries where family planning programmes have been unable to approach formulated objectives. In countries where in fact birth rates have decreased, infant mortality is at least twice as low as in underdeveloped countries without this decline.[27] The direct relationship between a high infant mortality and the difficulties to influence and decrease birth rates is understandable when considering that very few of the children reach adulthood.[28] In India, for instance, a man and woman statistically should have at least five to six children to be fairly sure that one son is still alive when they reach old age.[29] Demographically it would obviously be wrong to give a family in this situation the advice to limit the family size to less than six. If the pattern of mortality and morbidity in such a society does not change, family limitation propaganda will obviously meet fierce resistance. The political implications of this were clearly demonstrated in India during recent years and is discussed in other chapters in this volume.

A similar situation exists in Pakistan, where a survey in 1968 revealed that, on average, a woman should have at least five children in order to have a reasonable probability of her husband having at least one son living when reaching the age of 65.[30] There have been attempts to question the value of children in underdeveloped countries and to question the very basis for having large families in these countries.[31] In various calculations it has been tentatively demonstrated that a smaller family will more easily produce a surplus of labour during the married life of the couple. With a large family the surplus is argued to be far lower and the disadvantages of such a family would not disappear when the children grow old. That consumption far outweighs production in childhood can be debated. Incredibly enough in the same context it is written about adults that "consumption again outweighs production". Obviously this cannot be true and any actual experience of Third World realities will demonstrate that *in the marginal economies of subsisting poor families,* whether rural or urban, an additional child is most often a net benefit rather than the opposite, aside from considerations of security in old age.

The failures of family planning campaigns actualize one of the questions that were considered in the introduction: who is planning the family? Obviously the Indian rural family and the official family limitation propaganda have clearly divergent conceptions of the size of the ideal family. The experience from India is not isolated; in parts of Nigeria four children are seen as too few and an ideal number is seven or more children.[32] In Kenya it has been demonstrated that the number of children—above six—desired by an average family well corresponds to the average number of children actually existing in a Kenyan family.[33]

The insecurity of the single family regarding the survival of their children to the extent desired contributes to the difficulties to plan the future at all.

The Uncontroversial and the Controversial Family Planning

There is a disease in the Third World which is seldom regarded as a disease in the usual sense but which has an immense mortality. It affects only women and the poorer the women the more dangerous is the disease. The disease has no ordinary medical name but can be termed "illegal abortion sequelae".

The prevalence of this disease is not well known but it is quite obvious that it is widespread in some countries. In Latin America there are some estimations of its prevalence: in Santiago de Chile in

1967 the number of illegal abortions was estimated at around 130 000 and the sequelae after these abortions were responsible for approximately 40% (!) of the total maternal mortality.[34] From the same source it was demonstrated that at least one illegal abortion occurred per every second birth. Interviews with women have displayed that about 25% of women in Santiago in the age range 20–44 years had gone through at least one illegal abortion and of these women about 75% had gone through four illegal abortions or more. A similar situation prevails in Colombia, where the number of illegal abortions has been estimated at around 100 000 per year.[35] Around 10 000 women in Colombia are expected to die each year as a direct consequence of illegal abortions. The social repercussions of this fact mean that the average woman forced to commit an illegal abortion is 25–35 years of age, usually with 4–5 children and with very low family income. In several regions in Latin America "the abortion disease" is one of the most common causes of death among women in fertile ages. Under such circumstances a woman's desperate "choice" of the most dangerous contraceptive method is a strong argument in favour of alternative methods. In this context the access to means of individual birth control is hardly controversial: here an extreme kind of desperation is at stake regarding the possibilities of women to participate at all in the necessary change of community structures, in which she is suffering from a double exploitation because of immense social injustice and male chauvinism.

When regarded as top priority, family limitation measures on a large scale in order to increase the wealth per capita in the Third World are obviously dubious and questionable. It is still not uncommon to meet the standpoint that family planning activities should be a precondition in an underdeveloped country before economic aid and assistance is to be discussed at all. Some years ago this standpoint was widespread and obviously constituted a marked pressure upon the utilization of aid offered to a country, sometimes approaching blackmail. In spite of notable efforts to give family planning programmes and campaigns highest priority in international aid the overall results of these programmes and campaigns have been poor in relation to the prognoses presented. Obviously, as demonstrated in other chapters in this book, the campaigns attract those who are motivated for individual birth control and few others.

The undue support of family limitation efforts at the expense of investments in basic family health is a characteristic feature of the view that mass poverty is caused by an uncontrolled procreation among the poor. The *investment per averted human being* corresponds to several months income of the poor family as quoted by Potts:

> It is difficult to argue, however, that the family planning budgets should consume a sum of money equal to or greater than that spent on health services. In 1956–1957, India was spending over 7000 rupees (US$1000) per birth averted; in 1958–1959 this figure fell to 700 rupees (US$100) and is now at the 200 rupees mark (US$30). Even current expenditure is equivalent to four months income of the average Indian.[36]

The tendency of *blaming the poor for their poverty* is inherent in the ideology of family limitation as a prerequisite for development. In a critical scrutiny of the underlying values Robert M. Park states:

> There is a much more damaging consequence of population control than the manipulation of people's fertility in relation to the material conditions of their life. This is the ideological function of "blaming the people" for the society's severely oppressive nature. The propaganda claims that population is the cause of people's problems: "You are the cause by your excessive irrational family size". Billboards advertise large families as the problem, not landlords, industrialists or foreign investors. Because there are "too many people" doing something meaningful about the overwhelming problems looming for cities like Calcutta, Djakarta or Manila means getting tough with urban squatters (former peasants forced off the land) by shipping them forcibly back to their villages (this has already been done in Indonesia). It does not mean expropriating landowners and setting up labor-intensive agricultural projects. Rather than encouraging collective consciousness and action on real problems, the ideology of population control instead proclaims the goal of individuals to be: have a small family and "get ahead", don't be like "them".[37]

In India the resistance to family planning among the impoverished masses is also well documented by Indian doctors.[38] A vast literature now provides ample evidence in favour of the recognition of fertility behaviour as a rational response to deprivation of basic survival conditions.[38]

The pioneering work carried out by Thomas Poffenberg and his co-workers on fertility determinants in Indian families clearly show the rationality in the prevailing fertility pattern. In concluding one of their research reports they state:

> When the cultural, social and economic realities of these village couples were understood and when the role expectations were known, with some understanding of the means by which individuals gained recognition and other rewards . . . their fertility behavior was "rational".[39]

Much recent research supports "the child survival hypothesis". In a recent survey by Taylor and co-workers it was stated that most evidence indicates that higher fertility is related to experience with or fear of child mortality and that their own data

> suggest that the measurable child replacement effect operates through subconscious expectations of child death. Parents do not seem consciously to link child mortality with higher fertility. Cross-tabulations show, however, that experience of child mortality is correlated with less favourable attitudes to contraception and reduced and delayed practice of family planning.[40]

The most controversial aspect of population growth control in general and of family size limitation in particular is the priority given to these activities in the field of international aid. With the massive experience available from the conspicuously bad outcome of family planning programmes in the Third World, it is striking to note the constant high priority given to such international aid within the USAID, particularly before the World Population Conference in 1974. The total American civilian international aid has not reached as low a level as in 1970 since 1945. In spite of this tendency a formidable increase in family planning assistance occurred from US$2·1 million 1965 to about US$75 million in 1970 and US$123 million in 1972.[41]

The tendency to isolate population growth from its social and economic determinants almost always arouses (a reasonable) suspicion among impoverished masses in countries receiving international aid. Sometimes the prejudice in our moral and political guardianship can be revealing; in 1973 the following quotation by Carl Wahren of the Swedish International Development Authority (SIDA)— presently Secretary-General of the IPPF—is significant:

> To get oneself a child should rank equal to get oneself any consumption commodity. And therefore taxes on children should be introduced. At the marriage or when two people in any way decide to live together they will receive two coupons. These entitle the couple to get themselves two children either on their own or by adoption. If the couple would like to get themselves more children they will have to get another coupon by an exchange from a couple content with one child or from a bachelor etc. One can also imagine a situation, in which a car coupon is changed with a child coupon. It is my resolute standpoint that restrictions of this kind will be gradually established in e.g. Sweden. Sooner or later we shall face this situation. And this is a better alternative than if we shall be forced into hunger disasters and the like. Of two bad things one has to choose the least bad one.[42]

The quoted IPPF official is primarily referring to Sweden but the reference to "hunger disasters and the like" must mean that he also advocates the introduction of a coupon system in underdeveloped countries. In that case we have to look forward to an absurd and disgusting future of coupon and child trade.

The coupon ideology appears so out of touch with realities and so isolated in the serious family planning debate that it is tempting to neglect it totally. The tendency to consider the population growth in a narrow and biased sense and as something separated from the community where it occurs is, however, to be found even among top officials within SIDA. Ernst Michanek, the former head of SIDA, a few years ago inaugurated a seminar on sex education with the following words: "To influence human sexual behaviour and thereby the family size is a question at long sight but the most important of our generation".[43]

The population growth should thus be attacked by attempts to influence the sexual behaviour of the individuals. Again, the obvious attempt to isolate procreation from the economic setting where it takes place must be offending for those who are to be blamed for their behaviour.

In countries where population growth is a steadily growing menace against the rich minority of the country, desperation within this minority is growing accordingly. The well-known failure of the proposed compulsory birth control programme in India meant a bringing down of the sitting Government, the only Government in India to have supported compulsory birth control. What happened in India validated the statement of a known demographer that: "efforts at coercion in the developing world would be more likely to bring down the government than the birth rate".[44]

The desperation within the rich minority in India is obvious in several ways. One of the most cynical attempts to isolate the exploited poor family struggle for survival from its social and economic context—by having large families—was presented in a post-Bucharest conference in 1974 in Stockholm by Dr D. N. Pai. The notorious idea presented by Dr Pai was based on the fact that sex determination by amniocentesis (examination of the amniotic fluid after its aspiration through the abdominal wall by a needle) is possible in early pregnancy. Since in India the value of sons is much greater than that of daughters it would thus be possible to tell an early pregnant woman that her foetus is female or male. By telling her the sex of the foetus she is expected to be easily persuaded to undergo abortion directly upon sex diagnosis in case of a female foetus. Dr Pai seriously seems to believe that selective abortions of girls will contribute to the solution of the problem of mass poverty in India. An alleged advantage of this idea would be that the value of each woman will increase because the number of women will decrease. One is tempted to ignore and neglect this incredibly cynical idea but it is important to realize that the idea is deeply rooted within the Indian family planning establishment and has obviously already been considered by the WHO. Abortion after sex selection is one of the most explicit examples of the desperation prevailing in countries like India where the explosive situation due to economic injustice calls for fundamental political change.

What Should be our Attitude Towards the Global Population Growth?

People questioning population control campaigns and family planning activities as highest ranking priorities in the struggle against underdevelopment, are often in a simplistic way accused of a cynical belief in revolutionary upheavals as a basis for their critical attitude towards population control. However, it is obvious that the social implications of accelerated population growth do not mean potential revolution in itself: India, Bangladesh, Haiti and many other countries with extreme and continuing impoverishment would not have existed if overpopulation as such were an important precondition for insurrection. Overpopulation often means perpetual and stagnant oppression as in Haiti and maintenance of "law and order". Naturally, facilities to help individuals to plan their future should always be welcome unless these facilities represent a false way out of poverty and misery. Diminished population growth in itself does not mean any guarantee whatsoever that poor people acquire more wealth: in several sparsely populated parts of the world, impoverishment is still continuing, e.g. in Paraguay, Malaysia, Ethiopia and Bolivia.

The world population growth is obviously a concern of great importance: it is indisputable that the growth of the world population has gone up if regarded in a historical perspective. But a continued, undiminished growth rate is impossible and therefore not to be expected. Up to now almost all measures undertaken have been largely inefficient—except one. This single successful measure is not cheap since it implies redistribution of wealth. But the overconsuming rich countries have not been willing to mobilize the massive solidarity that this measure would require to support the poor countries in the Third World in such a way that at least prerequisites for economic justice are soon created. Among other things this should no doubt mean a—virtually controversial—choice of recipients for international aid and assistance:

> In general terms, this would mean contributing to struggles in underdeveloped countries for economic security and better employment, especially for women, and for better health care (including birth control): it would also mean fighting reactionary ideologies like population control, racism, sexism and elite technology. Serious progress in modifying the material and cultural bases for family size would have potentially far greater consequences than would the ruling classes' population control programs, including possibly removing some ruling classes. In contrast, the argument that population control is now a top priority clearly assumes the changes listed above will not be realized.[45]

Obviously it would be immoral to act according to the prevailing pattern: first "aid" with the purpose primarily to control population growth in the poor countries and then economic assistance for development. Except that all experience shows that this is an unscientific belief in the isolated effect of contraceptive distribution, this belief also means an unacceptable attitude of guardianship. The question of the world population growth must not continue to be a discussion of distribution of contraceptives. All experience has displayed that a quick population growth is characteristic for those poor countries, where for instance illiteracy and infant mortality are ranking high. Either we recognize the root of this bad in "the sexual behaviour" or we recognize the setting in which impoverishment occurs and thereby understand the dependency of population growth on other factors than the copulation frequency.

This is a more important political commitment in which the issue of population growth today is one, and only one, part.

Notes

1. WHO Report (1975). "The Epidemiology of Infertility", Technical Report Series No. 582, Geneva.
2. Adadevoh, B. K. (1974). (Ed) "Subfertility and Infertility in Africa". Caxton Press, Ibadan.
3. Lawson, J. B. and Stewart, D. B. (1974). "Obstetrics and Gynecology in the Tropics and Developing Countries". Arnold Ltd, London.
4. WHO Report, op. cit.
5. Chatfield, W. R. *et al.* (1970). The investigation and management of infertility in East Africa. A prospective study of 200 cases. *East Afr. Med. J.* **47,** 212–216.
6. Pradervand, P. (1971). The ideological premises of Western research in the field of population policy. "African Population Conference". Accra, December 9–18.
7. Nyman, A., personal communication.
8. WHO Report, op. cit.
9. Eraj, Y. A. (1969). Family planning, the control of population growth and economic development. Seminar on population growth and economic development. Nairobi, December 14–22.
10. Vittachi, T. (1973). Making the invisible visible, "CERES" (FAO), p. 36. November–December.
11. Pradervand, P. (1970). Family planning programmes in Africa, OECD, Paris.
12. Pradervand, P. (1972). Les politiques de population en Afrique francophone de l'ouest—obstacles et possibilités. Doctoral thesis, Paris.

13. Modawi, O. (1976). Infertility in the sub-Saharan Africa with special reference to Sudan. Khartoum.
14. Brenner, M. H. (1973). Fetal, infant and maternal mortality during periods of economic instability, *Int. J. Health Services* **3**, 145–159.
15. Himes, N. E. (1963). Medical history of contraception.
16. Tanzania Second Five Year Plan, Dar-es-Salam 1969, p. 12.
17. Suyin, H. (1970). Family planning in China, *Jap. Quarterly* **17**, 433–442. Suyin, H. (1973). Population growth and birth control in China. The conference Board Record, pp. 51–57. Suyin, H. (1974). The Chinese experiment. UNESCO Courier pp. 52–55, July–August. Djerassi, C. (1974). Fertility limitation through contraceptive steroids in the People's Republic of China. Studies in Family Planning, January. Faundes, A. and Luukkainen, T. (1972). Health and family planning services in the Chinese People's Republic. Studies in family planning, July.
18. Santpur, S. S. *et al.* (1977). Poverty and resistance to family planning, *IPPF Med. Bull.* **11/3**, 1–2.
19. Santpur, op. cit.
20. Fucaraccio, A. (1973). Birth control and the argument of saving and investment, *Int. J. Health Serv.* **3**, 133–144.
21. ILPES-CELADE: Elementos para la elaboración de una política de desarollo con integración para América Latina. Sintesis y conclusiones. ILPES, INST/S4/I.2, 1969.
22. Fucaraccio, op. cit.
23. Stewart, D. L. (1968). Family planning, prejudice and politics: an analysis. California Medical Center. September 14 (mimeo).
24. Podyaschikh, P. (1968). Impact of demographic policy on the growth of the population. *In* "World News of Population Problems" (Ed. by Szabady, I.), pp. 231–251. Budapest.
25. World Population Year Bulletin No. 5, 1973.
26. Potts, M. (1974). The implementation of family planning programmes, *J. Reprod. Fert.* **37**, 475–485.
27. Pradervand, P. (1970). Obstacles to and possibilities of family planning in francophone countries of West Africa and the republic of Congo. "Family Planning Programmes in Africa", OECD, Paris.
28. Pradervand, 1970, op. cit.
29. May, D. A. and Heer, D. M. (1968). Son survivorship and family size in India—a computer simulation. Quoted by Poffenberger, T. in *Demography* **5/2**, 765.
30. Park, R. M. (1974). Not better lives, just fewer people: the ideology of population control, *Int. J. Health Serv.* **4**, 691–700.
31. Espenshade, T. J. (1977). The value and cost of children, *Population Bull.* **32**, 3–47.
32. Lucas, D. and Ukaegbu, A. (1977). Other limits of acceptable family size in southern Nigeria, *J. Biosoc. Sci.* **9**, 73–81.
33. Bondestam, L. (1972). Population growth control in Kenya. Research Report No. 12, Scand. Africa Institute, Uppsala.

34. Chile, Country Profiles, Population Council, October 1970.
35. Stycos, J. M. (1971). Ideology, faith and family planning in Latin America, New York.
36. Potts, op. cit.
37. Park, op. cit.
38. Santpur et al., op. cit.
39. Poffenberg, T. et al. (1975). Fertility and family life in an Indian village. Michigan Papers on South and Southeast Asia, 10, Ann Arbor, The University of Michigan.
40. Taylor, C. E. et al. (1976). Interactions between health and population, Studies in Fam. Plann. 7, 94–100.
41. Population Programme Assistance, USAID, Bureau for Population and Humanitarian Assistance, Washington DC, December 1972, p. 4.
42. As quoted in Västervikstidningen, October 11, 1973.
43. As quoted in Press Release from SIDA Information Department, April 10, 1972.
44. Notestein, F. W. Population change, freedom and responsibility. Lecture delivered at the University of Kentucky, February 18, 1971. Mimeo, quoted in Family Planning Digest 3, 5, 1977.
45. Park, op. cit.

People are Precious—A Critical Look at the Population Control Movement[1]

Pierre Pradervand

It is indispensable, if one wishes to have a relatively clear understanding of the ideas circulating among those who in the sixties wanted to control world population, (and this appears to mean especially the rampant population growth of the poor countries) to give a brief historical glance backwards.

When people refer to Thomas Robert Malthus today, they rarely bother to situate him socially. This is regrettable, for Malthus's ideas are far more the ideas of a class, than of an individual. The tremendous success of Malthus's ideas was due mainly to the fact that he made the poor responsible for their own plight. Poverty was the natural result of the fact that sooner or later population outstrips the food supply. Furthermore, by having large families, workers occasioned an over-abundance of cheap labour which drove down their salaries until their numbers receded and equilibrium was again established. All this, was ascribed to natural laws ordained by God. The only hope for workers was sexual restraint, abstinence or delayed marriage.

Malthus's ideas did not go unchallenged. William Goodwin, an early socialist, was to contest the Malthusian analysis and claimed—as most socialist oriented thinkers have since then—that the basic causes of poverty resided in the organization of society, and that this organization was what was needed to be changed, rather than eliminating people. This debate was to continue almost uninterrupted from the early years of the nineteenth century until today. History was to repeat this debate twice—in the latter part of the nineteenth century: first between the neo-Malthusians and the socialists and nascent labour movement (especially in Britain); and again from the 1950s to the early 1970s, with the birth of a truly world-wide movement of population control impelled by the West and especially the United States.

The neo-Malthusians—an expression coined to describe themselves by the militant disciples of Malthus who undertook to actively spread his ideas in the latter half of the nineteenth century—differed from Malthus in one important respect: they actively propagated "artificial" methods of birth control. But otherwise, they were strictly faithful to his thinking. From 1880 onwards, the British neo-Malthusian movement published a newspaper entitled *The Malthusian* the subtitle of which was, "A Crusade against Poverty". The neo-Malthusians saw themselves *first and foremost* as crusaders against misery, (at a later stage, eugenic arguments compended their sad philosophy by encouraging the procreation of the rich and the diminution of the poor, supposedly eugenically "less fit"). One of the pioneers of the movement, C. V. Drysdale, mentioned that the first aim of birth control was to diminish the birth rate until it came into balance with the means of subsistence, "in view of eliminating misery or absolute poverty". The same author wrote that "remuneration of labor depends on demand and supply, and *the only really effective means of improving the position of the workers lies in their restricting their numbers*"[2] (italics mine). The eugenic note was later added when Drysdale wrote that it was important to introduce birth control among the poor, because "the poor, improvident, mentally and physically inferior types flood society with weakly and defective offsprings".

Another apostle of the movement, F. B. Sumner, was to write: "A sort of Gresham's law[3] prevails in the multiplication of human beings. Evidence from a wide range of sources shows that roughly speaking the fertility of the various elements of our population is inversely proportional to their mental, moral and social worth. . . . If we grant, as we must, that these differences in worth are, in part at least, hereditary, the case for racial deterioration seems complete". Having made such a diagnosis, the author comes to the necessary conclusion that "to slow down reproduction among the relatively inefficient—the 'exploited' classes if you chose—would be at once the greatest possible single step in the improvement of their condition and an equally important boon to the human race of tomorrow".[4] By a strange coincidence, these "exploited classes", at least in the United States, were mostly poor blacks, poor Irish or dark-skinned South European Catholics, East European Jews, etc. . . .—certainly not middle class, white, Anglo-Saxon Protestants.

Even as remarkable a person as Margaret Sanger, who started her career as a quasi-anarchist feminist, as her birth control movement started attracting middle-class respectability and support, claimed that "the chief issue of birth control is more children for the fit, less for the unfit".[5]

The scene is ready for "broadening" the horizon, and the "dangerous" (or "inefficient" or "exploited") classes will slowly take on a darker hue, and be situated less in Manchester or New York, but more and more in India, China, Africa, Latin America. It is very important to realize this link between the birth controllers of the early twentieth century and many population controllers of the 1960s. Many of the latter ones spoke of dependence ratios, KAP surveys, (knowledge, attitude and practice of family planning), growth rates and the like, but below the veneer of scientific phraseology one found too often the same motives, the same fears, the same will-to-power in the form of controlling other people's numbers rather than one's own consumption.

Thus, in 1917 already, Dr A. Robinson, in a preface to the book by A. Moore aptly entitled "Uncontrolled Procreation, or Fertility against Civilisation" wrote:

> There is an important point we have to keep in mind. It is our duty to preach birth control in our own countries, the countries we like to call civilised. But we have an equal, if not greater duty, to disseminate the principle and practise of birth control in the backward nations, the nations with higher birth rates. It is of the greatest importance for the future of mankind that the Gospel of birth control be preached incessantly to the peoples of Russia, China, Japan, India, Mexico, etc. . . . . It is not good for the civilised nations to reduce their birth rate to the desired minimum and the backward races to breed without restriction. Troubles would certainly ensue in the following years. It behooves us to communicate with minds that understand us in different countries and to exhort them to become apostles of the religion of birth control. If we cannot find indigenous apostles, we shall have to send our own.[6]

Which is what effectively happened! Everywhere in the Third World, apart from China, family planning programmes—especially in the 1960s, but as early as the 1920s in India—were the result of Western influences, and most often of the direct intervention of Western experts ("apostles").

Birth control was seen by many as the solution to the *economic* problems of the colonial countries. It is no coincidence that it was in

Puerto-Rico, a former American possession, that birth control was first introduced on a large scale in the Third World. The *Birth Control News* of July 1937 quotes the acting governor of the island as stating that "the island, for a long time probably, would continue to be essentially agricultural with no industrialization in sight to provide work for the present unemployed. The inevitable conclusion, the Acting Governor said, was to *attack the evil at the source* through sane and humane birth control. He said the island's budget could not now provide elementary schools for all the children and that the number unable to go to school was increasing" (Italics mine).

Contraception rather than jobs: who took that decision? The formerly devoutly Catholic Puerto Rican people? Hardly.

The same pattern, with slight variations, was followed in many other territories.

As social reforms and anti-poverty measures were growingly adopted by the legislators of the Anglo-Saxon and Western European nations—and, also, as birth control came to be adopted on a growing scale for its individual and health advantages—the neo-Malthusian movement petered out. The movement—but not, of course, the thinking. For the problems were basically the same, and the issues of stark poverty were, as affluence spread in the West, to move to the former Western colonies (Africa, Asia) and zones of economic influence.

The white man's burden became the white man's fear.

As the balance of power slowly, very slowly, changed, and ex-colonial territories acquired at least a veneer of "independence" (albeit very formal, as is now openly acknowledged), and as the widespread application of various cheap public health methods dramatically lowered death rates in these countries, new problems arose. The local elites, put into power by the former colonial occupant or tied to Western economic interests by monied chains, could be relatively easily controlled. But the "stirring masses" resulting from the so-called "demographic explosion" (one of the greatest misnomers of modern history)—especially if they were hungry or jobless—could raise thorny problems. They could revolt. They might even "go communist" (and there were rather unpleasant examples of this evolution all too readily available: China, North Vietnam, Cuba, to a lesser extent Algeria and others). This would not only upset the balance of power but could—a much more serious problem—lead to decreasing access to cheap raw materials, raise their prices . . . who knows, even cut off their supply? The whole basis of Western affluence would instantaneously crumble.

This was, by and large, the reasoning which originally prompted powerful groups to encourage massive Western involvement in population control. A small group of people in the most conservative circles of American society started disseminating the idea of the urgent need for population control in the Third World. (A rather large number of books printed in the late 1940s and 1950s in the USA stated this very crudely.) Thus, in a book with the revealing title "Too Many Asians" published in 1959, J. Robbins candidly wrote, "there are too many Asians for their own good. They have been breeding trouble for themselves—and for the world as a whole". . . . "When the sun goes down on an Indian village, the people are left in darkness. They have no books, no movies, no television. There is only one thing to do—go to bed. There they find their sole source of recreation and amusement, their brief escape from the hours of hard work of the day. At the root of Asian's problem of population is copulation".[7]

Not poverty, drought, poor government, cheap prices for raw materials are the problem. . . . No, but some rampant libido unleashed on the Third World.

Much more sophisticated authors, even world renowned demographers, vehicled basically the same message, albeit in more acceptable tones. Thus K. Davis in a paper entitled "Population and Power in the Free World" wrote in 1958, "If it be granted that the demographic problems of the underdeveloped countries, especially in the areas of non-Western culture, make these nations more vulnerable to communism, the question arises: what population policies can the free world pursue? It would appear that an appropriate policy would be the control of birth-rates, the lowering of death rates, the provision of technical assistance and economic aid, and the formation of military alliances".[8]

Foundations and institutes were founded with the sole aim of studying the "population problem" (one never spoke about the poverty problem or drought problem; as for overconsumption, it did not even exist—to hint at it would have then drawn immediate ridicule). University centres received large sums of money to train specialists—the training being oriented more and more in neo-

Malthusian terms, even if the language used stayed scientific. (You can starve a man to death and state with "scientific objectivity" that "The interruption of signals on the electroencephalograph appears to have resulted from considerable diminution of the intake of daily calorie requirements"). Many sincere demographers in the population establishments have protested strongly against such accusations levelled against them by more radical population specialists, accusing the latter of being "un-scientific", when in fact the radicals were simply refusing to accept the very definition of the "population problem" and "demographic inquiry" made in the name of science by the leading population institutions.

Given the immense weight of the United States in world scientific research and the dominance of English in the field of scientific publications, given the availability of abundant scholarships in the field of population, the resurrected neo-Malthusian way of thinking rapidly spread in the 1960s to most of the Western World, and even many developing countries, not to mention international organizations. Anyone who has seriously studied the population literature of the 1960s—as this author did almost daily for eight years—can but be struck by the amazing (and—ultimately boring) similitude of analysis, concepts, language, in hundreds of publications.

Some misinformed radicals saw a world-wide "conspiracy" in all these developments. This strikes me as somewhat ridiculous. Everything has happened in a very open, public manner. The facts are there for anyone—with time and funds—to analyse. That the rebirth of the neo-Malthusian movement started in the United States was normal, given the role this country assigned to itself after the Second World War as guardian of the West against communist subversion. That the intellectual monolithism of the population establishment was built up so rapidly and on such a world-wide scale is of no surprise either, in a world of almost instantaneous communication. Today, scientific ideas catch on almost as easily as the hula-hoop, and travel as fast.

In the ideology of the neo-Malthusian movement—for clearly its contentions are more ideological than scientific, given the fact that they are refuted by numerous recent historical examples—in this ideology, population becomes an independent variable (i.e. one that has a powerful force and influences other factors like employment, health, crime, etc. . . . rather than the other way round). During the

1960s, a growing number of "scientific" studies and prestigious individuals pinpointed "population" as the number one enemy of development. Quotes of this type could fill pages, but two will be enough: the very prestigious Pearson report, published at the end of the 1960s, proclaimed that "no other phenomenon casts a darker shadow on the prospects for international development than the staggering growth of population".

And the President of the World Bank, Robert McNamara, went on record as saying that: "To put it simply: the greatest single obstacle to the economic and social advancement of the majority of the peoples in the underdeveloped world is rampant population growth". (It is to his credit that he considerably altered his position later on.)

The solution to the problem became thus immediately apparent: population control (euphemistically named "family planning"). "Scientific" surveys had shown that most of the women in these countries were apparently eager to limit their families. Large scale programmes, usually designed by Western experts who knew almost nothing of these countries save their luxury and air-conditioned villas, were designed to promote recently discovered, low cost contraceptives. When it appeared that women were not adopting these methods as rapidly as the surveys showed they should have done, more experts, better administrative methods, more surveys, and more efficient contraceptives, better mass communication programmes were urged—and adopted. In some cases, programmes were designed with the sole aim of urging women to adopt family planning without changing a single thing in their environment of dismal poverty, (as in an experiment run in the late 1960s in Tegucigalpa, capital of Honduras). Experts were dropped via helicopter on unsuspecting Himalayan villages in Nepal (1970), Moslem women coerced into buses to have loops inserted without any explanations (Tunisia, mid-1960s), young women given contraceptive injections against their husband's will (various African countries).

The result?

Measured by the hopes and expectations of the neo-Malthusians for rapid fertility declines in the mid-1960s, it appeared as a fairly costly failure, at least in some major countries.

A leading family planner stated in New York in 1964 that he expected the loop would "change the history of the world". World history has not changed much since then. Many people are much poorer, and getting geared up for the radical social and political changes some population controllers had hoped to avoid. In the countries where birth control has worked well (Taiwan, S. Korea, Singapore, Malaysia, etc. . . . .) a growing number of specialists concede that the successes have mainly been due to many other factors apart from the programmes themselves, that many people would have adopted antinatalist measures all by themselves. In the countries where positive results have come much more slowly, like India artd Pakistan, poverty has fast been recognized as the main obstacle.

Needless to say, none of these comments should be implied as a critique of family planning *per se*. In terms of womens' emancipation, individual freedom, family well being and health, family planning, if correctly presented, can be of immense value. But these were not the reasons which motivated most population controllers to promote family planning.

The one country that in the 1950s and 1960s did not use Western experts, roundly condemned Western theories, took a road diametrically opposed to the one promoted by the neo-Malthusians (social revolution and structural change leading to new antinatalist motivations and hence birth control, *rather* than birth control to prevent revolution)—China—is acknowledged as being on the way to solving the problem. Yet neo-Malthusians were writing of China as late as 1960, "China—quite literally—cannot feed more people. . . . The greatest tragedy that China could suffer, at the present time, would be a reduction in her death rate. We have watched Wong die, his agony past, by the side of the road. . . . Millions are going to die in the same way. There can be no way out. These men and women, boys and girls, must starve as tragic sacrifices on the twin altars of uncontrolled human reproduction and uncontrolled abuse of the land's resources".[9]

Today, China feeds three hundred million more people, well. Her death rate appears to be the lowest of the large developing nations, by a long way. Her land resources are being admirably exploited and will produce much more in the near future. Most people in China, it would appear, is literate, has a job and easy access to good health care. Clearly something was wrong (in the Western prophecies and the Western analysis) for China to have succeeded so well.

It is rather interesting that in the 1960s not a single socia..ɔɩ country in the Third World considered it had a "population explo-sion"—or even a "population problem". Some of them even rudely upset Malthusian theories by managing astonishing economic "take-offs" despite population growth rates of 3% p.a. (e.g. Albania). At least one vigorously encouraged population growth, despite already high rates of population growth (Outer Mongolia). Nearly all of them offered—and of course still offer—family planning integrated in maternal and child health programmes, to the extent that WHO gives some of them support (e.g. Cuba).

Could it be that these countries which, taken together, were no better off than others, might have a lesson to teach the rest of the Third World?

The World Population Conference held in Bucharest in the summer of 1974 was a major turning point in the field of population. The slogan "The best pill is development" summarized one of the strong currents of thought at the conference. At the same time, this point of view having been more and more widely acknowledged, a growing number of Third World countries have since then turned to family planning (often for very mixed motives to be sure). And a growing number of people in the West, given the growing strength of the ecological movement, are pointing to the importance of issues of consumption.

For is not the main "explosion" problem today Western consump-tion, which implies a very distorted distribution of world resources? I believe that the "population problem"—as traditionally defined in earlier Western treatizes on this issue—may well prove to have been the greatest red herring in the field of development. By stressing it in such a biased simplistic manner, *neo-Malthusian thinking delayed the solving of the number one development problem—which is popular particip-ation in development.* If twenty years ago India had undertaken massive structural changes, a real land reform, distributed services and resources more equally instead of trying to coerce illiterate women to adopt the rhythm method using coloured beads, it would not have attempted its disastrous flirtation with compulsory steriliz-ation in the mid-1970s; it would not have been admitting that a larger number of people were worse (not better) off than fifteen years ago (cf. the famous Dandekar study on poverty in India, in the early 1970s).[10] At the root of India's population problem is not "copulation" but an alliance of middle and upper class interests opposed to radical social, economic and political change.

Aaron Segal in his study "The Rich, the Poor and Population"[11] has admirably summed up the real issue involved in the field of population. He writes:

> The road back to population sanity involves a few simple, unpleasant truths. These are:
>
> 1. Fertility does not cause poverty, war, or social unrest although it can, combined with other variables, contribute to any or all of these occurring.
> 2. Reducing fertility may leave the poor just as materially poor as before unless other kinds of assistance are provided and changes made.
> 3. The task of reducing fertility will have to be done by members of particular societies and outsiders can only play a marginal role.
> 4. The determinants of fertility at the individual, societal or global level are complex and mutually interdependent and the problem is not primarily one of bringing to bear the heavy artillery of post-coital contraceptives.
> 5. We had better find some more meaningful reasons for helping the poor than fear of what they may do to the rich, if we really wish to eliminate poverty.
> 6. Trade, aid, immigration, income distribution, and maternal health may have as much or more to do with reducing fertility than furnishing contraceptives. For instance, if we want to help some countries reduce their fertility we might start in the U.S. by not recruiting a majority of their trained medical personnel to solve our own shortage; accept as permanent immigrants some of their unskilled young, (much as Europe's population problems of the 19th century were partly relieved by the export of more than 50 million unskilled young persons to North and South America, Australia and elsewhere); give poor countries a chance to sell us cheap manufactured goods which are labor-intensive, especially products which depend on employment of women, and be willing to pay more for their agricultural exports. . . .
> 7. We concern ourselves with the real causes of poverty within our own rich countries and do not rely on birth control as a form of conservative social control.
> 8. We do not ask others to do what we say rather than what we do. Until rich societies themselves adopt and take seriously population control policies they should lay off advising poor

countries to do so. Instead they should wait for governments to take the initiative and keep external population inputs limited. The Chinese are in a better position, morally and materially, to convince Africans to take population problems more seriously than we are.

9. We abandon the pursuit of coercive means of birth control. If we cannot, at home or abroad, help create conditions in which individuals will want to voluntarily reduce their fertility then we have no moral right to coerce.

10. We re-examine our own immigration policies so that we reduce the damage we are doing to poor countries through the brain drain. This primarily means creation of incentives to encourage the skilled to return to their home-countries, enjoying opportunities to go abroad. Where possible (e.g. USA in respect of the Caribbean, and European Economic Community in respect of North Africa), we should pursue immigration policies permitting a regular, permanent, legal immigration of young unskilled persons and their families, rather than the present illegal and temporary male migrant patterns. [11]

Simply the publicity pages of the Sunday edition of the *New York Times* magazine consume enough paper to print all the school books in the African state of Cameroon. Yet, we prefer using these pages to peddle the 57th make of whisky, cigarettes which are an acknowledged health risk, cars that pollute our streets and distort our urban planning, cosmetics that perfume our vanity, sick "porno" movies that distort our vision of love, "defensive" weapons that deepen our fears, rather than scale down our consumer *hubris* to more modest proportions—which, incidentally, would enable us both to start tackling problems of quality in our Babylonian citadels *and* have more resources to pay for the raw materials of the poor countries at decent prices. A full page advertisement for a 1974 Pontiac in the October 1973 issue of *Ebony* magazine (USA) read: "Obviously, we are out to make you dissatisfied with whatever you have".

What a ferocious irony in that word, "obviously": the rich countries economic system (because the USSR is closely following in our tracks) acknowledging that its aim is to create dissatisfaction. In the meantime, a berber tribe in North Mali was reduced in 1973 from 8000 to 16 (sixteen) people in 5 months while we were busy slimming excess weight due to overeating and over indulgence.

A basic motivation behind earlier Western drive to "control" the population of the Third World seems to have been fear. There are many others, of course, including a few authentic humanitarian ones and quite a few smelling of Victorian charity. It came out (and still occasionally does) in the language used daily to describe the rising world population: "The anthills of the Caribbean" (Le Figaro, Paris), the "rampant rate of reproduction", of the Third World countries, the "staggering" rates of population growth, etc. Graphs still depict the burgeoning population as a Hiroshima-like A-bomb cloud, and even such superb scientists as Nobel-prize winner Norman Borlaug could write about staring over his shoulder at the "relentless frightening advance of the population monster". Speaking of the Indians, he even wrote about "the population monster growling (sic) behind them".

In all this earlier talk about population, it seems that one fairly basic truth had been forgotten: population refers to *people*. If we claim that there are too many people on earth, then can we be so sure *we* are not the excess ones? We Westerners who individually consume and pollute as much as fifty or more African peasants? In all my years in the field of population, I have never once heard a member of the population establishment say there were too many upper-middle class white Anglo-Saxon Protestants in the world (they form the original "core" of the neo-Malthusian movement), but two such people have openly told me there were too many blacks, and countless others have implied this, be it in their writing or conversations.

Yet fearful attitudes have never helped build a better world. Fear has never built cathedrals, or empires, created art, fed the poor, opened the doors of prisons, cared for those in need, started revolutions—and there are many types of these. Fear of people still less than all the others.

We live in a world of growing economic, social and political interdependency (as the so-called "energy crisis" has only too aptly shown). One of the greatest dangers of today are parochial, selfish, ethnocentric attitudes which blind us to the realities of the world. Ultimately, our fate is bound to that of the Bengali rickshaw driver or Congolese peasant women as much as to our own job or country. We forget this at our own peril.

We need a broader, clearer vision. We need to see people as infinitely precious, infinitely beautiful, and not in terms of "negative dependency ratios", "frightening growth rates", and other similar heartless expressions. Are we afraid of our mother, or child, or neighbour, or husband? Then why are we afraid of Mohamed, Vijeya, Liu or Carita?

In the world of Genesis, Cain could say about Abel, "Am I the guardian of my brother" and at least hope to get away with it. In today's world of globalized economies and thinking, the Western Cains can no longer say the same. *Today, Cain will have to learn that he can only guard himself if he guards his brother.* The future of humanity rests upon this realization more than any other.

The cement of a higher humanity must unite mankind in a higher vision of its common destiny. If we want to survive, clearer vision and greater compassion, not better pills, is what is most urgently needed.

Notes

1. This article is a revised version of "How to Delay the Adoption of Family Planning", which was published in *New Internationalist*, 1974.
2. Drysdale, C. V. *et al.* (1925). Small or large families. *In* "International Aspects of Birth Control" (Ed. by Sanger, M.), Vol. 1. 6th International Neo-Malthusian and Birth Control Conference. American Birth Control League (inc.), New York.
3. An economic thesis of 1857 which concerned the value of money (editor's note).
4. Sumner, F. B. (1926). Is the voluntary control of population an idle dream? *In* "International Aspects of Birth Control" (Ed. by Sanger, M.), Vol. I, p. 76. 6th International Neo-Malthusian and Birth Control Conference. American Birth Control League (inc.), New York.
5. Sanger, M., ibid.
6. Preface by Robinson, A. (1917). *In* Moore, A., "Uncontrolled Procreation, or Fecundity Against Civilization", p. 9. American Birth Control League (inc.) New York.
7. Robbins, J. (1959). "Too Many Asians". Doubleday, New York.
8. Davis, K. (1958). Population and power in the free world. *In* "Population and World Politics" (Ed. by P. M. Hauser), p. 213. Free Press, Glencoe.
9. Vogt, W. (1960). "People, Challenge to Survival". William Sloane Associates, New York.
10. See, for instance, Dandekar, V. M. and Rath, N., Poverty in India. *In* "Economic and Political Weekly", Bombay, Vol. II, Nos. 1 and 2, 2 and 9 January 1971.
11. Segal, A. (1973). The rich, the poor and population. *In* "Demography in India", Vol. II, No. 1.

Is There a Population Problem in the Industrialized Countries?

Erland Hofsten

It has become popular in recent years to maintain that there is a population problem not only in the so-called "developing" countries but also in the industrially developed countries. The following quotation by B. Johnson (*People*, October 1973) is typical:

> The population explosion is a global problem, and it is socially, economically and scientifically absurd and dangerous to see it only as a problem of poor nations whose consumption of world resources and output of pollution is relatively slight. This opinion . . . insists that, despite their relatively small annual increase, the richest nations account for an important part of the population problem because their resource-use and environmental impact per head is between 30 and 60 times that of the average south Asian peasant.[1]

A similar thought, although expressed in a more cautious way, is found in paragraph 19 of the World Population Plan of Action, adopted by UN World Population Conference in Bucharest in 1974:

> Recognising that *per capita* use of world resources is much higher in the developed than in the developing countries, the developed countries are urged to adopt appropriate policies in population, consumption and investment, bearing in mind the need for fundamental improvement in international equity.

It is seen that the latter quotation also talks about consumption and investment. There is no reason to enter into a discussion about these items here, but what is the implication of these statements as regards population?

Both statements quoted above in fact imply that population is held responsible for depletion of resources, as well as for pollution and other environmental problems. The essence of the statements is that population growth should be reduced or stopped also in the developed countries and that this would have a favourable effect on the environment.

In my view, it is completely wrong in this way to blame population growth for diseases of society and to create the impression that a reduced number of births might help to solve environmental problems. That this is so may be gleaned already from the fact that in industrial countries the use of resources in the past have increased at a rate which is much more rapid than the rate of population growth.

Ever since the time of Malthus in the early part of the nineteenth century it has been popular in certain groups to blame population growth for defects in society. Malthus himself threw the blame on population growth for the genesis of mass poverty in England in his time. During the 150 years after Malthus one can observe that as soon as unemployment has occurred on a mass scale there have been those who have wanted to apportion population growth the main blame. As an example, after the end of the First World War the well-known Swedish economist Knut Wiksell wrote that the explanation of the considerable amount of unemployment around 1920 in Sweden was the discontinuance of emigration to the United States during the war years.

But arguments of this kind are misleading. The fact that two phenomena have run parallel cannot be taken to imply that the one has caused the other. There is no reason to believe that a slower population growth would in any way solve the problems of unemployment or, for that matter, of energy waste, resource-use or pollution.

What has just been said should not be taken to imply that the importance of population growth factors for society and its development should be denied. An analysis of this complex, however, requires more than simple Malthusian comparisons.

The main reason why the above arguments in favour of a reduced population growth in the developed countries have been brought up in recent years is no doubt because representatives for developed countries in their contacts with countries of the Third World so often have encountered arguments according to which the family planning ideas are racist-imperialist, in other words, the supposed reason why Americans and others are so fond of preaching family planning is because they fear that the peoples of the Third World will become too numerous and that as a consequence political and economic power will be lost to them.

By maintaining that a reduced population growth is considered relevant to developed countries as well, the family planning advocates hope that it shall be easier for their contacts in the Third World to accept the Malthusian arguments about the necessity for family planning measures. This is also a way by which it may be possible to divert opinion from the real issue, exploitation of the poor by the rich. This implies that the argumentation is dishonest.

In some countries—in the first instance United States, Great Britain and the Netherlands—the interest in favour of family planning has given rise to political movements, aiming at attaining "zero population growth". How should we look upon these movements?

There is no reason to deny that there may be developed countries with a very dense population, for which there would be obvious advantages if the present population growth could come to a stop soon or which would even benefit from a population size smaller than the present one. It should be remembered that with modern technology man sometimes requires much more space than in an earlier period. Not least motor cars claim much space.

As every demographer knows, it takes a long time before new demographic tendencies become manifest. This is why population growth in the developing countries will remain rapid, even if efforts to promote family planning were successful. In a similar way, even if the number of births in a population is considerably lower than is required in order to maintain the population size in the long run, it will take a long time before this tendency becomes evident in the form of a decline in the population.

With present low mortality from birth and up to the end of the reproductive period (40–45 years of age) the average number of births required per woman in order to maintain the population size amounts to some 2·1–2·3. Not even this low figure is however attained in many cases. In Sweden where mortality is so low that only 2·1 children per woman are required for reproduction, the present generations of women in the reproductive ages do not give birth to more than some 1·6–1·8 children. Although the number of children born to Swedish women has now been below the number

required for reproduction for many decades, the population has
continued to grow, even though at a very slow rate. The main
explanation for the above-mentioned fact is that it takes such a long
time for new demographic tendencies to become manifest. In
addition, reduced mortality in the higher age brackets, as well as
immigration have played a role. It is only now that the time has
come when a population decline may become revealed rather soon
(unless counterbalanced by migration).

The situation is similar in many other Western European countries. In a number of such countries the crude birth rate is so low that
a negative natural growth rate is expected to occur within a decade or
two. In the Federal Republic of Germany this has already come
about: since the early 1970s the crude birth rate has been lower than
the crude death rate. The "zero population growth" will therefore
automatically be realized in many cases.

The situation is similar in Eastern Europe. In most countries in this
region, including the European parts of the Soviet Union, the birth
rate has now for decades been so low, that it cannot be sufficient for
the reproduction of the population. This is a fact that has caused
anxiety, specifically with regard to the future development of the
labour force, and has led to pronatalist measures which have resulted
in a certain rise in the number of births in some of the countries
concerned.

From the experience gained in the 1930s and 1940s it is known that
it is necessary to be very cautious in drawing conclusions from
population data for short periods. Judging from period data it may
look as if reproduction is well below unity, but the deficit may be
caught up through the birth of children that have been postponed
during years of economic recessions. This is what occurred in the
1940s as compared with the 1930s when the economic depression
made reproduction look extremely low. At the same time, age at
marriage was reduced and the intensity of marriage increased.

Something similar may obviously occur once more. In other
words, the present extremely low birth rates may be followed by a
new "baby boom" in the 1980s. Although this possibility should not
be excluded, it is far from certain that it will appear. In fact, there are
factors which support the view that a repetition of what happened in
the 1940s is not to be expected. Thus, it is relevant to ask the
question, what is going to happen in a country where the rate of

reproduction for a long time remains below unity and where consequently each new generation is smaller than the former one. Without a considerable amount of immigration this tendency must, sooner or later, become manifest in the form of a decrease in the total population.

As has already been pointed out above, countries with a very dense population may welcome the prospect of a future population decrease in the country. However, it is never satisfactory to speak in terms of the total population only. Before accepting this conclusion we must therefore analyse what is occurring with regard to the age distribution of a declining population. If the rate of reproduction is so low that each new generation is—say—20% smaller than the previous one, the consequence will be that the proportion of old people in this population will be considerably higher than if the population reproduces itself. This will cause problems with regard to the maintenance of the society and—still more—the care of the old. The age composition of the labour force will also be a different one, with important consequences for the labour market. In a diminishing population there will be a higher proportion in the age groups 40–65 years as compared to the age groups 15–40 than will be the case in a stationary or a growing population.

The conclusion will thus be that a rapid decline in population may give a country serious problems of an economic nature. Also in the psychological sphere a decline in a population may have obvious drawbacks. If every generation is 10 or 20% smaller than the previous one, this will make it difficult to create a belief in the future potentialities of the population. It would seem that in most cases the ideal is a population which neither increases nor declines.

The relation between a decline in the population and immigration should also be considered. If a net natural decrease of a population shall really lead to a reduced size of the population, it is of course necessary that there is no immigration which offsets this net natural decrease. If the failing children are replaced by immigrants, no reduction in population size will obviously occur. It would seem that this is the way it often works. If the new generations in a population are small, the consequence will be a stream of immigrants.

The social composition of the immigrant population will always differ considerably from that of the home population. There will be a tendency for the immigrants to fill the occupations which require less training, implying monotonous work etc. Under such circumstances the social integration of the immigrants will be slow. Sooner or later there will be an obvious risk of antagonism between the immigrants and the home population. The more numerous the immigrants are, the more obvious these risks will be. In order to avoid such a situation a country may prefer not to let the number of births decline too far.

Let us assume, however, that a country accepts a birth rate which gives a reduced population size and that it keeps its borders closed to immigrants. Will this automatically reduce the pressure on energy and resource-use and lead to a reduced amount of pollution?

According to the *ceteris paribus* way to argue this will be the case. In other words, if all other circumstances remain the same, a reduced population will lead to reduced energy consumption, less resource-use and less pollution. This is no doubt true. But *ceteris paribus* arguments are never valid in the social sciences. According to UN sources, consumption of energy in coal equivalents in 1975 amounted to 10 999 kg in the United States and to 221 kg in India. But if energy consumption can thus presently be fifty times higher in the USA than in India, it could very well in the future be one hundred or even two hundred times higher. There is hardly any limit to the amount of energy consumed, the resources used or the pollution caused per person in a country which is dominated by the kind of economic and political structure which gives the present technological development. We must realize that it is not the size of the population which determines the level and character of the technology of a society.

In the short term a reduced number of children may in fact lead to an increased use of energy etc. This is because environmental problems have so much to do with luxury. Families with children, especially small children, do not have the time required, nor the amount of money needed, in order to dedicate themselves to the kind of luxury consumption which implies environment damage.

To conclude: it is completely false to insist that the attainment of zero population growth or even of a reduced population in the industrialized countries will lessen the consumption gap between these countries and the underdeveloped ones, or will contribute to a solution to pollution and other environmental problems. The responsibility for capitalist overproduction and its effects rests with political and economic realities and not with the growth of population.

Political Economy of Population Control in India

Debabar Banerji

Population Control Policies and Programmes in India

India was the first country in the world to have a state sponsored population control programme. It has also perhaps the most extensive network of birth control agencies, along with extensive programmes of mass communication, training and research. In terms of investment on family planning as a percentage of national income, it also occupies a pre-eminent position in the world. Perhaps it has also the distinction of being the first country in the world which proclaimed population control to be so urgent that it cannot await improvements in the social and economic fields. Indeed, it has often been asserted that changes in social and economic fields could take place only after the growth of the population is curbed.

As a logical corollary to such a policy, use of pressure, force and monetary enticements had come to be accepted as a "legitimate" means to "motivate" people to take to birth control. There has been a steady escalation in the use of coercive means to make people accept birth control. This trend culminated during the emergency period of June 1975–March 1977 in the use of naked force to physically catch hold of individuals and forcibly sterilize them on a scale which is perhaps unprecedented in human history.

The government of India's claim of attaining a sterilization performance of 7 635 396 in the nine months from April 1976 to January 1977[1] provides a staggering account of the degree to which the entire might of the government machinery was let loose on hundreds of millions of helpless people, most of whom belonged to the weaker sections of the society, to round them up and forcibly sterilize them.

Many agencies from outside the country have often played critical roles in shaping India's population control policies and their implementation since the very inception of the programme. It is significant that the President of the World Bank, who visited India during the emergency, "paid tributes to the political will and determination shown by the leadership at the highest level in intensifying the family planning drive with a rare courage of conviction".[2]

If population policy implies taking active steps to relate population size to issues such as migration, urbanization, manpower requirements, employment, education, social security and health services, such a policy was never given even a serious thought. At best it can be said that any policy in this field was confined merely to what can be called population control policy or, more appropriately, a birth control policy.

At the time of launching the national family planning programme, in the early 1950s, the government of India had enunciated what was termed as "guiding principles" for development of the programme.[3] These were:

(1) The community must be prepared to feel the need for the services in order that these may be accepted, when provided.
(2) Parents alone must decide the number of children they want and their obligations towards them.
(3) People should be approached through the media they respect and through their recognized and trusted leaders, and without offending their religious and moral values and susceptibilities.
(4) Services should be made available to the people as near to their doorsteps as possible; and,
(5) Services have greater relevance and effectiveness if made an integral part of medical and public health services and specially of maternal and child health programmes.

A decade and a half later, when the family planning programme had reached a distinct watershed, a new policy was formulated which underlined the need for having concurrent social and economic development as an important element of a population control policy. Health, nutrition and family planning was visualized as a single package which, in turn, formed the bigger package of the Minimum Needs Programme of the Fifth Five Year Plan[4] (p. 2).

The then Union Minister of Health asserted at the World Population Conference held at Bucharest in 1974[4] (p. 5):

Population policy is thus one of the several vital instruments for securing comprehensive social development and it cannot be effective unless certain concomitant economic policies and social programmes succeed in changing the basic determinants of high fertility. It has truly been said that the best contraceptive is development.

This policy was strongly endorsed by the then Prime Minister Indira Gandhi in her address to the National Population Conference held in the same year[5] (p. 4):

All workers of the family planning movement do not always fully appreciate the integral relationship between general development and family planning. When we reapportioned some funds to strengthen our rural health services, and there was a reduction in the percentage of the funds allocated under the serparate head of family planning, there was an outcry. This was misrepresented by the international press to suggest that we were giving up our family planning programmes.

Yet another population control policy was formulated in April 1976 in the wake of the declaration of the national emergency.[6] This included setting aside 8% of the central assistance to state plans specifically against performance in family planning, freezing of the representation of the central and state legislatures on the basis of the 1971 Census for the next 25 years, raising the age at marriage to 18 for girls and 21 for boys, higher graded monetary compensation, hirher priority for girls' education up to the middle level and to child nutrition. For the first time the Union Government allowed some states, which felt that the facilities available to them were adequate to meet the requirements for compulsory sterilization, to exercise their legislative powers to pass legislation for compulsory sterilization.

There was yet another policy change following the March 1977 elections when the new government categorically ruled out the use of force or coercion in any form, in implementing what is now called the family welfare programme. The government's views were expounded by Prime Minister Morarji Desai in April 1977 in the following words:[7]

The policy of the population control is to be vigorously pursued but purely on a voluntary basis. During the past two years the programme became a sort of "menace to the people", but in any programme of health, coercion will not help. When the people take to it willingly the programme will show much better results and the adoption will be in a more effective manner and it will also result in greater welfare of the people. The name "family welfare programme" is, therefore, far more suitable and meaningful.

As in several other social and economic fields, the actual programmes concerning population control differed widely from the enunciated policies. Since its very inception the birth control aspects received an over-riding priority over the other aspects of the programme. Even when this programme was integrated, it grew at the cost of the health services, because health workers were pressurized to attain family planning targets. Health work thus suffered as there were no targets set for such work. Significantly, foreign agencies, both bilateral as well as multilateral, have played important roles in actively promoting this pattern of growth of the family planning programme. The first United Nations Evaluation Mission (1966), for instance, recommended that[8]

> The Directorate (i.e. of family planning) should be relieved from the other responsibilities such as maternal and child health and nutrition. It is undoubtedly important for family planning to be integrated with maternal and child health in the field, particularly in view of the loop programme; but until the family planning campaign has picked up the momentum and made real progress in the states, the Director-General concerned should be responsible for family planning only. *This recommendation is reinforced by the fear that the programme may otherwise be used in some states to expand the much needed and neglected maternal and child welfare serfices.* (Emphasis added)

Despite giving such an overriding priority to the birth control aspects of family planning programme during the past twenty years, the then Minister of Health and Family Planning had to admit in his national population policy statement of 1976 that the prrrogramme had thus far been able to touch only the fringe of India's population problem. The subsequent drive of forcible sterilization during the emergency did yield 8 106 639 sterilizations, according to the data provided by the government at that time.[9] It has, however, to be presumed that the data produced by the government are reasonably reliable. Over and above, there is the question of the demographic profile of the acceptors of family planning under such conditions of duress. A nationwide study of community response to the intensified family planning programme[10] has revealed that a substantial proportion of the acceptors belonged to demographically dubious classes, such as those with high parity, those with grown up children and those with wives above the reproductive age. There were also cases where the lure for money or the pressure for meeting targets led to sterilization of the spouse of a previously sterilized individual, sometimes even repeat sterilization of the same individual.

The backlash of use of force on such a large scale has been even more devastating. The entire programme—the family planning as well as health aspects—has suffered very serious loss of credibility. The sterilization performance data for the first six months of 1976–77 reveal that, compared to the 1975–1976 figure for the corresponding months, sterilization performance has gone down by as much as 90·8%.[11] Another significant feature of these data is that this decline has been very pronounced in all the states, including southern states of Andhra Pradesh, Kerala, Karnataka and Tamil Nadu, and the state of Maharashtra.

Value Orientation of the Decision Makers

India's population control policies and programmes should be studied in the context of the value orientation of the decision makers. As has been repeatedly pointed out by Myrdal,[12] at the time of India's independence, most of Indian national political leaders were members of a privileged upper class. The leaders provided a great contrast to the impoverished masses. After independence, the new positions of responsibility and power were given to these leaders investing them with still greater privilege. Many who had borne heavy individual sacrifice in the independence struggle saw in their personal advancement a symbol of the national political revolution. As politics became increasingly concerned with practical issues and as the pressure of the leaders' own vested interest grew stronger, India developed a new type of politician: men with few ideological inhibitions over working for special interests invaded the political arena[12] (p. 291).

While these politicians felt compelled to commit themselves firmly to building an egalitarian society and they espoused such values as the right to work, to health, to special care for weaker sections of the community and to free compulsory education by 1960 for all children up to the age of 14 (see the Directive principles for State Policy of the Constitution of India,),[13] they were not prepared to effect the necessary social, political and administrative changes to attain such goals. They wanted to win a modern war with bows and arrows. They persuaded themselves that the values of a highly privileged class—values which had in the main been inherited from the colonial era—would not interfere with the making of a social and economic revolution in the country. Similarly, they also believed that they could usher in the revolution without changing the structure and function of a bureaucracy thoroughly soaked in colonial tradition.

Alienation of these national political leaders from the masses, their westernized values, their lack of competence in technical matters and their reluctance to come to grips with urgent social problems, along with pressure from certain powerful vested interests, both within the country and abroad, all combined to induce the leaders to depend heavily upon foreign agencies for "technical" and monetary assistance. The appeal of the Western conceptual approach drew added strength from the fact that it fitted in well with the rationale for opportunistic interests in developed Western countries and among the influential intellectual elite of developing countries[12] (p. 20).

Finding they were inadequate for the job, Indian political leaders, scientists and civil servants went out of their way to appeal to foreign experts for help. The latter generously responded.[14] A large number of foreign advisers were invited to play a dominant role in almost every facet of India's economic and social life—in the planning process, government administration, industry, agriculture, education and community development, as well as in family planning, medicine and public health. As a reward, Indian counterparts were offered what was perceived by them as glittering opportunities, such as fellowships in Western educational institutions, study tours and visiting professorships and offers of consultancies and of participation at seminars, workshops and conferences in foreign countries. This also served to give a powerful boost to their Western enculturation and earned them approval from their condescending mentors.

However, the country had to pay very heavily for these developments. Servility, conformism, mediocrity and a lack of initiative and enterprise became valued attributes of the civil servants and technical personnel in India. Strict adherence to the rules of seniority during a phenomenally rapid expansion of services ensured that many key posts demanding creativity, initiative and enterprise of a very high order were filled by persons who, even by colonial standards, were neither bright nor suitable. This led to virtual glorification of mediocrity. Foreign experts were left almost at liberty to shape the country's vital policies according to their own values and their own social and political interests. They also acquired considerable influence in the implementation of these policies.

Family Planning Movement in India

After Independence, in the very First Five Year Plan (1951–1956), the "urgency of the problem of family planning" was clearly recognized.[15] The findings of the 1961 Census dramatically brought home the explosive nature of the population growth in India and the urgent need for controlling it. Responding to it, in the Third Plan (1961–1966), the objective of stabilizing the growth of the population was considered to be the very centre of planned development. Following this, in the Fourth Plan (1969–1974), family planning found its place as a programme of highest importance[14] (p. 11). As a result of attaching increasing importance to the programme, there has been a very steep rise in investment in family planning in the successive Five Year Plans—from a mere Rs.1·5 million for the First to Rs.22 million for the Second to Rs.246·6 million in the Third, rising to Rs.3300 million in the Fourth Plan[14] (p. 11). The outlay for the Fifth Plan (1974–1979) is Rs.5600 million[16] (p. 253).

In the 1950s and in the early 1960s, following the traditions of the planned parenthood movement of Western countries, family planning clinics were established in urban and rural areas. When, however, it was realized that the range of such clinics is very limited, again taking the cue from the community development movement in the United States, an extension wing was added to these clinics by establishing an enormous network of family planning extension workers.[17] Substantial additions were again made to the programme in the mid-1960s when some foreign consultants projected the intra-uterine device (IUD) as the miracle device and succeeded in persuading the decision makers in India to undertake a massive programme to popularize the use of this device.[18] When, however, the IUD programme also failed, it became a "target oriented time-bound programme, adopting the cafeteria approach". This involved[14] (pp. 16–17): (a) offer of "monetary incentives" to the doctors, the motivators and to the acceptors; (b) mobilization of law and order and tax collection machinery for family planning work; and (c) exerting administrative pressure on field workers to ensure that they attain certain predetermined family planning targets.

Adoption of the Mass Vasectomy Camp Approach in 1971 represented a high point in the escalation of the use of coercion, administrative pressure and monetary enticements in family planning. Under the leadership of the divisional commissioner and the deputy commissioner, the entire staff of a district, numbering in thousands, were threatened with dire consequences if they failed to attain certain family planning targets.[19] These persons were let loose on the people and they were allowed to use (or misuse) all their powers and patronage to round up people for the mass camps. Unfortunately, despite taking recourse to such extreme measures it was not possible to get any lasting results.

Failure of extensive use of the mass vasectomy camp approach indicated to the decision makers that there was very little scope for further pressurising people into accepting birth control measures. This failure, in fact, impelled them to recognize, in early 1974, the need for concurrently improving the health and nutrition status of the people. This realization also made them more aware of some other social and economic determinants of promotion of a small family norm among people—for example, education, employment and social justice, including an equitable status for women. About this time, the Planning Commission also came up with what it called the Minimum Needs Programme in the draft of the Fifth Five Year Plan to make "a frontal attack on poverty". The Minimum Needs Programme included the package of integrated health, nutrition and family planning services suggested by the Union Ministry of Health and Family Planning. "Development is the Best Contraceptive", became the new watchword of the family planning programme. Even as late as in January 1976, in the report for 1975–1976, the Union Ministry of Health and Family Planning asserted that[20] (p. 75):

The year under review also happened to be the second year of the Fifth Five Year Plan which, for the first time, seeks to launch a direct assault on the problems of underdevelopment. High fertility rates have been identified as more a function of poverty than of anything else. The Family Planning Programme which is expected to tackle the problem of high growth rates of population has, therefore, been linked with the basic problems of poverty so that it is not run in isolation from social realities. As a social welfare programme, family planning is taken as a component of development. Hence, it is linked with the Minimum Needs Programme which has the basic aim of improving the quality of life of a large section of our people who have long remained victim of poverty and underdevelopment. In fact, Family Planning has been recognised as the "inarticulate premise" which makes all the development efforts meaningful.

Implementation of this population policy required certain basic structural changes in the society so that it was possible to bring about a shift in the investment of additional resources and efforts to the poverty stricken sections of the population. This shift was required in almost all segments of the social and economic development programmes of the country. Specifically, within the limits of a Family Planning Programme, it required a virtual revolution, involving far-reaching changes calling for a total renovation of the entire decision making machinery and a thorough rejuvenation of the entire machinery for implementing the programme, including the critical areas for education, training and research.

It soon began to be realized that bringing about such changes at the political, economic, bureaucratic and professional levels needed much more effort than the leadership was prepared to make. The inadequacy of these efforts became palpably apparent in implementing the Minimum Needs Programme of the Fifth Plan.

Proclamation of the National Emergency on June 26, 1975, could have provided the necessary milieu to bring about the required changes to promote family planning as an integral part of a programme to improve the levels of living of the weaker sections of the population. Again this time, unfortunately, the forces which favoured retention of the status quo prevailed and they raised the bogey of population explosion to give another lease of life to the thoroughly discredited coercive methods of promoting family planning.

Indeed, the emergency conditions provided the exponents of this approach with almost unlimited powers to crush the resistance of th people to family planning. They had firm control over the media of mass communication. They also had under their command a massive police force and other forces of repression to enforce sterilization on those they desired to pick up. Emergency powers were also used to ensure that people have no access to any legal redress against the excesses perpetrated on them. Persons showing even the remotest semblance of resistance were threatened with immediate arrest for an indefinite period without trial or legal redress.

The country-wide study of community response to the intensified family planning programme,[10] covering the states of Gujarat, Haryana, Karnataka, Kerala, Rajasthan, Tamil Nadu, Uttar Pradesh and West Bengal within the emergency period (October 1976–January 1977), revealed that the entire machinery of the government, under the leadership of the deputy commissioner, with full backing from his superior officers, including the political leadership of the government, was mobilized to exert pressure on people to submit to sterilization. In many states procurement of cases for sterilization was tagged in almost as a precondition for getting assistance from a government agency of any kind. Issue of licenses for guns, shops, cane crushers and vehicles, issue of loans of various kinds, registration of land, issue of ration cards, exemption from payment of school fees or land revenue, supply of canal water, submission of applications for any job, exercise of food powers on shopkeepers, any form of registration, getting transfers, obtaining of bail or even facilitation of court cases are instances of services which were linked with procurement of cases for sterilization.

A high point in the application of pressure of this type was the allocation of sterilization targets to school teachers with threats of dire action if they failed to achieve the prescribed target. Interviews with these teachers revealed that imposition of such intense pressure on them posed acute personal problems and often caused co   e hardship to a number of them. This desparate demand
        a large number of very hard pressed government
        offer of monetary incentives for getting acceptors
       rm of middle man—a commission agent. A commis-
        out government officials in distress by procuring
        a price. He also carried out "business", with

or without collusion with the medical staff, by getting "non-eligible" cases operated upon for sterilization or by under-paying the acceptors.

In states such as Haryana, Punjab, Uttar Pradesh, Madhya Pradesh and Rajasthan, the police force was extensively used to overcome resistance to family planning. Parties consisting of personnel from health and family planning, revenue and development departments with police protection have raided villages, sometimes in the very early hours of the morning—predawn raids—to round up sections of people for sterilization. There were also reports of similar "raids" on public buses to catch people.

Even though the nature, the degree and the intensity of such raids varied considerably from state to state and even from district to district in the same state, it was possible to identify some of the notable features of such raids:

(a) The weaker sections usually formed the focus of the raids. Persons belonging to the more prosperous sections, even though eminently eligible for sterilization, were exempted. Some, however, had to buy their "release" by procuring substitute cases from the poorer classes.

(b) These organized raids created such a scare among the villagers that often almost the entire adult population of a village fled away to the fields at the very sight of any approaching vehicle. There had been instances when people hid themselves in the fields for weeks together.

(c) There were also instances of agreements reached between villagers and raiding parties to the effect that if the villagers made available a given number of "cases" for sterilization, the village will be spared from raids. These sterilization "cases" generally belonged to the groups that were vulnerable to pressure, i.e. the weaker sections.

(d) Some groups had succeeded in avoiding sterilization by successfully running away and hiding themselves or by threatening to offer violent resistance.

(e) More often the villagers had to give way. However, it was observed that in the later months as the efforts needed to overcome villagers' resistance had steadily mounted, these raids had declined in frequency and there were indications that this method might have been abandoned altogether.

The fact that there has been a precipitous fall in the number of vasectomies after the emergency in all the states provides evidence that coercive methods in one form or other was employed all over the country. Against an all-India decline of 97·8% in vasectomy during the first six months of 1977–1978 as compared to the number of vasectomies performed during the same period in 1976–1977,[11] in the states in which the ruling party was utterly routed in the parliamentary elections of March 1977, the decline was 99·9% in Uttar Pradesh, 98·9% in Bihar, 99·6% in Rajasthan, 99·9% in Madhya Pradesh, 98·7% in Haryana, 97·1% in Punjab, 99·8% in Himachal Pradesh and 99·6% in Delhi. In the southern states where the opposition parties in fact lost further ground during the March 1977 elections, the decline was 99·7% in Tamil Nadu, 94·6% in Karnataka, 90·7% in Andhra Pradesh and 88·7% in Kerala. These data underline the fact that the degree of variation in the use of coercive means in different states of the country was not as much as was assumed earlier, and that the degree of family planning excesses cannot entirely explain away the difference in the electoral behaviour of the northern and the southern states.

Because of the degree and the extent of the use of force to get family planning acceptance, family planning excesses form the darkest chapter in the history of the emergency excesses. Fortunately, the leadership which was associated with these excesses decided, for reasons that are not yet clear, to seek renewal of the people's mandate early in 1977. Taking political advantage of the deep revulsion of the masses and of their bosses towards such excesses, the opposition parties got together and gave a pledge to the people never to use force in any form in family planning (now called family welfare), restore civil rights and freedom of the press, provide employment in ten years and eradicate poverty. People gave them a massive mandate and the government which had been ruling the country for over thirty years was unceremoniously overthrown. India can thus claim yet another distinction of being the first country in the world where family planning became an election issue which was decisive in the overthrow of a national government.

It is now being revealed that the number of persons who lost their lives as a result of police firing could run into hundreds. Many more hundreds lost their lives as a result of complications from sterilization operations; many times more of this number had to suffer enormous disabilities as a result of complications arising out of the operations.

Present Status of the Family Planning Programme

While several radical changes in the programme have resulted in a number of additions to it, efforts to weed out the redundant components have been very inadequate. This has given a very humbled appearance to the programme[21] (pp. 61–87).[22, 11]

The urban population is served by a total of 1820 family planning clinics and 2333 other institutions which also operate family planning work. There are 5168 family welfare planning centres and 37 690 sub-centres providing services to rural populations. Conventional contraceptives, with the main emphasis on the condom (Nirodh), are being distributed through all family planning institutions. Condoms are also sold commercially at highly subsidized rates through over 220 000 retail outlets. One thousand four hundred and five rural and 1860 urban institutions are providing post-partum family planning services. There are also 2072 institutions for providing abortion services—the so-called medical termination of pregnancy. Family planning services are also being provided through agencies of the organized sector, such as government ministries and departments, labour organizations, industrial undertakings and the Employees State Insurance Scheme. All services except the highly subsidized sale of condoms are provided free of cost.

Positions for more than 75 000 full time workers have been sanctioned for direct extension work in the field. Over and above, there are 66 200 workers for supervision and technical assistance at various levels. Apart from extensive mobilization of all the mass media units of the Union Ministry of Information and Broadcasting and strengthening these units and establishing over 350 mobile audiovisual units for family planning, other media for mass communication, including the indigenous media, have also been requestioned to provide a massive communication support to the programme[14] (pp. 15–16).

As a disincentive, some states have withdrawn certain concessions, such as maternity leave to their non-industrial employees who do not adopt a small family norm. On the legislative front, the legal minimum age of marriage has been raised from 15 to 18 for girls and from 18 to 21 years for boys and the abortion law has been considerably liberalized (p. 17).

An extensive network of training institutions have been established to provide training to the very large number of family planning workers of different categories. Steps have also been taken to ensure concurrent and periodic evaluation of the programme by the Government as well as independent agencies. Support has also been provided to encourage research in the fields of bio-medicine, demography and "communication-action" research[14] (pp. 21–23).

Far reaching changes have also been introduced in the organization to sustain the programme. For instance, at the central level, family planning work was taken out of the Directorate-General of Health Services and in 1966 a separate department of family planning came into being in the Ministry of Health and Family Planning[14] (pp. 17–20). There have also been major organizational changes at the regional, state, district and block levels.

Thus, while claiming to have a new policy, essentially, the new government has not brought about any change in their approach to the family planning programme. Even more significantly, the very persons who had occupied leadership positions in the programme during the emergency have been asked to stay on to implement the new policy. There are very few new faces, very few new ideas and indeed very few new initiatives. It is almost like expecting blast furnaces to start manufacturing ice.

To lend his weight to the programme, Prime Minister Morarji Desai has pointedly joined his colleagues from the Ministry of Health and Family Welfare to assert, while launching family welfare fortnight on December 15, 1977, that his government gives the highest priority to population control. The communication media of the programme are also prominently projecting the September 10, 1977, statement of the much revered elderly statesman and the architect of the present government, Shri Jayaprakash Narayan. It states:[23] "I have all along been a supporter of family planning and I have expressed my support to this programme from the many platforms in the country and also through the Press. I consider Family Planning to be one of the most essential programmes to be adopted by our country for its general progress and prosperity. The only reservation I have made which I should like to repeat here is that no coercion should be used in the implementation of this programme".

Thus, once again, the population control programme stands precariously on a precipice. As on earlier occasions, in the absence of adequate organizational response, all policy assertions will continue to sound very hollow. Such situations are fraught with serious danger. In the absence of a proper understanding of the situation, in sheer desparation, the authorities might panic once again and take "drastic" steps against the people. But this time the people too may be aroused to take a still more drastic stand against their "authorities".

Conclusions: A Political and Social Interpretation of the Family Planning Movement in India

Perhaps an explanation for this approach to population control and heavy dependence on foreign agencies is to be found in the social and economic forces which have shaped the political system of the country. Despite all the egalitarian pronouncements, the political leadership in India not only retained but it actively reinforced the class structure of the pre-independence days. It did not keep its promise to eradicate illiteracy and to provide universal primary education by 1960, but it made heavy investment in higher education; gross social and economic exploitation of the weaker sections of the society by the upper classes have continued unabated till today, if, indeed, they have not actually increased in severity. Political leaders have also failed to improve the levels of living of the poor to any significant extent and the fruits of development have mainly benefited the upper classes; its record is equally dismal in the fields of land reforms, community development, health services and employment. The rich have become richer and the poor poorer, politically, socially as well as economically.

Fortunately, this lop-sided pattern of development is at least one of the major factors responsible for the rapid population growth in the country. This was recognized by the leadership as a serious threat to the entire social and political system which sustains them—it turned out to be the Achilles' heel of what otherwise appeared to be an impregnable system.

Instead, however, of bringing about the long overdue structural changes to honour the commitment it had made to the masses of the population of the country, as early as in the mid-1950s, the political leadership actually used the threat of population explosion to justify perpetuation of the system. The bogey of population explosion was not only used as a very convenient alibi to explain away its failure to keep its promises to the masses, but was also used to justify launching, with very active inspiration, support, guidance and often naked pressure from foreign agencies, a mass campaign which was specifically directed towards curbing births. While the upper classes continued to thrive at the cost of the masses, the masses were told that their lot could not be improved unless the population growth was curbed.

Propitiation of the privileged classes at the cost of gross neglect of the social and economic interests of the vast masses of the people, however, created one problem for the rulers. It generated amongst the masses a negative attitude towards family planning. To these people life is virtually an unending chain of misery, degradation and deprivation. They have no economic choice open to them, nothing to look forward to. A surplus of fresh human stock is the only tangible capital that can be invoked. They have thus no stake in the survival of the system and, therefore, no stake in curbing births. Indeed, it would not be too cynical to say that, if anything, these oppressed people have a positive stake in the destruction of what is to them a tyrannical system which causes them so much misery. They have little to lose if the system is blown up by a population explosion. Also, they have much to look forward to from the alternative political system that will emerge after the explosion.

In the early phases of the programme, attempts were made to overcome this negative attitude by launching campaigns to persuade people to accept family planning through education and motivation and mass communication. Recourse was taken to coercion and enticement following the failure of the persuasive methods. Failure of one coercive tactic to overpower people's resistance led to adoption of successively more intensive methods of coercion for attaining sterilization targets—coercion went up from mere monetary enticements, to employment of "touts" to procure cases for sterilization camps, to putting administrative pressure on health and family planning workers to deployment of the law and order and tax

collecting personnel and forcing them to attain a prescribed sterilization target. With the declaration of the emergency in June 1976, the
enforcement of control of population growth took the form of a
brazen class war when the entire might of the oppressive machinery
of the state, including the police force, was used to sterilize millions
against their will.

Fortunately, the oppressed people succeeded in thwarting what
appeared to be a relentless march towards the 1984 of George Orwell.
Taking advantage of the deep seated resentment against family
planning excesses, a new set of rulers have taken over from the previous
one, pledging never to use force in any form in family planning.

As the previous political leadership refused to bring about basic
social and economic transformation of Indian society which could
generate motivation for a small family norm among the masses, they
had to adopt ruthless measures to avert the impending disaster due to
rapid rate of population growth; the "demographic time bomb" had
to be defused for the very survival of the system.

Nor can the present political leadership fail to defuse the demographic time bomb. Having foreclosed its option of forcibly sterilizing people, the sheer demographic compulsions will force it to be put
into operation what the then Government of India had so loudly
proclaimed at the 1974 World Population Conference at Bucharest:
that development is the best contraceptive.

Social and economic transformation thus remains the only way to
defuse the demographic time bomb, this has thus turned out to be
the ultimate weapon in the hands of the oppressed masses. With this
weapon, they will wrest more and more powers from the exploiting
classes and ensure that social and economic prerequisites for a
nationwide adoption of a small family norm are met. The powerful
demographic compulsions and the abject failure of use of force to
have birth control provide ample grounds to take an optimistic view
of the political and economic future of India.

Notes

1. India, Government of, Department of Family Welfare (1977). *Centre Calling*, **XII**, 4–5, April–May.
2. India, Government of, Department of Family Planning (1976). *Centre Calling*, **XI**, 11, November.

3. India, Government of, Department of Family Planning (1968). "India: Family Planning Programme Since 1965", New Delhi, Department of Family Planning.
4. Singh, K. (1975). "Population, Poverty and the Future of India", p. 2. New Delhi, National Institute of Family Planning.
5. Sanyal, B. K. (Ed). (1975). National Population Conference: Proceedings, *J. Pop. Res.*, Supplement, January–June.
6. India, Government of, Department of Family Planning (1976). "National Population Policy", New Delhi, Ministry of Health and Family Planning.
7. Desai, M. (1977). Population control on voluntary basis, *Centre Calling*, **XII**, No. 4–5, April–May.
8. United Nations Advisory Mission (1966). "Report on the Family Planning Programme in India", pp. 8–9. New York, United Nations.
9. India, Government of, Department of Family Welfare (1977). Milestones, *Centre Calling*, **XII**, 7; July.
10. Banerji, D. (1977). Community response to the intensified family planning programme. *Economic and Political Weekly* **XII**, Annual No; pp. 261–266.
11. India, Government of, Department of Family Welfare (1977). "Monthly Bulletin on Family Welfare Statistics", May and September numbers.
12. Myrdal, G. (1968). "Asian Drama: An Enquiry into the Poverty of Nations", Vols. 1–3. New York, Twentieth Century Fund.
13. Basu, D. D. (1970). "Shorter Constitution of India", pp. 230–235. Calcutta, S. C. Sarkar.
14. Banerji, D. (1971). "Family Planning in India: A Critique and a Perspective", pp. 27–30. New Delhi, People's Publishing House.
15. Raina, B. L. (1968). Family planning. *In* "Encyclopaedia of Social Work in India, (Ed. by M. S. Gore), p. 311. New Delhi, Planning Commission, Vol. I.
16. India, Government of, Planning Commission (1973). "Draft Fifth Five Year Plan (1974–79)", Vol. II. New Delhi, Planning Commission.
17. Raina, B. L. (1963). "Family Planning Programme: Report for 1962–63". New Delhi, Ministry of Health.
18. India, Government of, Ministry of Health and Family Planning, Committee on Administrative and Financial Aspects of the IUCD Programme (1966). "Report", New Delhi, Ministry of Health and Family Planning.
19. Krishnakumar, S. (1972). Kerala's pioneering experiment in massive vasectomy camps, *Studies in Family Planning*, **III**, 177–187.
20. India, Government of, Ministry of Health and Family Planning (1976). "Report, 1975–76". New Delhi, Ministry of Health and Family Planning.
21. India, Government of, Ministry of Health and Family Planning (1973). "Report, 1972–73", New Delhi, Ministry of Health and Family Planning.

22. India, Government of, Ministry of Health and Family Planning (1973). "Family Planning in India: Programme Information 1971–72", New Delhi, Ministry of Health and Family Planning.
23. Jayaprakash, N. (1977). All along been a supporter, *Centre Calling* **XII,** 10, October.

Family Planning in a Tamil Village[1]

Göran Djurfeldt and Staffan Lindberg

The recent atrocities of forced sterilization of millions of people in India committed during the emergency of 1975–1977 is not a cruel exception to the general policy of the Indian Government during the last fifteen years. After a period of indifference or reserve a massive Family Planning Programme (FPP) was launched in the early 1960s.[2] The government's change of attitude towards the population problem seems to have been brought about partly through foreign pressure, mainly American, as a condition for future aid commitments. Since then the programme of population control disguised as family planning[3] has come to play an increasingly dominant role. In the official view population growth is often made responsible for the failure of the development policy and the growing impoverishment of the Indian people, reflected in the fact that the percentage of rural people living under the poverty line (Rs. 15s. per month in 1960/1961 prices; one rupee was at that time about 20 cents) has increased from 38% in 1960/1961 to 54% in 1968/1969.[4] This ideology of population control can be labelled neo-Malthusian, since its basic tenet is that population tends to grow faster than the economic resources by which it subsists.

The main goal of the family planning policy has been to persuade couples with more than two or three children to undergo voluntary sterilization. The operation is most commonly performed on men (vasectomy). In connection with delivery women can also be operated on (salpingectomy), which is a more complicated operation. The government has put less emphasis on other methods of birth control. Technical contraceptive methods are considered too complicated for "simple village folk". Encouragement of abortion has been included in the programme only recently, and then against the opposition of orthodox Hindus who consider abortion a sin. Likewise, the government has not made any serious efforts to raise the average age of marriage. According to law, a girl need only be fifteen years in order to marry.

Clearly the main motive for launching the family planning pro-gramme is a macro-motive: a reduced rate of population growth is considered by the government and the ruling classes as a national interest. To undergo sterilization is, then, a patriotic act. In a pamphlet available at most primary health centres, the former President of India, Zakir Hussein, addresses his countrymen in the following words:

> Brothers and Sisters!
> Our population problem is a colossal and pressing one. In my capacity of President of the nation and as a private individual I give high priority to this problem . . . Our family planning scheme will not be successful till the day our brothers and sisters come to realize the fact that having more than two or three children is not good, and act accordingly.

A variety of reasons for adopting FP are given in the pamphlet: the children must be fed, dressed and educated, and when they grow up they must get a job, which is more difficult in a family with too many children. The small and happy family makes for a happy nation. Another micromotive stressed in the propaganda is the concern for the mother. Pregnancies at too short intervals are a threat to the health of the mother.

What is the effect of this message in the rural areas where three-quarters of the population live? It is an irony that many people, at least in South India, do not know that they belong to a country called India. Only a minority know the name of the President of the country. On the other hand few people could have been ignorant about the FPP as such, even prior to the emergency. It has been widely propagated for by big advertisements and in the cinemas.

The Village

Thaiyur panchayat belongs to Chingleput District. It is situated some 25 miles south of Madras City near the coast and the Bay of Bengal. Thaiyur has about 5000 inhabitants and about 1000 house-holds belonging to 10 different hamlets. It has a peculiar caste composition, since nearly 90% of the population are Harijans of the ex-untouchable caste of Paraiyan. The caste composition is a conse-quence of the "dual economy" which is found here: the panchayat lies near to the Kovelam Salt factory in which a majority of t Harijans are employed for part of the year. The economy is "dual" in the sense that it is dominated by agriculture during half the year and by salt production during the other half. Despite this peculiarity one can draw conclusions from our study of the Thaiyur economy which can be useful also in a more general context.

Most people in Thaiyur are poor. In terms of cash about half of the households earn less than Rs. 1000 a year, and about 70% of all households can spend less than one rupee per consumer per day. On the other hand 15% earn more than 2000 rupees. The three richest households in Thaiyur earn about 10% of all incomes. Their income is about 50 000 each per year.

On the local level the Panchayat Union has the major responsibility of carrying out the FPP. The head of the Thiruporur P.U.—of which Thaiyur is a part—stressed "agricultural production and FP as the most important programmes for the future". The health inspector is the official in charge of the latter. According to him, the auxiliary nurses—midwives are instructed to propagate FP in the maternity centres. They encourage the women to adopt the loop system. Up until November 1969, the system had been adopted by 96 women, while the target for the year was 200. Likewise, in Thiruporur P.U., 286 vasectomy operations had been performed during the same period, whereas the target was 450. A partial reason for the latter failure was the lack of vasectomy facilities within the Union.

According to government instructions, propaganda should also be promulgated at public meetings. The extension officer for education is responsible for the arrangement of such meetings:

> . . . it is very difficult to have public meetings here, because the villagers will disturb them. For example, we were conducting one meeting in one village. Then one fellow got up and started to discuss the price of rice prevailing here. "Why can't you give one measure of rice (2 litres) for one rupee, as you are doing in Madras? If you do that, we may start to think about family planning."[5]
>
> Now, how can we conduct meetings when conditions are like this? These Harijans are lazy!

Thus, instead of public meetings the Union has adopted the policy of trying to motivate people through personal contacts and face-to-face communication. One of the main duties of the female village level workers is to teach the women FP methods and to convince them to try the loop. The male village level workers also engage themselves in family planning work. If successful it can be remunerative. The person who can convince another person to undergo an operation, and who arranges for it to be made, is entitled to ten rupees. The patient himself will get thirty rupees.

The villagers of Thaiyur are favoured in terms of medical facilities by a neighbouring Primary Health Centre. Moreover, a voluntary aid organization—called the Swallows and receiving funds and volunteers from Scandinavia—is working in Thaiyur. They have built a well-equipped health clinic in Thaiyur main hamlet concentrating on maternity and child care. The Swallows take a special interest in FP, but only during a short period has this been manifested in FP propaganda. In 1968 a Scandinavian volunteer midwife joined the project. Her special task was to carry out FP work. Her first attempt at propaganda was at a public meeting in Komancheri—a Harijan colony. Those who gathered around the Land Rover to listen to her proved to be so decidedly negative to family planning that the meeting had to be abruptly ended almost before it had started.

Despite massive efforts the voluntary FPP has been far from successful. By witnessing only family planning propaganda, a naive observer easily gets the impression that Indian women are almost continually pregnant. Such a distorted understanding of the demographic structure of rural India is quite common, especially among townspeople and Westerners. If we want to understand why F.P. has failed in Thaiyur, we must correct these distortions, by looking at some infrastructural facts of demography and household economy.

Family Size and Population Growth

By comparing the two population censuses of 1961 and 1969 and by sample surveys of vital statistics, we have estimated the rate of population growth in Thaiyur at 1·8%. This is close to the all-India growth rate of 2% estimated by Myrdal[6] though below the 1971 census estimate of 2·5% for the period 1961–1971.

The mean size of a Thaiyur household is 4·83 persons. This figure is slightly higher than the average for Tamil Nadu as a whole, which

is 4·57, but lower than the figure for rural India (5·20).[7] Table I
shows that very few families "swarm" with children. In a majority
of the households there are two children or less. Only about 20% of
the households have more than three children. Of course, these data
do not convey the whole truth: there are many young families with
few children; and there are many old families in which the children
have already left the nest. But those facts do not contradict the
general conclusion: the Thaiyur villagers do not breed "like rabbits".

A Thaiyur woman is likely to have gone through six or seven
pregnancies when she passes out of childbearing age, i.e. when she
reaches 50. Out of these children she is likely to lose about two. Six
or seven deliveries between marriage and menopause entails an
average space of five or six years between each pregnancy which is
far below the reproductive capacity of a woman. We may conclude,
then, that Thaiyur women already practice *birth spacing* or some
other method of "family planning".

TABLE I. *Number of Children Living in the Household.*

Number of children living in the house-hold	Number of households	
	(*n*)	(%)
0	162	17·2
1	192	20·3
2	232	24·6
3	167	17·7
4	101	10·7
5	52	5·5
6	25	2·6
7	8	0·8
8	3	0·3
9 and above	3	0·3
	945	100·0

The most common traditional method of birth spacing is prolonged lactation, which people know reduces the likelihood of a new
pregnancy. In Thaiyur, especially among Harijans, infants are

breastfed as long as they prefer. Forced weaning occurs only when the mother is pregnant again. The belief that prolonged lactation affects ovulation and menstruation after childbirth has been confirmed by many.[8]

Abortion is another way of preventing births. "Women often seek risky ways" to get abortions, according to one of our respondents. In Thaiyur a herbal abortifacient is available: the juice of the stem of the Yeruhachedi bush[9] is said to provoke abortion of the foetus.

The conclusion that one can make from the study of Thaiyur demography is that family size is less a result of blind sexual urges than most neo-Malthusians tend to think, and more a result of planning and foresight.[10] Thaiyur families are, as a matter of fact, to a large extent "planned" in the way actually intended by the FPP. The poor have less children,[11] which is evident from very marked differences in fertility between different agrarian classes.

TABLE II. *Number of Births Per Wife (of Head of Household), as Related to Agrarian Class.*

Agrarian class	Mean number of births per wife (of household head)
Big farmers (owning 20 acres or above)	5·15 ($n = 41$)
Middle farmers (owning 3–20 acres)	4·05 ($n = 216$)
Small farmers and landless labourers (owning less than 3 acres)	3·42 ($n = 558$)
Total for all households engaged in agriculture	3·67 ($n = 815$)

Note to the table: the figures are based on all wives in Thaiyur, many of whom are still of childbearing age.

It is also wrong to say that poverty goes together with high natality which is claimed to be a law by, for example, Berelson and Steiner.[13] It is not true for Thaiyur, and probably not for India as a whole. The Indian pattern is probably the same as that found in pre-revolutionary Russia and China, or in medieval England,[14] where family size and natality increased with increasing wealth.

On the Necessity of Having Children

The most important duty of children is to take care of their parents when the latter grow old. To an old person, having children is a matter of life or death. The tragedy of losing one's only son is an illustration of this: when one of our field workers saw an old woman lying on the road with torn clothes, he asked her:

> "Why are you lying here in the mud?"
> She answered: "I came a long distance because my son has gone away from our house. He is 18 years old, and he is my only son. So I am searching for him. I have searched for the past 15 days, but I cannot find him. I won't live in the world without my son".

Another illustrative case is that of an old married couple living alone in their house. A married daughter is living in a nearby hamlet, but they have nobody to take care of them. The old man is not able to work. The old lady is willing to work, but the landowners do not allow her because they think she is too weak and hence they drive her away from their fields. So the old couple do not get any income. Sometimes their daughter brings food to them, but mostly they are starving. "I was moved when I met them", our interviewer writes. "I gave them one rupee which I happened to have in my pocket. The old man accepted the money in an excited mood, and immediately gave it to his wife. She went straight to their neighbour's house to buy wheat".

If an old person has no one to care for him when he grows old, he will starve to death. He cannot count on the community to help him, neither can he trust his neighbours. According to the norm, he cannot even expect help from his married daughter. Most often she lives in another village with her husband, and her parents have no right to demand any help from their son-in-law, while he, in turn, has full authority over his wife. Or, in the words of a woman in Eri Ethir Vayil:

> I have no son. If I give our only girl in marriage to someone, who will then protect us? What will happen when we grow old, when we have no son? We can't go to our son-in-law's

house. Even if we give him our land to protect us, he may sell it and run away leaving us in the street."

Other advantages also accrue from grown-up children. If a man has a joint family with his grown-up sons and their wives living with him, as in 9% of the Thaiyur families, it will have definite economic advantages. He can, for example, build an irrigation-well on his lands:

—Once there is a well for us, there will be no suffering.
—Couldn't you dig a well yourself?
—The Government must do it. If we had been able to do it ourselves, we would not have expected help.
—But some people have managed on their own.
—Yes, in big families they will be able to manage. When there are many male labourers in a family, it is possible.

Likewise, it was said about one family: "All able-bodied members work hard to earn their living. So even during last year's drought, they were able to adjust without incurring any debts."

It is because of such advantages that big farmers want big families. Once grown up, his children will make his farm and family prosper. When they are small, the children are not too burdensome: they can easily be fed and clothed with the income received by a big farmer.

One of the most important goals in life, then, is to get grown-up sons. When trying to fulfil this goal, people must also consider the risk of losing one or more children. The infant mortality in Thaiyur is, according to our estimate, nearly 30%. An elementary exercise in probability calculus could run like this: let us say you have six children, three boys and three girls. Probably one girl and one boy will not survive their first year. Four children remain and have survived the most dangerous period in life. Their parents can be reasonably sure that at least one boy will live longer than they themselves.[15] The preference of boys to girls is reflected in the sex-ratio in Thaiyur: 978 women per 1000 men.[16]

We can now see that the Government's attempt to propagate the small family norm to the people in Thaiyur must fail. It is an attempt to persuade people to do something which most of them will perceive as contrary to their own interests. Whether the incentive be 30 rupees or a transistor radio, ordinary people are generally too clever to let themselves be cheated by their government and its foreign advisors.[17]

The small family norm originates from a Westernized urban, middle-class setting. In towns, the family has to subsist on the salary of the father only (town children are improductive consumers much longer than those in the rural regions) and as a consequence the living standard is inversely related to the number of children. Ideally, they should be put through high-school, and perhaps university; and their studies must be financed by the father's salary. The more children, the smaller the share of the cake for each child.

In the rural regions the economic position of children is different. That is not to say that they are a pure blessing. Small children are improductive consumers. In poor, landless families, they are a strain on the household budget, especially in times of crisis due to drought, death, or disease. But ordinarily, it seems, even small farmers and landless labourers are able to provide adequately for their children. When they are about ten years old they begin to contribute to the family income. Girls take care of their smaller siblings and relieve their mothers who can work outside the home and earn a daily wage. Both boys and girls graze cattle, either their own family's or those of some wealthy landlord. Children go fishing, and thus add valuable protein to the family diet. Boys participate in cultivation, for example in irrigation work, in watching the standing crop etc.

There is even a market for child labour in Thaiyur, although it is restricted. Apart from cattle grazing, child labour can also be used in the salt fields, in the commercial sector (shop attendants, waiters), and in the tertiary sector as, for instance, house servants; pumping cycle tyres is a children's speciality, etc.

To conclude, although children are a necessity and a blessing, most families are smaller than they could be, given the reproductive capacity of the women. Family planning is already practiced, but with traditional methods. Poverty sets the limit: the poor have less children than the rich, not because "a small family is a happy family", but because the poor cannot afford the number of children they would like.

The Response to Family Planning in Thaiyur

In view of the previous analysis it is not surprising that the FPP has failed to make headway in Thaiyur. Interviews on the topic proved to be a very delicate matter. Most people became angry. The aversion to the very words "Family Planning" is so great that people often started to quarrel with our interviewers as soon as they heard them mention it. As said in one of their reports:

> When the talk turned to the subject of family planning, there began a murmur of protests from the neighbours who were listening to the interview. Hence our conversation had to be abruptly ended.

The negative reactions show that people are not unfamiliar with the concept of FP. Some people plead ignorance, but rather as a means of defence, it seems. They lie, act stubbornly and even aggressively, sometimes because they fear compulsory sterilization. The question is, therefore, not whether people know about FP, but rather what they know about it.

One can say that for an ordinary villager, FP means an operation to sterilize him or his wife, in order to limit his family to only two children. People are not very familiar with contraceptives or with the loop system. Men know that "Nirodh" (the condom) exists, because of the slides shown at the cinema, but they may not know what it actually is. And condoms are not available anywhere near their place.

People's tendency to identify FP with sterilization is a direct consequence of the Government programme which almost exclusively stresses sterilization. The operation is intensely disliked by an overwhelming majority in Thaiyur. The most important reason for this aversion is simply that many people especially those with one child or less, want to have more children.

As reported about one man:

> He suffers so much for not having a child. He does not want any property, if only his wife could have a child. His wife cried at the time of the interview when I asked about their children. They both said that people in the village are ostracizing them because they have no children.

One old woman cried during the interview and complained:

My son is working all the time for the livelihood of his family.
He is honest and God-fearing, but he is not blessed with a child,
even though he has married three women. As a mother, I cannot
bear to think of his misfortune.

In this connection it is worth noting that a nurse and former
Swallows volunteer became famous in the village for her ability to
help women overcome infertility. During her time people came
from far away to be treated by her. Needless to say, such people have
little interest in family planning. Neither have people with few
children, as exemplified by this young woman:

> —I have no opinion about FP and whether it will be good or
> bad. I know about FP. My first child is three years old. I was
> feeding it until I conceived my second child.
> —But after how many children do you think it would be good
> to adopt FP?
> —I don't care. I will have as many children as I get.
> —But how will you be able to give food to all of them?
> —How can we know beforehand? How can we decide before-
> hand?
> —But there are temporary methods of FP.
> —I don't know about that. Why are you asking all these
> questions? We're not going in for it.

The woman expresses scepticism towards the questions put to her,
as they are hypothetical and concern a distant future. One would
wish that sociologists showed the same amount of scepticism when
constructing their attitude "items", like KAP-surveys.[18] They contain questions of the same vague and hypothetical nature as the above
interview. The answers to them can in most of all cases only be
artificial attitudes with little relation to real behavior, which denies
them their pretentious claims of being a basis for scientific
measurements.

When asked about it, people often refer to the infrastructure which
makes it necessary to have children:

> —If we had two or three children, FP would be good. If I myself
> had three children, I would adopt FP. But now I have only one
> child. My wife is pregnant with a second one.
> —But suppose you get three girls?
> —Then I would wait for a son. What is the use of having a girl?
> Only liabilities!
> —But isn't a girl as good as a boy?

—Only sons will protect their parents in their old age. The girls will go to their husband's place. That is why we want sons only.

People seldom considered religious questions of the following type: are not children the gift of God? Is contraception not infanticide, even if the infant is killed in its mother's womb, rather than after birth? God is giving me children—will He not also protect them? When religious and moral arguments are used, they often stand as rationalizations and legitimations of attitudes which are founded on more mundane realities: most people do not feel any need for birth control. When confronted with FP propaganda, they have to defend themselves. If they cannot simply ignore it, or threaten the propagandist, they have to develop rationalizations as a means of defence. A common counter-argument is the assertion—an incorrect one—that sterilization is dangerous. One woman specified:

> —Nobody in the village will undergo that operation because it is dangerous. One man in Komancheri, one in Thaiyur, and one in Periapilleri died after they had undergone that operation.
> —Did they die immediately after the operation?
> —No, they died some time afterwards due to hard work. A person who undergoes that operation should refrain from hard work and eat good nutritious food.

As we saw above, only a minority of the families in Thaiyur are in fact in need of FP, particularly when the mother is weak because of too frequent pregnancies, and/or the parents think they have too many children.

We met only a handful of people who said that FP was good. They immediately added that most people were against it. In a few cases the family had decided to try FP. One example is Ponnammal's daughter, a tuberculosis patient. Every week she gets an injection at the clinic, and she is very grateful to the people there as they are helping her very much. Some six months ago she had an unnatural abortion. She did not want to have a child at that time, so she took some medicine to get it aborted. She became very ill and the clinic people took her to a hospital in Madras. At that time she was willing to undergo sterilization. But according to her mother she refused at the last minute, giving her weakness as a reason. The doctors also refused to operate on her because they thought she was too weak. When she recovered and came back to Thaiyur, the clinic people advised her to avoid conception. But she became pregnant again. The clinic people told her: "You said you didn't want a child. Now you are pregnant again, just two months after the abortion. How can we believe you?" Now she says that she will definitely go to hospital for the delivery and undergo sterilization.

In cases like this the operation fails to come about even though the woman is willing. One reason for this may be that her husband objects to it which is reason enough in a society with a heavy male dominance.

In one case sterilization was actually performed (extract from report):

> At this stage of the interview one lady appeared and started to tell something. She has given birth to four children. Then she was sterilized in a hospital. But now only one of her children is alive. So she is very unhappy at having been sterilized. "Everybody asks me why I have done it", she says. "At that time I was in Gosha hospital. I had three days of labour pains. Then the doctor asked my husband if I could be sterilized after the birth, because otherwise the fifth child could cause my death. My husband agreed to it. And I was suffering so much that I did not know what to answer, so I agreed. Then my fourth child could not open its mouth after four months so it died."

Because of incidents like this, the FPP is backfiring. It creates hostile attitudes among people alienating even those couples who are potential adopters of contraceptive practices.

Family Planning as a Social Phenomenon

An area can be defined as *absolutely overpopulated* if the means of subsistence potentially contained in it do not suffice to feed its population. The approximately 1000 households in Thaiyur have to subsist on 2500 acres of tilled land plus pastures, lakes etc. At present this is more than sufficient. Thaiyur agriculture produces more than is needed for its own consumption requirements. Still agriculture is "underdeveloped": it does not utilize all its productive potentials. The average yield per acre in paddy production is only about 500 kg. Modern high-yielding varieties produce more than 3000 kg under ideal conditions. *If the productive forces of Thaiyur agriculture were fully*

developed, the village could easily accommodate twice its population.
Thaiyur can consequently by no means be considered as absolutely
overpopulated.[19]

Still there are indicators in Thaiyur of what a neo-Malthusian would
call overpopulation: starvation, misery, landlessness, unemployment,
urban migration, etc. But this is a *relative overpopulation*: people do not
starve because there are too many to share too small a cake. They starve
because they are exploited and denied their just share of the cake.
Landlessness and unemployment are only two symptoms of a system
which denies people not only their means of subsistence but also their
means of production and even their very participation in social
production. And it is largely as a consequence of this exploitation that
the cake is not growing. The current agrarian system thwarts rather
than promotes the growth of the productive forces.

The tendencies inherent in the economic system continuously
produce a relative over-population which the neo-Malthusians mistake for an absolute one: tenants are evicted from their land; small
farmers are expropriated; the employment opportunities for agricultural labourers are decreasing while the proletariat is increasing. (We
make a full analysis of these phenomena in our work on the economy
of Thaiyur panchayat—"Behind Poverty".)[20]

The class-basis of the ideology of population control is obvious:
the ruling classes who reap the benefits of the current system
obviously have no interest in abolishing it. They rightly sense that
the growing relative over-population is a most serious threat to their
position. When they say that the curtailment of the population
growth is a matter of national interests they are ascribing their own
interests to the nation as a whole.

Intellectuals of similar persuasion have expanded this class-
perspective so that it has become an all-encompassing ideology
which, masked as scientific theory, is capable of explaining everything. Even the resistance of the people who generally have no
interest in contraception, is interpreted and explained by this ideology not as a rational and reflected opinion, but as an irrational
reaction stimulated by religious obscurantism, illiteracy and super-
stition. One of our field-workers interpreted the popular resistance
to family planning in the following way:

> It was evident from their resistance that they had a very peculiar
> attitude towards FP. They still believe that it is their bounden

duty to accept any number of children offered to them by God in the midst of suffering. . . . The essential background is their misunderstanding of life and its purpose. The reason may be found in their illiteracy. Perhaps education and self-understanding can rejuvenate them.

Ordinary people, thus, lack the intellectual capacity to understand what is best for themselves. The small family *is* a happy family, even if people refuse to realize it. People must be manipulated into striving for their own self-interest. Such is the patriarchal and authoritarian tone of the Indian FPP.

This is most evident in its choice of methods. Sterilization has been given priority, because it is the most effective means and because other contraceptive methods are said to be too complicated for villagers to use. In other countries sterilization has only been used on a large scale with animals and with mental patients. In Sweden a man was until recently forbidden to have himself voluntarily sterilized. The sterilization policy is symptomatic of the attitudes of the Indian upper and middle classes towards the working classes. Professor C. D. Rajeswaran is only going to the logical end-point of this authoritarian scale; at a seminar held at the Madras Institute of Development Studies and attended by the academic establishment of Tamil Nadu, he suggested that:

> . . . we have to take note of the quality of the population and see what percentage of our population are unwanted. In this country owing to the influence of certain beliefs a sizeable section are not producers while they have to consume to exist.[21]

He then went on to propose that professional beggars, mental patients, patients suffering from communicable diseases and habitual criminals should be compulsorily sterilized:

> If we want to develop into a full scale welfare state which is our aim, we should also see that these classes of people are not allowed to contribute to the increase of our population and it is very necessary that these classes of non-producing consumers are slowly eliminated. (*loc. cit.*)

According to a short protocol, no member of the distinguished seminar protested to this proposed policy.

Perhaps Samir Amin is right in his rather gloomy prediction:

> The world-wide birth control campaign in the developing world expresses the fears of the "developed world" in the face of

the danger of a radical challenge of the international order, by the peoples who are its first victims. In the extreme case the development of the spontaneous trends of the present system would require the *reduction* of the population of the periphery. The contemporary technical and scientific revolution within the context of this system, in fact, excludes the prospect of productive employment of the marginalized masses in the periphery. The failure of "voluntary" birth control methods must thus lead to considering much more violent methods, ultimately coming close to genocide.[22]

The FPP is a growing failure. It is doomed to remain a failure as long as the motivations of individual couples conflict with the goals of the programme. No reforms, no tactical reconsiderations can make the programme a success. Its unfeasibility can even be demonstrated by means of mathematical deduction as Agarwala has done.[23] Working with figures from the 1961 Census, he has shown that if the Government wants to reach its goal of zero-growth of population by 1991, and of bringing down the birth rate to 16 per mille in that year (equal to the predicted death rate):

> . . . roughly 4 million sterilizations have to be performed annually during 1961–66. The number of annual operations will increase to 10 million during 1986–91. In other words, while all the currently married females of the reproductive age above 42·5 or their husbands will have to be sterilized in 1961, all those above age 22 will have to be operated upon in 1991.

This shows, as Agarwala says, that the programme is "beyond the limits of feasibility" (*loc. cit.*).

The failure of the FPP evidently increases the danger of a fascist reaction along the lines predicted by Samir Amin above. This prospect makes it imperative for the progressive forces in India to fight the neo-Malthusian ideology of population control, and to fight for a FPP with democratic objectives and working methods. Such a programme could be linked with programmes for maternity and child care. It should aim at assisting families with too many children and a felt need for contraception, and families where further pregnancies are a health hazard to the mother. Its objective should not be a drastic reduction in birth rates, because this can probably not be achieved without a change of the economic roles of children. The necessary reconsiderations of the present policy are indicated by these reflections made by a Swallows volunteer midwife after two years of work in Thaiyur:

> They have not been receptive to family planning propaganda. They have said that they "have no guarantee that their children will survive". So what should be done is to create such a guarantee. If that can be done through preventive medicine, then I think family planning is all right. But, for example, when they get a loop they start bleeding. They and others get afraid. You cannot force them to adopt it. One must create the readiness. Sometimes the men resist. I don't know if it is true that one should strive to tell them that they would get a higher living standard by having fewer children. They are perhaps happier with children than with a radio. The wealth of the poor are their children.[24]

As long as the Government cannot create an economic and social structure which stimulates a reduction in birth rates, where other social institutions can take over the functions now fulfilled by the children, it cannot expect the people to abstain from producing the children which, in the present social situation, are their only security.

Postscript

During the emergency 1975–1977 our pessimistic prediction about a fascist reaction was borne out. Though the sterilization campaigns were not as repressive in the South as in the North, they were still effective in a state like Tamilnadu. In Thaiyur many poor farmers were operated on. The main means of bringing about this result was to coerce the teachers and village-level-workers. They were forced to bring a certain quota of patients during each campaign, otherwise they would forego salary increases or be transferred to another district. The monetary incentive to the patients was more than doubled and the campaigns were conducted in the agricultural off-seasons when the poor peasants and landless are semi-starving and are easier to motivate by remuneration in cash.

Despite all this, the programme did not reach more distant villages; there was still huge resistance in many villages and many government officials passively sabotaged the programme. The resistance was reinforced by cases of death due to lack of proper postoperative treatment. Most labourers also complained about loss of working ability as a consequence of the operation. A large proportion of old men were sterilized, it seems, so the effect on the birth rate cannot have been as dramatic as demographers expected.

The massive anti-Congress verdict in the 1977 elections was to a large extent due to widespread resistance and resentment against the sterilization campaigns. The change in government has brought the Indian people a respite from the class-war waged on them by the ruling classes—but for how long?

Notes

1. This essay is a shortened and modified version of Chapter 9 in our study, "Pills Against Poverty—a Study of the Introduction of Western Medicine in a Tamil Village", Curzon Press, London, 1975. Most of the information refers to the situation in 1969–1970. We have chosen to retain the "ethnographic present" except in the introduction and in the postscript. We are grateful to Lars Bondestam for constructive criticism.

   Mr G. Kasturi, Mr M. Paramasivam and Mrs K. Sundari worked as research associates in the study. The study was sponsored by the aid organization the Swallows and financed by SIDA (Swedish International Development Agency). The economic and political structure of the village has been presented in our study, "Behind Poverty—the Social Formation in a Tamil Village", Curzon Press, London, 1975.

2. Samuel, T. J. (1966). The development of India's policy of population control. *Milbank Memorial Fund Qu.* **44,** 49–67.

3. It is desirable to make a clear distinction between family planning and population control. The latter includes all attempts to administratively regulate the growth pattern of a population, while the former refers to the strivings of individual families to voluntarily plan their size, space between births, etc. In a way, one could say that this essay deals with the perversion of family planning which results from its being subjected to political interests in population control. As will be evident, the terms family planning and Family Planning Programme, when used by the Indian Government, actually stand for population control.

4. Bardhan, P. K. (1973). On the incidence of poverty in rural India of the sixties. *Econom. & Polit. Weekly* (Bombay), **VIII,** 245–254.

5. The D.M.K. Government won the 1967 elections partly due to their promise to sell subsidized rice for one rupee a measure to the people.

6. Myrdal, G. (1968). "Asian Drama: An Inquiry into the Poverty of Nations", p. 1400. Pantheon, New York.

7. "Census of India 1961", Vol. I, India, Part III (ii), Household Economic Tables. Government of India Press, New Delhi 1965, pp. 40–41.

8. See, for instance, Perez, A. O. (1971). "Timing and sequences of resuming ovulation and menstruation after childbirth." (Cited in *Current Anthropology*, April 1972, p. 253). Quoted by de Jonge and Varkevisser 1972, p. 5.

9. Probably *errukka cedi* which according to the *Tamil Lexicon* is Calotropis giganthea, i.e. henbane. (*Tamil Lexicon*, University of Madras, Madras 1934).

10. Similar conclusion have been drawn by:
Bondestam, L. (1972). "Population Growth Control in Kenya." Research Report No. 12. The Scandinavian Institute of African Studies, Uppsala, p. 37 ff.
Douglas, M. (1966). Population control in primitive groups. *Brit. J. Sociol.* **17**, 263–273.
de Jonge, K. and Varkevisser, C. Fertility in two rural areas in Tanzania: a dependent variable. Paper presented to the Seminar on Population and Economic Growth in Africa, Afrika Studie-Centrum, Leiden 18–22 December 1972.
Konter, J. H. The implications of family planning in the changing socio-economic structure of the Nyakyusa Rungwe district, Tanzania. Paper presented to the Seminar on Population and Economic Growth in Africa. Afrika Studie-Centrum, Leiden 18–22 December 1972.
Mamdani, M. (1972). "The Myth of Population Control: Family, Caste and Class in an Indian Village", Chaps 4–6. Monthly Review Press, New York and London.

11. Schenk, H. (1973–1974). India—poverty and sterilization. *Devl. & Change* **V**, 36–53.

12. Douglas, op. cit., de Jonge and Varkevisser, op. cit. and Sahlins, M. (1972). "Stone Age Economics", pp. 34 and 49 n. Aldine-Atherton, Chicago.

13. Berelson, B. and Steiner, G. A. (1964). "Human Behaviour. An Inventory of Scientific Findings", p. 478. Harcourt Brace and World, Incorporated, New York.

14. Shanin, T. (1972). "The Awkward Class. Political Sociology of Peasantry in a Developing Society, Russia 1910–1925", p. 63 n. Clarendon Press, Oxford.

15. A similar calculation has been made by de Jonge and Varkevisser: "Gradual decline in infant mortality in Rungwe/Tanzania/has been insufficient to ensure parents who have experienced the sudden death of children in their childhood that they have a living son in their old age when they need support unless they reproduce to the limits of their capacity. To be reasonably certain (80%) of the survival of one son when the father is 65 years old, a couple must bring seven children into the world. It is hardly controversial to assert that no reduction in fertility is foreseeable before dramatic improvement of health services". (de Jonge and Varkevisser op. cit., p. 3).

16. In the West the common pattern is the reverse, i.e. an overweight of

women. But in India, as in pre-revolutionary China (Hinton, W. (1966). "Fanshen: A Documentary of Revolution in a Chinese Village", Monthly Review Press, New York), there are more men than women. There may be many explanations for this, but the preference for boys is one plausible cause. The common explanation (cf. e.g. Mandelbaum, D. (1970). Curing and religion in South Asia. *J. Indian Anthropolog. Soc.* **5,** pp. 171–186, p. 183), is that girls, although they are not intentionally neglected, tend to get slightly less attention and care than boys. On the aggregate level, this may result in a slightly higher mortality for girls than for boys.

In a personal communication, Bertil Pfannenstill, Lund, pointed to an alternative explanation: the sex-ratio can be a product, not of a differential mortality for boys and girls, but of an uneven balance already *at birth*. Since boys are preferred to girls, families who have already got boys tend to abstain from further children. But those families who have only got girls have to continue producing children. Therefore, there are more boys born than girls. Unfortunately, we have no Thaiyur demographic data against which these alternative hypotheses can be tested, but the latter interpretation is ruled out in an article by Dandekar, K. (1975). Why has the proportion of women in India's population been declining? *Econom. & Polit. Weekly* **X,** 1663–1667.

17. Instead people will cheat the government. Many will let themselves be sterilized when they have already passed their reproductive age. (Mandelbaum, D. (1973). Social Components of Indian fertility. *Econom. & Polit. Weekly,* Annual Number 1973, **VIII,** (p. 153).

18. Cf. the article by Pierre Pradervand in this volume.

19. Samir Amin states that there are only a few areas in the Third World which are absolutely over-populated according to his definition. These are the West Indies, the Nile Valley, the delta regions of Asia and Java. Most other areas, including the southern part of the Indian subcontinent, cannot be considered absolutely over-populated. Amin, S. (1972). Under-populated Africa (originally presented to a meeting of experts on population—education—development in Africa South of the Sahara, Dakar, November 29 to December 4, 1971). Reprinted in "Family Planning in Ethiopia", No. 3, Ethiopian Nutrition Institute, Addis Abeba, pp. 86–97, p. 89.

20. Djurfeldt-Lindberg, op. cit., chaps 4–7.

21. Rajeswaran, C. D. (1972). Application of scientific methods and family planning, *Monthly Bull.*, Madras Institute of Development Studies, **II,** pp. 52–76, p. 74.

22. Amin, op. cit., pp. 93–94.

23. Agarwala, S. N.(1966). The arithmetic of sterilization in India. *Eugenics Quarterly* **13,** 209–213. Quotations from p. 213.

24. Similar views have long been presented by the opponents to the neo-Malthusian dominance in the family planning movement, de Leeuwe, J.: N.V.S.H. and I.P.P.F. and Population Policies. Paper

presented to the Seminar on Population and Economic Growth in Africa, Afrika Studie-Centrum, Leiden 18–22 December 1972. Compare also the following statement by the Indian delegates to the WHO Regional Committee, 1969: "Family Planning becomes a controversial issue as soon as it is identified with population control; but there is no difficulty in introducing family planning as a normal activity of a maternal and child health programme designed for the protection of mothers and children. In fact the integration of FP into maternal and child health services represents the best and more rational approach". "Health Progress in India". As presented by the delegates to the WHO Regional Committee, 29 September to 9 October 1969, *India J. Pediat.* **36** (1969), pp. 490–494, p. 494.

Japan's Abortion Laws and Birth Control Ambitions in the Underdeveloped Countries in Asia

Bo Gunnarsson

Listening to the debate in Japan on the population situation in the Third World, one does not need to be possessed of metaphysical powers to discern the phantom figures of dubious motives. Seldom is any distinction made between family planning and population control and many speak of the latter as though they envisioned a fight against the plague.

Three persons in authority with whom this author spoke reflect the opinions of the party in political power and of industrial and business leaders:[1]

> —People shouldn't be allowed to have children in such circumstances as in Calcutta. They have no dignity anymore. Vasectomy must be made compulsory, enforced by law, on humanitarian grounds (Nobusuke Kishi, former prime minister, leader of the Parliamentary Committee on Population Issues, President of the Japan Organisation for International Cooperation in Family Planning, JOICFP, a private organization, financed by donations from industry, and special adviser to UNFPA; see also below and footnote).[3]
> —Our security is best served not by strengthening our military forces but by helping the Asian nations to control the population explosion (Saburo Okita, expert on aid to developing countries, former President of Overseas Economic Cooperation Fund).
> —The labor explosion in developing nations in Asia may keep the wages on a low level but who will provide all the jobs needed? This situation will sooner or later create social chaos and even anarchy. Not only our investments will be threatened but also our imports of natural resources (Kogoro Uemura, former president of Keidanren, The Japanese Federation of Industries).

In Japan, poverty in the developing countries is generally explained as a matter of there being too many mouths to feed and too little to feed them. Despite the fact that Japan herself rose from bombed ruins to her present position of world power economically speaking within a span of twenty years, there exists among its leaders little or no faith in the ability of the poorest countries to make any such progress. One reason for this is probably a latent racism; another is that a higher demand and consumption within the raw material-exporting countries are eyed more and more as a threat to Japan's own welfare. The statistical survey made by the Club of Rome on the earth's limited resources has been taken at its word in Tokyo.

Mr Okita calls this reaction "self-preservation". He says that Japan is a very small country, an island in a double sense, surrounded by 1600 million and impoverished and hungry people, all of whom are seeking a better standard of living. Mr Kishi shares his apprehension: "Japan's population will probably decrease in about 50 years but with our few natural resources we will still face a food crisis. Our supplies will be endangered by the massive growth in India and elsewhere".

Japan's dependence on import is steadily increasing and in 1977, according to the Ministry of Trade and Industry, it reached about 59% for grain (despite an overproduction of rice), 90% for most minerals, 75% for lumber and lumber products and 99% for gas and oil. More than half of this import comes from the Third World. Nevertheless, Japan's efforts in the area of population have been rather limited to date. "We have a historical handicap to overcome", says Mr Kishi.

Militarism's strong bonds to Malthus's theories contributed to the fact that Japanese family planning aid was taboo up until 1973.[2] Anti-Japanese feelings still run high in Southeast Asia and a direct action within the population sector would be altogether too provocative. Chojiro Kunii, head of JOICFP, states, "The question of aid is of a very sensitive nature. Other nations can easily misunderstand our intentions since population control is a matter of reducing childbirths. It is, as it were, a form of intervention . . .".

Moreover, the time is not yet ripe, partly because of the personages leading "the movement" in Japan. Nobusuke Kishi, Ryoichi Sasagawa and several others of the major propagandists for population control held key posts during the days of militarism and were sentenced to prison at the end of the war, under suspicion for war crimes.[3] After a study tour of i.a. Calcutta, Kishi formed his

Parliamentary Federation for Population Issues which now has over 150 members in the Diet. The group, which receives financial support from business and industry, purports to build up a strong public backing for its cause; it does lobbying and strives to create an international programme of action on the highest political level. Kishi's relations with various dictators in Asia and Latin America are well-known. With the Government's tacit approval, the federation, with Kishi at the stern, undertakes diplomatic crusades in various parts of the world, donning the cloak of Japan's conscience in the developing countries. In the fall of 1977, visits were made to Washington and Latin America and President Carter received advice from Kishi in person to direct great attention to population expansion which "threatens many of the national and international aspirations of our two governments".[4] Mr Kishi warned, "This problem has so far been one for the scientists but now it is one for top-level politicians and parliamentarians to deal with".

During later years, Japan has been urged more and more often to take on a role in the struggle·against population expansion in the Third World. Immediately prior to the population conference in Bucharest, General William Draper (died 1974, known for his intimate relations with Kishi and the right wing ever since the beginning of the American occupation of Japan) argued:

> The very fact that Japan has been the only nation in Asia to solve its population problem and that it has achieved such an unparalleled economic development, leads to the conclusion that the Japanese government and people are now facing a great and friendly challenge and unusual opportunity to help their Asian neighbours to solve their problems for their own good, for the good of Asia and for the benefit of the world. A large number of Japan's legislators now realize that the world population problem must and can be solved. It gives real promise that Japan and the Japanese government are beginning to assume real leadership in Asia in the effort to bring birth rates into reasonable balance with today's much lower death rates.[5]

Rafael Salas, the Executive Director of UNFPA, who lauded Kishi as a "progressive statesman", has officially besought Japan to give more support to population control. The wishes of various dictators in Southeast Asia have been expressed more discreetly. It is thus important to ask—what degree of general applicability does the

Japanese experience have and what credentials, besides its wealth, does Japan have for taking a very active part in the population growth control in the Third World? Is Japan a model for the developing countries to pattern themselves after?

The historical background of Japan's present population policy is of interest in this connection:

> In a sense the Japanese have got a step ahead of Malthus. The reasons are not clear. One factor may have been the combination of feudal patterns of inheritance in which man had only one heir and the Japanese practices of adoption which made it unnecessary for this heir to be his natural child. As a result, a man didn't need a large number of children for financial security and family continuity and usually found a big family more of a liability than an asset. During the Tokugawa period 1650–1865 peasants practised infanticide to keep down the number of mouths to be fed and the population did remain static for a century and a half despite the growth of the economy.[6]

When Japan broke her long isolation in 1870 during the Meiji restoration, the ideas of Malthus swept in on the waves of everything else Western that invaded the country. Dr Takuma Terao, Chairman of the Japan Family Planning Federation, remarks, "Those in power in the Japanese Empire interpreted Malthus in their own peculiar way. Instead of dealing with the food shortage through population control, the leaders created the cult of the 'hinterland' and later the "'Greater Asia Prosperity Sphere' for an expanded Lebensraum".[7] The rice riots of 1917, when millions of people revolted, were taken by the powerful as still another substantiation of their conviction that the country was overpopulated. A socialist-dominated popular movement for family planning took shape but was driven underground when the military took over.[8] Abortions were made a criminal act by law for the first time already in 1880, and in 1940 the National Eugenic Law purported to stimulate childbirth and to "protect the quality of the Yamato race". The aim was to increase the numbers available for labour and warfare. Premiums were paid to women who gave birth to more than 10 children.

The repatriation of 6·2 million soldiers returning from war and emigrants returning from the colonies had brought the population up to 80 million. The Eugenic Protection Law of 1948 allowed abortion on economic grounds as well. Amidst the then prevailing poverty and housing shortage, the law was met with strong response. The devastation caused by the war was immense, but the infrastructure and the high level of education remained intact. The economic development, and all of its integral parts which spurred it onward and upward—the Korean War, low wages, urbanization, rapid rises in childcare costs, cut-throat competition in the schools and exploitation of women as cheap labour—caused an intensification in birth control. The absence of social reforms gave rise to a feeling of insecurity in the face of the future, to which the Japanese people responded in general by putting more of their money into savings accounts. This accumulated capital could be invested in industrial expansion. Thus, Japan cut her birth rate in half within 10 years—from 33·5 in 1948 to 17·2 in 1957, and the population increase has been stabilized at around 1·2% per year since then.

The main purpose of the Japanese population policy is still under dispute. Is the goal of the policy and of the seemingly progressive laws passed in its context really to attain widespread birth control and thereby to reduce population growth or is the goal instead to master the social chaos and to stop the ever threatening leftist front? A Japanese sociologist writes: "To be sure, women should be able to have abortions. But the Eugenic Protection Law is by no means a part of the struggle for their welfare or that of their families. It is meant strictly to create optimal conditions for business and industry".[9] The most important factor behind the demographic "revolution", then, is that the wielders of power have succeeded in creating a social structure which renders it impossible for the poor to have more than one or two children even if they should so desire. That the poor have undergone so many abortions is the real explanation for Japan's achieving the very remarkable, drastic about-face in her demographic statistics. The number of pregnancies *begun*, around 2·7–3·0 million per year, has not changed during all these years. According to an extensive investigation, well-paid Japanese have more children on the average than workers with relatively low wages.[10] Condoms and abortion are the most commonly used forms of contraception. Despite pioneering efforts towards the development of the IUD in the 1930s, it was not approved for general use by the Ministry of Health until 1974, most likely then as a gesture toward the UN conference in Bucharest.[11] Besides, a doctor's charge for insertion of the P-ring is roughly US$100. Birth control pills are still not legalized. The official line is that the pill "has yet to be scientifically evaluated". But, since so much of the other medicine already on the market has been subjected to less testing and is less safe, the real reason would seem to be another: The Japan Society of Obstetricians and Gynecologists does not want to relinquish abortions as its best source of income.[12] At least six Japanese drug companies are permitted to export birth control pills to developing countries. One of them also unloads prostaglandin pills on developing countries. These pills have not yet been approved in the rich countries.[13]

Toward the end of the 1960s when it seemed as though a shortage of young members of the labour force threatened (these workers earn less than older ones), demands were raised by pressure groups from industry for a revision of the abortion laws. Slogans such as "Respect for life", "End the shame of having Japan called an abortion paradise" and "Have babies, increase your prosperity" rang through Parliament. Others expressed a newly found concern for health hazards faced by women or for moral degeneration.[14] An investigation by the Ministry of Health's Population Problem Council proclaimed in 1969 that a higher birth rate was desirable. Under pressure from industry, the conservative party in power introduced a bill for the removal of the clause covering "economic grounds" from the Eugenic Protection Law. They argued that the standard of living had risen and thereby the situation which had made the clause necessary had been eradicated.

Various people's interest groups, led by radical women's groups and the handicapped,[16] protested vehemently. The women's section of Sohyo (The General Council of Trade Unions of Japan) expressed the will of the people in their petition to the Government demanding that measures be taken to solve the social problems which force women to seek abortion. This should be done instead of changing the abortion law, they reasoned.

It is undeniable that abortions can endanger a woman's health. According to an investigation. 42% of all married women in Japan have undergone one or more abortions (7–8 was not an altogether unusual number).[17] More than 20 million women have been forced to submit to abortion during a 30-year period due to pressing economic needs. To make the law more restrictive would only make their situation more intolerable.

Family planning organizations and neo-Malthusian conservatives also raised their voices, emphasizing that the population, even with a stable growth rate, would increase by about 30 million during the next 20 years. Saburo Okita expressed himself in alarmist terms: "Controlling the population is important for us in maintaining the present patterns of consumption of natural resources and food in the future. If we do not exercise control we may be inevitably forced into war against other countries to feed our population".[18]

What decided the matter in the end was most likely the fear that people might get the wrong idea—especially in Southeast Asia and in the developing countries, considering as they were the liberalization of their own abortion laws. The revision was passed twice in the Lower House but was never brought to a vote in the Upper House. The pressures from industrial interests died down. They came to realize that the poor countries of Asia could offer a surplus of ideally cheap labour and that Japan had more to gain by moving the labour-intensive low-wage sector southward.

Can Japan export her demographic "revolution" to regions which are experiencing a "population explosion", then? No. Abortion is a drastic means of contraception which can never be established as a general practice except under very special circumstances. Such circumstances have prevailed in Japan, which even before the Second World War was an industrial nation with a high level of education, and they prevail today in a very few developing countries, e.g. South Korea and Taiwan. Aside from the strictly moral objections to the mere recommendation of a "Japanese solution", the importation of their methods in the absence of an infrastructure and a population strongly motivated to practice birth control can have only a marginal effect. Despite this, Japan Medical Association is negotiating with the Government of Bangladesh on the opening of an abortion clinic in Dacca.

Another Japanese phenomenon which has stimulated great interest among family planning administrators in developing countries is the commercially-based distribution of condoms. India's Nihrod Programme and Thailand's Community Based Distribution System are among two of the efforts which have copied the Japanese model to a large extent. But, here again, a strong motivation must reign if men are to use condoms—crowded conditions constitute but one of the many factors to the contrary—and, in the absence of motivation, an increased availability of these contraceptives can have but an insignificant effect on the birth rate.

Japan's credentials to take a more active part in the efforts towards birth control in Asia are nothing more than a matter of financial resources. Analyses of the problem have remained on a primitive level and what the people in Japan and in the developing countries are faced with is in fact a network of myths.

Mr Okita emphasizes that he for one prefers a "clinical solution" for population planning and would not put priority on economic development. He argues, "One day's delay in implementing effective family planning may mean decades of grave results". Referring to president Lyndon Johnson's immortal remark, he says, "One dollar invested in family planning equals 100 dollars invested in economic development. The vicious circle of poverty and high birthrates must be broken".[19] (Even those who have so many good things to say about socio-economic development as a prerequisite for birth control mean by "development" something quite different from what the poor and oppressed in the Third World are striving to obtain.)

The asserted adverse effects of population growth on the environment is an often recurring theme in the population debate. A new concept, pollution per capita, has come into being. Mr Kunii says, "We do not want what has happened in Japan to be repeated in the poor countries. Our fishing areas are polluted, our air is at times hazardous to health, and people have died from poisoning. The basic cause is overpopulation".

The food situation is viewed in the same manner. The rice harvest per hectare is 4–6 times greater in Japan than in, e.g. India. Still, many talk as though the food supply in India cannot increase in volume and as though every single little newborn child bears a responsibility for the hunger crisis. Dr Tsutomi Ouchi, Tokyo University, said in an interview, "I shudder to think of the degree of environmental pollution which would ensue from putting as much fertilizer and as many pesticides into the rice-fields of Southeast Asia as in Japanese paddies. I also do not think that there is enough water in Indonesia to water all paddies adequately".[20]

The UN conference in Bucharest turned into a bitter lesson for Japan. No one had anticipated the fierce opposition to the World Action Plan. Pronouncements on the compromise to which the delegates had to resort pendulated between "regrettable" and "tragic". Special lament was expressed for the fact that the proposal to set up a quantitative goal (a reduction of the birth-rate by 5–10 per 1000 before 1985) was forced out of the plan. Japan and a number of Asian nations sustained a counterattack and succeeded in including a passage characterized as "a revival of zero population growth", the concept which had been infused throughout the original plan.

"Thanks to this constructive compromise, the UN conference was saved from turning into a fiasco", commented Toshio Kuroda, the grand old man among Japan's demographers and head of the Institute of Population Problems under the Ministry of Health. "Those who live outside Asia cannot readily understand how serious the situation is since they lack first-hand experience."

Five months later, a new optimism was ignited. The 21 member nations of Economic and Social Commission for Asia and the Pacific region (ESCAP), at a meeting in Bangkok, made a number of additions to the World Action Plan which were termed "most appropriate to conditions prevailing in Asia". "All nations in the region are united in our conviction that we must exercise an energetic birth control program in the future. We could agree on proposals which were unthinkable in Bucharest", Kuroda declared.[21]

The trump card was the establishment of population control goals, the proposal which had been crushed in Bucharest. And India—whose delegates at the UN conference had asserted that "development is the best pill"—plunged back into the antinatal camp and stated her aim to be zero population growth by the year 2000. Another proposal which was passed was a call to the member nations to consider a liberalization of abortion laws for the purpose of protecting women's health. The subject had previously been taboo.

Since 1973, Japan has increased its aid to developing countries for family planning purposes more than sevenfold. During 1978, UNFPA is stated to receive 14·5 million dollars from Japan. Additional funds will go to IPPF and bilateral aid. Part of this aid is administered by private organizations, primarily JOICFP. Aware that the impoverished of Southeast Asia have not forgotten the brutal occupation of the Japanese Imperial Army, JOICFP has launched its own version of "humanistic family planning". It consists of, in short, a semi-annual deworming, a programme which alone naturally cannot raise the standard of living, but which does show originality in its cynicism and reveals the Japanese elite's exaggerated and unwarranted faith in the power of technology to solve everything. Mr Kunii explains,

> By distributing deworming agents, we establish a personal contact and thus better relations with the local populations. About 60–90% have intestinal worms. Since parasite control means better public health, we anticipate a more positive attitude toward family planning. We shall also provide information on nutrition and health. It is important to win the trust of the people and our program can be a milestone in the struggle of humanity against the population explosion.

JOICFP, which has pilot projects under way in South Korea, Taiwan and all ASEAN countries, has received a certain amount of criticism at home for its "integrated" programme. "What you are doing is the opposite to population control since you are helping the people increase their numbers even more", cry certain of the most fervent Malthusians.

The demographic transition in Japan from high mortality/high birth rate to low mortality/low birth rate has indeed inspired great admiration abroad. The Japanese are proud, they too, and often remark that their present material well-being owes its existence to the "population revolution". But this "revolution" in Japan was accomplished without any radical social changes. It arose as a response to extremely adverse conditions which themselves could be interpreted simplistically as resulting from a period of a pronatal policy. At the same time, the Korean War meant an economic upsurge for Japan. It was not the birth control programme which gave the Japanese economy the wind for its sail. No matter how one looks at the population problem, one cannot remove economic development as an absolute prerequisite to family planning. And, even then, if family planning is practiced in the absence of equal efforts in the social sphere, as we can see in Japan, South Korea and Taiwan, the problems of the population will remain as unsolved as ever.

Notes

1. Interviews and talks, 1974–1977.

2. Eighteen million Asians, most of them civilians, and three million Japanese soldiers died during the Imperial Army's warfare in China and Southeast Asia.
3. Kishi was, 1938–1940, one of five of a team who ruled the occupied Manchuria. He later was appointed minister in General Hideki Tojo's cabinet. After the Japanese defeat, he spent two years in Sugami prison, suspected for war crimes, class A. He was prime minister 1957–1960 and is still extremely influential as a "Kuromaku" (power behind the scenes). Sasagawa was also jailed, suspected of war crimes, but, like Kishi, released without standing trial. In 1939, he went to Rome with a military escort and negotiated with Mussolini on the formation of a civil axis between the two countries. He is now the leader of Japan's extreme right wing. Through his organizations, Japan Shipbuilding Industry Foundation and Japan Science Society, he has donated at least four million dollars for family planning projects sponsored by JOICFP, UNFPA, WHO, Draper World Population Fund and various Asian dictators. He is now a "special adviser" to UNFPA and, as a "philanthropist", he is also received with open arms at the White House.
4. "Mainichi Shimbun", 17 September 1977.
5. Japan Population Conference, 2 July 1974, Tokyo.
6. Reischauer, E. (1977). "The Japanese", p. 71. Tokyo. "Infanticide was regarded as a quite proper process and was known as *mabiki*, which is the word used of thinning a row of vegetables by uprooting. Conversely, in order to secure a supply of children without expenses of bringing them up, farmers were known to buy children kidnapped in large towns by regular traffickers, known as 'child merchants'. Before Tokugawa times infanticides seem to have been sporadic and to have followed natural calamities like famine and plague but by the middle of the eighteenth century they were prevalent throughout Japan and had reached alarming proportions". Samson, G. B. (1973). "Imperial Japan", p. 24. Pantheon Asia Library.
7. *Mainichi Daily News*, 18 March 1975.
8. Huddle, N. and Reich, M. (1975). "Island of Dreams", p. 314. Autumn Press, Tokyo, New York. The Japanese Government in 1922 tried to prevent Margaret Sanger from landing but finally permitted her entry on the condition that she would not give any public lectures.
9. Othake, Y. (1975). *Human*, No. 2.
10. "Population Revolution in Japan", published by *Mainichi Newspaper*, 1969.
11. The Ota-ring, designed by Dr Tenrei Ota in 1930. Criticism was based on the common belief that it was against medical common sense to wear a foreign object in the body. *JOICFP News*, No. 4, 1974.
12. Wagatsuma, T. Tokyo University School of Medicine.
13. Nagano Y in *AMPO*, No. 17.
14. Prime Minister Eisaku Sato 23 March 1970 proclaimed to Parliament: "Respect for life is being ignored in these times—as symbolized by the

confusion in sexual morality. . . . We have to preserve the sense of nurturing the embryo as our own child, a gift from heaven . . . not for the labor supply, but in relation to the social disorder, we should revise the Eugenic Protection Law which is the fundamental cause of social vice".

15. Different women's groups argued that the aim of the revision also was to shift the blame for abortion from the society (which in itself necessitates abortions for economic reasons) to the individual woman (*AMPO*, No. 17).

16. Handicapped young people strongly opposed the first article in the Eugenic Protection Law which says: "This law is instituted so that (we) may check the birth of inferior descendants as well as protect the life of mothers from the eugenic viewpoint". The 1974 White Paper on Population states: "Population quality with mental and physical health is our main national goal even more than economic growth. . . . The purpose of population policy is to improve inherited qualities and to exclude inferior hereditary factors. Superior hereditary qualities should be conveyed to the next generation as a property . . . making use of the Eugenic Protection Law, it is important to check inferior inheritance and to spread information for this purpose" (*Human*, No. 2, 1975).

17. Opinion survey by the Prime Minister's Office, 1976.

18. *Human*, No. 2, 1975.

19. *Human*, No. 2, 1975.

20. *Asahi Evening News*, 18 August 1973.

21. *Mainichi Daily News*, 30 January 1975.

Race Ratios: The Politics of Population Control in South Africa

Madi Gray

Introduction

To understand population politics in South Africa one needs to take a look at the recent political history of the country. Since the present white nationalist minority government gained power thirty years ago, it has systematically been implementing its party programme of *apartheid*. Rooted in earlier legislation, the apartheid policy is designed to deprive the majority of the population of all political and economic rights. As the regime has entrenched its own power, the non-white (black) population has been subjected to increasing oppression, exploitation and terror. The UN General Assembly has designated the obnoxious apartheid system as "a crime against humanity" and declared 1978 as the International Year Against Apartheid.

Control of Population Movements

Even before the Union of South Africa was formed in 1910 the movements of Africans and Asians (Indians) were controlled. Asians could not cross from one province to another, and African workers had to have a legitimate permit or "pass" before they could obtain employment. In the 1920s and 1930s attempts were made to extend the pass system to all Africans over sixteen years. Years of militant struggle led by women throughout the country forced the government of the day to exempt women from carrying passes.

In the 1950s, with the present government firmly in control and with more sophisticated demands from industry, a new law was promulgated. Called, ironically, the *Abolition of Passes Act*, the regime changed the name of the requisite document to "reference book" and all Africans had to carry them or be liable for arrest.

Again women throughout the country were mobilized. Led by the Women's League of the African National Congress (ANC) and its allies in the Federation of South African Women, nationwide protests culminated in the capital city of Pretoria on 9 August 1956. Twenty thousand women of all racial groups sang out their defiance of the racial laws and presented sackfuls of petitions. Only after extreme brutality including threats, mass arrests, the burning of huts and crops, deportations and murders, was the women's resistance finally crushed.

The effect of these laws has been to divide families, separating parents from their children and husbands from their wives, and arrests of more than 800 000 people annually for "technical offences" against the pass laws.[1]

These harsh effects on the lives of the black people have been worsened by another series of laws. Africans are only allowed to own land in the so-called reserves, 13% of South Africa's overgrazed and least fertile areas. The reserves were originally proclaimed in 1913 and 1936, but the present government renamed them "bantustans", claiming it was prepared to grant "independence" to one "territory" after another. Ten such bantustans are planned. The first two "independent" bantustans, Transkei and Bophutatswana, after consolidation consist of three and seven separate pieces of land respectively. Like the other projected bantustans they are overcrowded, have no natural resources or minerals, and are economically entirely dependent on South Africa.

More than nine million Africans were in "white" areas in January 1975, according to the Deputy Minister for Bantu Administration (now called the Department of Plural Relations). The statistics were incomplete, added the Deputy Minister, as they did not account for those who had evaded census officials.[2] Thus, more than half of the African population continues to live and work in the "white" urban and rural areas, where they are subject to grinding poverty, mass arrests and forced removals.

The population of the bantustans is heavily dominated by women, children, sick and aged people, who are declared "unproductive units" or "superfluous appendages".[3] The ablebodied, on the other hand, cannot find work in these areas and are forced to sign contracts binding them to work in the mines and industries, where they live in squalid, overcrowded single sex hostels, and meet their families on average three weeks per year.

Officially, South Africa's population of over 25 million (1975) is divided into four racial groups. The largest is the African population (71·2%). Two other groups who do not have any meaningful political rights whatsoever are the coloured people (9·3%) and the Asian people (2·8%). These three groups regard themselves as black, a term popularized by the Black Consciousness Movement in a deliberate attempt to counter the systematic efforts of the regime to divide the groups they themselves call non-white. The white minority constitutes 16·6%, a decline since 1970 of 1·3%.[4]

Swart Gevaar—Black Danger

South Africa has her own doomsday prophets. Philip H. Moore predicted in 1959:

> Towards the end of this century there will be about 27 million natives (Africans) in the Union (Republic of South Africa). From 1950 to the year 2000 the increase will have been threefold! The Bantu areas (bantustans) will be impossibly overcrowded and the inhabitants will be short of food. Will it be possible to prevent these concentrations overflowing into the less settled European (white) land, and if this should take place, then not only the Bantu but all the people of South Africa will find themselves forced to starvation level.[5]

Because of their everpresent fear of being outnumbered by the black majority also on the local level, the whites promulgated the Group Areas Acts of 1950 and 1966. Under these laws, established communities have been torn apart and separate townships created for each of the population groups in each area. The pattern is to surround the white areas by a buffer zone of townships for the coloured and the Indian people, with the poorest section of the community, the African, living furthest away from the centres of work. Thus far 600 000 people have been forcibly removed and resettled in segregated townships. Only about 7 000 are white, the vast majority, more than 550 000, are Asian and coloured people.[6] Up to 1978 the staggering figure of 2·15 million Africans had been removed mainly to "resettlement camps" in the bantustans. It is planned to remove a further 1·73 million Africans to such "camps". There is no proper housing, no sanitation, often no water within easy reach, high prevalence of disease and of malnutrition, and no work. Consequently, mortality rates among children are so high that the policy of forcibly removing 15% of the population seems deliberately genocidal.

Population—Yesterday, Today and Tomorrow

The prospect of becoming an evershrinking proportional minority appalls the whites. Not only do they fear being outnumbered and overwhelmed by the black majority, a phobia as old as the colonization of South Africa, but the most reactionary section also fears that this may mean that even African labourers may have to be taken into skilled jobs. For years a strictly enforced colourbar reserved the skilled work for whites. Now the demands of industry are changing. To fill the jobs formerly done by whites a process of restructuring is underway. This includes an increased mechanization, job fragmentation and an expansion of especially lower-level skill training for Africans.

TABLE I. *Population Census Returns, 1936–1976 (in Thousands).*

	1936	1946	1951	1960	1970	1975	1977
Africans	6 617	7 851	8 594	12 187	15 058	18 136	19 370
Coloureds	772	931	1 008	1 501	2 018	2 368	2 438
Asians	221	286	368	477	620	727	765
Whites	2 009	2 380	2 647	3 088	3 751	4 240	4 373
Total	9 619	11 449	12 719	16 003	21 449	25 471	26 946

Sources: 1936–70—"Africa South of the Sahara", 1972, p. 707; Industrial Development Corporation of South Africa, "Yearbook 1972", p. 41.
1975–77—Official estimates from Department of Statistics, Pretoria.

Table II illustrates how the rapid expansion of the black sections of the population force statistical predictions to change. These statisticians are, of course, white, and their predictions are coloured by wishful thinking. They have always tended to overestimate the growth rate of the whites and to underestimate that of the blacks. One of the most glaring examples of such wishful thinking was an estimate produced by the Industrial Development Corporation based on the 1970 census. They assumed that the white population would virtually double itself by the year 2000, to reach 7·5 million, which would imply an annual growth rate for whites of 2·4%.[7]

TABLE II. *Predictions of Race Ratios to the Year 2000.*

	Predictions made in		
	1966	1970	1975
African: white	4·0:1	4·4:1	5·2:1
Black: white	5·0:1	5·2:1	6·1:1

Sources: "Statistical Yearbook", RSA, 1966; IDC, "Yearbook", 1972, p. 43; SAIRR, "Annual Survey 1976", p. 32.

In fact, figures going right back to 1911 show that only once, in 1951, during the international post-war baby boom, did the annual rate of natural increase for whites rise above 2% p.a. During the 1970s the rate has fallen below all previous levels, to 1·45% in 1971 and 1·42% in 1972.[8] Due to immigration, the actual growth rate for the white population during these years is somewhat higher—a point we shall return to later.

Since 1950 the ratio of whites to the black sections of the population has declined rapidly, from about 1:3·8 in 1951 to about 1:5·0 in 1975. In most industrial countries one sees similar trends of falling natural growth rates. The continuous rapid growth of the blacks in South Africa is a pattern one is conversant with from most underdeveloped countries. That these two phenomena can exist side by side in one and the same country reflects the political realities in South Africa, a country in which colonizer and colonized live side by side under totally different socio-economic conditions.

The Asian and coloured sections of the population are in a slightly different position, compared to the Africans. In the ten years between 1968 and 1977 the registered birth rate for the coloured people fell from 42·0 to 27·2 and that of the Asian section of the population fluctuated, rising from 31·0 in 1968 to 33·7 in 1971, since when it declined to 26·5 in 1977.[9] The rapid spread of family planning clinics, often attached to factories and other places of work, may have contributed to the declining birth rate, especially amongst the coloured section. But economic factors play an important role. It has already been mentioned that these two groups are forcibly moved to townships where they form a physical buffer between the Africans and the whites. Economically, and politically too, the regime has placed them in a buffer position, so that these two groups should not identify with the most oppressed and largest section of the population, the Africans. Thus, the coloured and Asian workers, employees and professionals get higher wages and salaries than their African counterparts—though substantially lower than their white counterparts. Their parallel trade unions have the right to negotiate on their members' behalf, whereas African or multiracial trade unions have no legal bargaining power. On the whole, the housing provided for the coloured and Asians is of a higher standard than that provided for Africans, though nowhere near the standard provided for the whites. Today the coloured and Asian people have no real political power. Nevertheless, the all-white electorate gave the ruling Nationalist party a landslide victory in the elections held at the end of 1977 on a platform which, *inter alia*, offered greater political influence to the coloured and Asian people.

The obvious aim behind these marginally better conditions is to separate the coloured and Asian people from the African majority. For many years the regime lived in a fool's paradise, believing it had succeeded. But since the nationwide uprising which began in Soweto in June 1976, it had to rethink. The coloured and Asian people sided with the African initiators of the uprising. Coloured and Asian school children joined the demonstrations, coloured and Asian university students destroyed their campuses, coloured and Asian workers heeded the call for general strikes. The human buffer policy was a dismal failure, with the coloured and Asian people identifying their own oppression as being essentially the same as that of the African people, thereby identifying themselves politically as part of the oppressed black majority.

A comparison of the death rates for these two groups is also interesting. The death rate for the Asians is about two per thousand lower than that of the whites. This probably reflects a greater socio-cultural stability of the Asian community—South African whites have among the highest social instability figures in the world, with high divorce, suicide and accident rates, as well as suffering from the diseases of overabundance. The death rate for the coloured people, on the other hand, is about five per thousand higher than the white rate.[10] This reflects both a greater social instability due to their marginal position, being treated as illegitimate stepchildren of the whites, as well as their greater poverty and poorer living conditions. There are no statistics available for African birth and death rates, infant mortality rates cannot be found, and this in a country with one of the most sophisticated and punitive apparatuses for controlling the movement of people. Can it be that there are no financial advantages to be gained from ensuring that African natality and mortality figures are accurate? Can it be that such statistics would be too embarrassing to reveal—studies conducted at two hospitals in Durban would suggest that this is the case.

For example in just taking tuberculosis in Durban in 1973 one can compare the incidence per thousand of population: for the whites 0·29, Asians 1·11, coloureds 2·24 and Africans 4·08.[11] Death as a result of gastrointestinal and nutritional diseases in whites between the ages of one month and ten years is virtually unknown, but approximately 55 and 30% respectively of African and Asian children admitted for treatment of these two diseases in Durban, die.

Immigration and Emigration

For the first twelve years of Nationalist Party rule immigration was not encouraged. In the aftermath of the 1960 Sharpeville massacre and the wave of sabotage which followed the country experienced the largest exodus of whites and of international capital in its history. But foreign banks, especially in the US, reversed the capital outflow, and a massive public relations campaign, spearheaded by the South Africa Foundation, which is financed by a consortium of business interests, persuaded both finance and people that South Africa was a country with a bright future. The regime decided during the 1960s, when the decline in the ratio of white to black became apparent and alarming that it would have to develop an active immigration policy. The effects are shown in Table III.

At the height of the 1960s propaganda campaign to attract immigrants the growth rate of the white population was boosted by 0·7–0·9% p.a. But by the early 1970s the flow of immigrants began to drop and only picked up temporarily again during 1974 and 1975.

TABLE III. *Immigration and Emigration of Whites Per Year*, 1930–1977.

Year	Immigration	Emigration	Net gain
1930–1944	4 500	2 600	1 900
1945–1959	16 300	10 300	6 000
1960–1964	25 100	10 300	14 800
1965–1969	39 000	9 900	29 100
1970–1974	34 000	6 800	27 200
1975	50 500	10 300	40 200
1976	46 239	15 641	30 549
1977	24 822	26 000	−1 178

Sources: "Statistics of Immigrants and Emigrants 1924–64", Report No. 286, 1965; "Bulletin of Statistics", June 1974, Tables 1.3.3 and 1.3.6, and Sept. 1974, pp. 1.9–1.14; "SA Institute for Race Relations Annual Survey"—citations from Dept. of Statistics; Colin Legum, *African contemporary record*, 1976; *Rand Daily Mail*, 28 January 1978.

Most of these immigrants came from the former Portuguese territories of Mozambique and Angola, both of which gained political independence during those years. Immigration figures started falling and legal emigration rose at the end of 1975, when it became known that South Africa had invaded Angola. This trend became even more accentuated after the Soweto uprisings. A new factor has also entered the picture since the Angola fiasco: illegal emigration, or desertion, of young white conscripts. The capital outflow which followed the Soweto uprisings was less dramatic than in the 1960–1962 period, largely because of much tighter government control of capital export. But the foreign reserves sank, the foreign debt of South Africa rose, and a number of observers believed that the country was on the brink of a very serious economic crisis. Thanks once again to actions taken by private banks in the US and West Germany, as well as a rise in the free price of gold, South Africa survived—at a cost of galloping inflation and rising unemployment. But in early 1978 it was still virtually impossible for South Africa to obtain longterm loans—even her best friends were only giving short and medium term loans at high rates of interest.

The decline in immigration is likely to continue. In 1978 a new law was passed, the effects of which are to force automatic South African citizenship on all white immigrants between the ages of 18 and 25 years. According to the Secretary for the

Interior the consequence of the law "will be to make young immigrants liable for military training".[12] It is most unlikely that immigration can be boosted again as happened in the 1960s. When Namibia and Zimbabwe achieve real independence white refugees can be expected to stream to South Africa, but we do not know to what extent they will be welcome. Plans that were revealed in early 1977 to transfer some 150 000 people of Dutch and German descent from Southern Africa to Bolivia may further counter the South African white interests.

The capitalist crisis in South Africa and the continuing uprisings, including the armed struggle led by the African National Congress (ANC), are not conducive to attracting new immigrants. Furthermore, the political climate towards South Africa has hardened. Public opinion even in the UK, the main source of immigrants, is more informed today of the iniquities of the apartheid system. Active anti-immigration campaigns have grown up in the very countries that traditionally provided the largest number and the most acceptable immigrants, and demands for economic sanctions have grown. In 1977 the Socialist International, representing the social democratic and labour parties of the Western countries, declared itself in favour of stopping all new investment in South Africa and against immigration there.

Figures for African migration are not available as it is illegal (except contract labour migration). With the changed political face of Southern Africa, brought about by the liberation of Mozambique and Angola and the struggles in Namibia and Zimbabwe, it is likely that illegal immigration is falling off. Emigration, however, is rising rapidly. Thousands of young blacks, some only eight years old, have fled their country since the ruthless mowing down of young people, the mass detentions and naked police brutality began in June 1976.

In 1970 the Chamber of Mines employed some 400 000 migrant workers, three-quarters of whom came from neighbouring countries.[13] Five years later the number of migrants who were employed in mining and quarrying had gone up by 60%. Just over half of them were foreign migrants. All in all some 3 685 000 South African migrant workers and 415 000 foreign migrants were registered in South Africa in June 1975.[14]

During the 1970s there has been some pressure to cut down on the proportion of migrant workers, and to establish a more stable workforce. This demand apparently goes against the prevailing apartheid and bantustan policy. Political expediency, however, requires a shift in strategy. On the one hand, bantustan administrations must be seen to take over more of the repressive functions of the Pretoria regime. Thus the Transkei "legislature" introduced onto its own statute books the notorious "terrorism" laws, and Bophutatswana "courts" have put alleged ANC guerilla soldiers on trial. On the other hand, there are feverish attempts to rapidly increase the number of blacks with middleclass aspirations. Mining and industrial magnate, Harry Oppenheimer, put it most succinctly when he said: We must show the blacks that they have a stake in the capitalist system if we are to avoid a socialist revolution.

So it is, that areas like Alexandria, zoned for single-sex hostels in the 1960s, are being rezoned for family housing. 99-year leases are being offered in some African townships—to heads of families who accept "citizenship" in a bantustan. Some companies are building family housing for a tiny proportion of their most privileged African workers.

Economic hardships for the majority are increasing. Estimates of African unemployment in May 1977 were as high as two million. In Durban and Johannesburg a survey showed that the unemployed had either been born in the area or had lived there for a long time. Neither the new face of apartheid, nor the high unemployment rates, threaten the migrant labour system, the cornerstone of the bantustan policy.

Family Planning

Attitudes to birth control among the ruling white minority are often contradictory, and until the 1960s the conservative attitudes to family planning prevented all but the most privileged sections of the population from easy access to methods of birth control. One would have thought that despite religious objections to modern methods of family planning, the great white fear of being numerically dominated by the black population groups would have led to ready access to and indeed encouragement of birth control among the most oppressed sections of the population. In fact, this only happened in 1972–1973 when the pill began to be distributed free, through municipal family planning clinics.

The Dutch Reformed Church (DRC) is the most conservative and the largest church in the country. It is also the theological and ideological powerbase of the regime. In 1960 a DRC spokesman on moral questions said, "The Church is generally opposed to birth control amongst whites on Christian and ethical grounds, and I suppose the same would be applied to Africans. This aspect has never been discussed by the church. But we do not consider the argument that the population may become too large is valid. Science and technology will cope".[15]

Some decade later, when the decision was taken to distribute the pill freely, DRC theologians reacted: "It is the duty of the whites to 'multiply on the earth . . . and thus keep the increase of the white population high'. They (would like to) ban the pill for all white women. The pill . . . leads to promiscuity and prostitution. However, 'the bantu . . . could be given the pill with an easy mind. . . . The morals of the blacks have already sunk so low that promiscuity could not be any greater'".[16] These "men of God" not only distort the truth, but totally disregard the havoc wreaked in the family life of the African people by the ramification of the pass laws, bantustan system, etc. In Natal in 1968 it was noted that "two ministers of religion each devote one sermon a month to family planning and hand out FPA literature at the services".[17]

It would be simplistic to portray the white population as a unitary body all engaged in preserving race purity, all regarding the pill as immoral and sinful and the gravest threat to family life among white communities in South Africa. There have, for instance, been women's groups, admittedly dominated by whites but having black members, who have declared that it is a woman's right to control her own fertility and to make her own decisions about contraception and abortion.

The African reaction is perhaps best summed up in a statement made during the debate in the late 1960s: "The white man has thought of something to decrease the African nation. I therefore believe that the birth control pill is outstandingly fatal to the African nation".[18] At the same time white women are constantly being plied with inducements to raise large families.

Some whites are conscious of black fears that population control measures may be forced upon them. As early as 1963 a social anthropologist at the University of Pretoria attacked free distribution of the pill at a large industrial concern on the grounds that

Africans might feel that the growth of their race was deliberately being limited.[19] Some Africans do express feelings of distrust at the stream of white sponsored birth control propaganda. A clergyman in Soweto thought that whites were needlessly causing suspicion in the minds of Africans "when they keep telling us how we should control our birthrate".[20]

But not all objections from Africans to birth control derive from fears fostered by white racism. Some black people object on medical grounds, and others use religious and moral arguments. Social factors working against the use of modern contraception among African men include loss of social status in the community and loss of the bride-price. Women fear the anger of their menfolk, should secret use be discovered. In the past, at least, many women have not been able to gain access to contraceptives because of a belief, often justified by the practice of the local clinic, that they need the man's consent.

As in other parts of the world, most of those in South Africa who argue in favour of family planning, both black and white, regard it as a cure for the high rate of illegitimacy, the misery in the urban and rural ghettos, the mounting crime and vagrancy rates, and do not consider the part played by the capitalist economic structure in destroying family life and bolstering oppression. They prefer to emphasize the benefits of smaller families and play down white desires for fewer Africans. They do complicated calculations to show that health, education and welfare facilities, meagre as they are, cannot possibly expand, let alone improve, at a rate fast enough to keep pace with population growth. The point they miss is that if the wealth of the country were fairly distributed among all people, then health, education and welfare facilities would receive high priority and would be expanded to cater to the needs of all people, irrespective of race or socio-economic status.

From Taboo to Acceptance—the Role of the Family Planning Association (FPA)

The FPA was started as early as 1932 to provide voluntary birth control services. They joined the International Planned Parenthood Federation (IPPF) in 1953, and for a number of years battled against resistance to family planning methods at all levels of society. In 1966 their fate changed dramatically when they received their first government grant, an event which signalled the legislation of contraception. In the six years to 1972 the FPA transferred all of its 229 clinics to local authorities as soon as they had been established. After 1973 the FPA was to provide primarily educational and informational services.

South Africa was one of the testing grounds for injectibles, like the controversial Depo Provera, which was, of course, not primarily directed to white women. According to studies carried out in 1969, in the Cape Town municipal family planning clinics both oral contraceptives and IUDs lost favour, whereas experimental injections of Depo Provera showed a corresponding remarkable leap in popularity, from 9% among previous attenders to 28% among women who attended for the first time. Although white women constituted about 6% of the attenders, they only formed 1·3% and 2·5% of Depo Provera acceptors.[21] Today South Africa is among the 76 countries in the world which, according to an IPPF-list, "have approved Depo Provera for contraceptive purposes or for the suppression of ovulation".

Much attention has been paid by the FPA to coloured women. In the urban areas of the Cape factory clinics were started in order to cope with the high drop-out rate of coloured women. The above-mentioned study in Cape Town showed, however, that coloured women had the lowest drop-out rate of all groups. Moreover, 81% of the women who attended FPA clinics during 1969 were coloured, and they also had the highest number of revisits during the year, 4·3 per patient compared to 3·2 for African and 2·9 for white women.[22]

The birth rate among coloured women has declined rapidly in various centres where FPA has been active. Between 1962 and 1966 the birthrate for coloured people fell in Cape Town from 42·5 to 39·5 per thousand, in Johannesburg from 41·1 to 28·6, and in Port Elizabeth from 45·0 to 34·3. As already noted, also on the national level the coloured people do have the fastest declining birth rate of the three population groups for which figures are available.

Services are provided separately for each of the four population groups. Since the municipal and other local authorities have taken over the clinics no statistics on consolidated attendance data have been forthcoming. In 1969, however, at the FPA clinics the attendance rate per thousand of population was for Africans 3·0, coloureds 5·3, Asians 23·1 and whites 1·5.[23] These figures make one wonder if the falling birth rate for the coloured people is indeed connected to the efforts of the FPA, or whether there are other, socio-economic, factors which play a greater role. As for the comparatively high attendance rate for Asians, it is noticeable that in the very same year, 1969, the Asian birth rate reached a peak of 33·9 per thousand.[24] The number of family planning clinics and mobile units had risen to 2045 by 1975 since local and central government agencies have taken over. Great efforts are being expended on reaching African women. A 240% increase in the number of African women attending family planning clinics was noted in December 1975 compared to the same period the previous year. The increase over the December 1974 attendance figures was for whites 38 400, coloureds 5600, Asians 11 800 and Africans 361 000.[25]

Abortion and Sterilization

Legislation on abortion is highly restrictive, which is not surprising considering the attitude of the Dutch Reformed Church and the bulk of the ruling Nationalist Party. Abortion has always been virtually illegal prior to the passing of the 1975 Abortion and Sterilization Act. Of course there has always been a high illegal abortion rate, with backstreet abortionists providing the services thousands of desperate women needed. According to the Abortion Reform Action Group, 14 abortion cases were daily being seen at the all-African Baragwanath Hospital outside Johannesburg. Of the 80% of cases which were illegal 40% had gone septic.[25] This means that one hospital alone treated over 4000 illegal terminations annually, which casts doubt on the police figures for the whole of Johannesburg for the six years period 1959–1964 of only 302 deaths from illegal abortions.[26]

It is mainly the better off white women, who have so far been able to take advantage of the complex law on abortion. According to the Department of Health, in 1977 only some 500 legal abortions were carried out, of which 75% were on white women. Thus, early safe terminations are difficult to obtain, and many doctors called for more liberal abortion legislation.[27] Under stances one can hardly take for granted that illegal e decreased—despite the harsh penalties for such ac- the highly dubious figure of 21 000 cases for the was calculated.[28] The illegal abortion rate has almost certainly increased during the 1970s, partly because of the work of family planning motivators, and partly because of the growth of pro-abortion groups in many of the large centres, which for the first time have challenged traditional dogma and allowed for some individual thinking and discussion of the problems revolving round abortions.

Both abortion and sterilization are surrounded by shame, guilt and myths, and it is difficult to perceive an accurate picture of what is really occurring. That sterilization was legalized in the same act that concerned abortion has not calmed those who tend to question the motives of South African lawmakers. But fears that abortions may in certain cases only be granted to those who consent to sterilization may as yet be groundless, as in 1977 fewer than 100 sterilizations were legally performed.

The most oppressed sections of the population tend to be well aware of the dangers of forced sterilization. In a Natal bantustan area in early 1970s a mobile clinic suspected of sterilizing women was mobbed and destroyed. And during the uprisings from June 1976 several mother and child health clinics were razed to the ground, because they were suspected of the forced sterilization of mothers. With such violent reactions occurring, one has to question the reliability of the figure of 15 sterilizations performed on Africans during 1977 which was reported by the Department of Health.

A new organization, the Cape Provincial Association for Voluntary Sterilization (CPAVS), has been formed. The very official sounding name coupled with well produced propaganda material seems to have been successfully infiltrated especially into black sections of hospitals and family planning clinics in many parts of the country. The authorities were said to be unaware that their own staff were using the material, which sets out to persuade both women and men of the benefits of sterilization in those families which have "enough" children.[29]

Health and Medical Services are Inadequate

Only if family planning advice, services and supplies are incorporated into a genuine and holistic health programme, rooted in a democratic society, will there be no grounds for suspicion against birth control. Medical statistics show an extreme bias in favour of the whites. In 1970 the doctor–patient ratio was 1:400 for whites and 1:44 000 for Africans,[30] and in 1970 the nurse–patient ratio was 1:256 for whites and 1:1581 for Africans.[31] The number of hospital beds per 1000 of population in 1972 was 10 for whites, 5·6 for blacks in white areas, and for Africans in the bantustans only 3·5.[32] (We have already noted that it is precisely in these areas where the need for health care is greatest—the dumping places for the aged and infirm, the women and children.)

Hospital conditions even in the cities are often appalling. A report on the Livingstone Hospital in Port Elisabeth in August 1977 revealed that 11 000 births a year are handled by this over-crowded maternity section of the hospital, catering for all the black population groups. At the same time there are often empty beds in the whites-only maternity section of the Provincial Hospital. Among other things the report revealed that often four or five women had to share the same labour room, that there are "long rows of women lying on trolleys in passages and foyers which in places were draughty and cold", and that "toilet and bathing facilities were described by one doctor as 'crude and primitive' while another said they were 'unhygienic'".[33]

Life expectancy figures reveal the effects of the vicious system of exploitation coupled with inadequate health care and grinding poverty. In 1970 J. L. Sadie estimated life expectancy for Africans to be around 45 years.[34] Whites, on the other hand, could expect to reach around 70, coloureds 50 and Asians 60 years.[35]

The same picture holds for infant mortality rates. Between 1963 and 1974 the infant mortality rate for whites fell from 29 to 18 per thousand live births, and for coloureds from 128 to 115 per thousand. The Asian people, allowed a life less interrupted by the apartheid system, experienced a steadily falling infant mortality rate, from 56 to 32 per thousand during the same period.[36] Vital statistics for Africans are, of course, not available, but studies have shown that about 40% of children in the Transkei die before the age of 10 years, whereas in Sekukuniland, a dumping ground for people who have been forcibly removed to "resettlement camps", about half of all the children born do not live to see their fifth birthday.[37]

In 1966, the last year in which kwashiorkor was a notifiable disease, official figures mentioned 11 000 cases of this often fatal protein-malnutrition disease. The same year it was calculated that serious protein-calorie deficiency occurred in 43 000 children.[38] Deficiency diseases are more common in rural than in urban areas. Nevertheless, "at least 80% of schoolgoing children from Bantu households in the capital of Pretoria suffer from malnutrition and undernutrition".[39]

Health care for the majority of the population has deteriorated, and no serious attempts are being made to improve conditions. Showplaces are built, admittedly, but there is no attempt to grapple with the fundamental problems. The words of the head of the Hospital Services in the Cape Province are revealing: "We are trying our best to alleviate the overcrowding, but with the funds at our disposal we have not been able to keep ahead of the population explosion".[40]

At the same time as money is being ploughed into the different forms of family planning, as the forced removals of economically inactive Africans continues, as the bantustan areas are granted a sham independence, so the authorities are breeding hundreds of thousands of African babies whose chances of a full life are stunted already in the womb. A malnourished woman cannot produce a healthy child. The central nervous system of a developing baby is the area most sensitive to the effects of malnutrition. So many black children are born as second-rate citizens with prenatal deficiencies. Severe protein-calorie malnutrition during early childhood also affects the development of the brain.

The violence of the white society can be expressed in many forms—from ruthless shootings of unarmed children to this far more insidious stunting of the capacities of a people. Whatever form it takes, the whites have made it clear that only by countering their brutal violence with revolutionary violence will the South African people be able to have healthy children, control their own movements and establish a democratic and egalitarian society in which basic human rights are respected.

Notes

1. *Apartheid Quiz* (1976). International Defence and Aid Fund, p. 19.
2. *Survey of Race Relations in South Africa 1975*, South African Institute of Race Relations, p. 38 (henceforth referred to as *SAIRR*).
3. Bernstein, H. (1975). *For Their Triumphs and for Their Tears: Conditions*

and Resistance of Women in Apartheid South Africa, International Defence and Aid Fund, p. 16.
4. Derived from offical statistics, quoted in *SAIRR 1976*, p. 31.
5. Moore, P. H. (1961). "South African population problems", abridged version in *The Natal Mercury*, June.
6. Bernstein, op. cit., rev. ed. 1978, p. 15.
7. *Yearbook* (1972). Industrial Development Corporation of South Africa, Johannesburg.
8. *SAIRR 1975*, p. 39.
9. "Africa South of the Sahara" (1978), p. 830. Europa Publishers, London.
10. Ibid.
11. Annual Report of the City Medical Officer of the City of Durban, Durban 1973.
12. *Guardian* (Britain), 27 February 1978.
13. *Power, Privilege and Poverty* (1972). SPROCAS Publ. No. 7, Christian Institute of South Africa.
14. Derived from *SAIRR 1976*, p. 284.
15. *Southland Daily News* (New Zealand), 6 June 1960.
16. *Sunday News* (Tanzania), 9 December 1973.
17. Hill, H. (1968). Family Planning in South Africa—a Report to the IPPF.
18. *Long Island Press* (New York), 3 January 1967.
19. *Pulse* (London), 4 January 1969.
20. *The Star* (Johannesburg), 25 February 1969.
21. Robertson, I. (1971). Report on family planning clinics conducted in Cape Town municipal area from 1960–1969. *South Afr. Med. J.* **45**, 13 March 1971.
22. Ibid.
23. "Consolidated Attendance Data", Year ending 31 December 1969, FPA of South Africa.
24. "Africa South of the Sahara", op. cit.
25. *Newsletter*, Abortion Reform Action Group, Durban, 7, April 1975, p. 9.
26. Strauss, S. A. (1968). Therapeutic abortion in South African law. *South Afr. Med. J.* **42**, 20 June 1968.
27. Westmore, J. (1977). Abortion in South Africa and attitudes of Natal medical practitioners towards South African abortion legislation, University of Durban.
28. Spilhaus, P. (1977). Report on a symposium on the population explosion in South Africa, Pretoria, October.
29. *Daily Dispatch* (SA), 11 July 1977.
30. Derived from *SAIRR 1976*, pp. 382–4.
31. Derived from *SAIRR 1973*, p. 355.
32. *SAIRR 1973*, p. 352.
33. *Sunday Times* (SA), 7 August 1977.
34. Sadie, J. L. (1970). An evaluation of demographic data pertaining to the non-white population of South Africa, *SA J. Econ.* **36**, 1 February 1970.

35. *South African Statistics 1970*, Bureau of Statistics, Pretoria 1970; *SAIRR 1971*, p. 302; and *SAIRR 1976*, p. 32.
36. *SAIRR 1971*, p. 302; and *SAIRR 1976*, p. 32.
37. Reid, J. V. O. (1971). Malnutrition, *Some Implications of Inequality*, SPROCAS Publ. No. 4, South Africa Christian Institute, Johannesburg.
38. Cosmas Desmond, "African Resettlement", *ibid.*
39. Reid, op. cit.
40. *Sunday Times*, op. cit.

The Foreign Control of Kenyan Population

Lars Bondestam

Attempts to control the growth of the Third World population can be seen as one of many components of the upper class strategy to divert attention from the actual causes of poverty. Dubious measures of development serve to prove an inverse correlation between population and economic growth and hence a need to control the former. They hide the inequalities and the concentration of power and means of production to the wealthy, i.e. to those who seek to monopolize the interpretation of underdevelopment and its causes in their own favour.

Any idea of development *by* the people would threaten the hierarchical order between the centre and the periphery as well as within the respective countries. Consequently, development is defined as *for* the people—the fewer the people the easier it is to help the few that are left. The ideology of "development for the people", however, is a guarantee for a continuous underdevelopment. The strategy implicit in this ideology aims at the symptoms of underdevelopment rather than at its causes. The contradiction between "the green revolution" and the need for land reform is one glaring example. Another is the biased allocation of resources towards the cities, despite that urban problems emerge in rural areas. A third example is the focusing on population by trying to artificially reduce its birth rate, although the fertility pattern is known to reflect the socio-economic conditions. This is why "the green revolution" yields not only more wheat and rice but also eviction of poor peasants, and this is why urban slums do not cease to expand and deepen. This is also why population growth remains high in regions untouched by proper development. Numerous studies prove these general reflections to be applicable to most of the periphery, including Kenya.

The Background

During the colonial period the British controlled politics and large scale commercial activities in agriculture and industry in Kenya. The Asian minority, who were restricted from playing any role in farming, controlled the distributive sector of the economy. The Africans remained in the subsistence economy or served as suppliers of cheap labour. The uneven growth of the economy, by region and by ethnic, racial and economic groups, should be seen in the light of Kenya's role as supplier of goods for the European market—economic growth was concentrated to those profitable areas which produced goods for export. By 1960, some three million hectares of the most fertile land, mainly in the so-called White Highlands, were held by less than 4000 European settlers.

The Kenyan economy was tied to Europe, with its booms and depressions. The crisis of the 1930s turned a labour shortage in Kenya into a surplus, and in 1933 the Carter Commission warned that "the future of the next thirty years or so may be imagined as a race between the tendency of a growing population to congest the land and a growing skill to make the same land support a larger population".[1] When capitalism temporarily recovered after the Second World War, the East Africa Royal Commission transferred the joy to the colonies: "There is no evidence to suggest that up to the present, the general rate of growth of the African population has exceeded the overall ability of the economy of the three territories (Kenya, Uganda and Tanganyika) to support it. Indeed, we believe that the recently accelerated growth of population is in part both a cause and a consequence of the greater economic opportunities which are open to the indigenous population".[2] Thus, optimism and pessimism in Kenya went hand in hand with the ups and downs of the economy in Europe.

Kenya was subject to more thorough penetration by colonial capitalism than most other territories of the continent, so the degradation of the British bureaucracy in 1963 implied a crisis of confidence—white settlers started leaving Kenya, would-be foreign investors hesitated to show up, and economic stagnation was imminent. The restoration of confidence became a prime task to win back the western capital. The replacement of white rule by African nationalism paved the way for the petty-bourgeoisie and for the emergence of a strong comprador class, that turned out to be an effective tool for the transfer of colonialism into neo-colonialism. "When national independence was achieved the political aim of taking over the economy became merged almost imperceptibly with individual aspirations to take over the jobs, positions and life styles which the economy made possible." (ILO, p. 87).[3]

The reliance on a capitalist development was expressed in a weighty document of 1965, Sessional Paper No. 10,[4] according to which "the only permanent solution to Kenya's problems rests on rapid growth". The Western influence has grown stronger since then. Over-generous concessions for foreign businesses were granted right from the first years after independence and much of Kenya's new industries between 1964 and 1970 were foreign owned or controlled. Virtually all the policies formulated the first three to four years after independence were contrived and executed by foreign advisers in ministries. Population control became a part of the extended modern brand of the colonial policy in Kenya.

The Population Council Report

The Family Planning Committee of Mombasa and the Family Planning Association of Nairobi were formed in the 1950s with support particularly from the Pathfinder Fund (USA). The two groups were amalgamated in 1961 to form the present Family Planning Association of Kenya (FPAK). It claimed to be multi-racial but the African component was just a black mask. The driving force behind FPAK was Dr J. McAllan who gained recognition of the Association by the International Planned Parenthood Federation (IPPF), which today is the main financial source. He was backed by J. G. C. Blacker, government demographer in the Ministry of Planning and Development (MPD). According to Kivuto Ndeti, former member of the Department of Sociology at University of Nairobi,

> The neo-Malthusianism of Blacker and his cohort of foreign advisers caught like wild fire among some policy-makers and some short-sighted academics. The foreign experts utilized the crisis of confidence and seized the opportunity to plug-in whatever programme was in line with their thinking or the agency they worked for. Thus, the foreign experts made sure

that family planning was incorporated in the Sessional Paper No. 10. A large part of this important report, which set the goals for the further planning of Kenya, was written by foreign experts outside the country—less than two years after independence. When the document came out in 1965, it contained all Blacker's demographic-economic rationales, together with his population projection to the year 2000. . . . In the eyes of the world, this act was synonymous with the Kenya government's policy on population. In conclusion the Sessional Paper No. 10 stated: "A high rate of population growth means a large dependent population, reduces the money available for development, lowers the rate of growth and makes exceedingly the task of increasing social services". This declaration represents the wicked-success of foreign infiltration in Kenya's development management. Now, that the final break-through had been made, the next logical measure was for the MPD, headed by Tom Mboya, to ask Population Council for an American mission to come to advise the government on the population problem.[5]

The Population Council came to justify what was already decided many thousands of kilometres away. Their study was mainly limited to interviews with people in key positions, with little or no understanding of the role of population in the total development process. After a three-week visit the delegates had become experts on Kenya and returned to USA to recount their tale. The arguments, as given in the Population Council's report,[6] are crucial since they were used in the Government's final decision to embark on a National Family Planning Programme (NFPP). The basic reasoning of the report can be divided into three steps:

Use of the intrauterine device (IUD or loop). "One must mention one of the most encouraging aspects of all: the availability of the IUD . . . its potential is almost revolutionary. . . . At present the mission believes that the IUD has the widest applicability and will be successfully used in all but about a fourth to a fifth of the women who try it". (pp. 13 and 28)

A 50% decrease in fertility within 10 to 15 years thanks to the advantages with IUD. "A realist current target for a national programme would be a planned build-up within five years (i.e. by 1972) of a structure that would introduce birth control at a rate that would cut fertility approximately in half within 10 or 15 years. . . . To achieve the above result would require the organization of a programme that at the end of five years could introduce 150 000 IUDs each year, and provide supplies and advice on other methods of contraception to an additional 50 000 couples. . . . Assuming 50% reduction in fertility, the population of Kenya would by the year 2000 total about 19 million, women reaching 50 would have had an average of about 3·5 children, and the population would be growing at about 1·8% per year. (p. 10)

Economic and social benefits from a decrease in fertility. Education: "If fertility were to be reduced by 50% in 15 years, the proportions enrolled would rise at an accelerated pace, reaching 100% shortly after 1985" (p. 4) (compared to 62% participation rate in 1990 if fertility remained unchanged). Employment: "A reduction in fertility would make the employment problem much less acute. Thus, by the year 2000, if fertility had been cut in half, the number of males in the principal ages of economic activity would increase from 2·2 million to 5·2 million, rather than 6·9" (p. 5) (if fertility remained unchanged). *Per capita income:* "During the first 20–30 years after initiating a reduction in fertility, the total national product would increase more rapidly than would be the case if the birth rate were unchanged". (p. 5)

This reasoning is not realistic. The expected future use of IUD, on which the optimism of the mission is based, is a belief in plastic-technology as a short-cut towards development. The estimated 50% decrease in fertility is nowhere nearly justified even by the simplest calculation. Economic development is wrongly assumed to be negatively affected by a growing population. School participation rate is likewise wrongly assumed to be a function of population growth only. Reasons for the high unemployment are not even touched upon. Unless distribution of welfare is taken into account, which it is not, GNP per capita has limited significance as a standard of development. The report concentrated on "the problem of population growth", whereas only one page (out of a total of 45 pages) is devoted to the "Benefits of fertility reduction to health and to the individual family".

Birth control is needed, because "The population of Kenya, now about 9 million, would, at the current rate of increase, reach 144 million in less than a century. But, in fact, the almost certain continued decline in mortality would cause the population to grow at an even higher pace unless fertility were also reduced" (p. 3). This doomsday-argument is aimed at frightening the policy-makers. There is no reason to believe that the present high birth rate will remain constant in the next century. Fertility is treated as an independent variable and the possibility of a decrease in birth rate as an effect of rising living standards, more and better education, and other fruits of would-be development is not discussed in the report. It simply implicitly assumes that a family planning programme (FPP) is the only means to reduce fertility.

The report contradicts itself on a very important point. It says that "the goal would be to have every pregnancy the result of a voluntary choice" (p. 10), and that fertility can be reduced by 50% in 10–15 years. But this would imply that Kenyan women actually prefer to have not more than 3·5 children, on average. Several studies have shown, however, that the average desired number of children in Kenya is above six, i.e. almost twice as many as falsely assumed in the report. One may ask: whose voluntary choice—the women's or the Population Council's?

Let us finally quote the sum and substance of the recommendation of the Population Council (my comments in brackets):

> On the basis of our review of the situation in Kenya (which has been neither analysed nor even reviewed), and considering need in relation to economic growth (which has not been considered) and public demand (which has not been investigated), we strongly recommend that Government embark on a programme directed toward a decrease in the rate of population growth. Without such a programme we see little hope of decreasing the gap between the people's aspirations (which have not been defined, let alone understood) and realisations in regard to economic development (measured in GNP per capita), social progress (not yet defined, although we are on page 40) and family welfare" (which does not necessarily follow from a population growth control programme). (p. 40)

Population Council's report still infects the discussion in Kenya—not least manifested at the Bucharest Conference on Population in 1974, where Kenya broke away from the anti-Malthusian African standpoint and joined the Asian line. After that neo-Malthusian piece appeared, the debate has been dominated by foreigners and dominated by the view that population is to be blamed for an inadequate socio-economic growth. The correlation between these two characteristics is significant: more than two-thirds of the writings by foreigners (up to late 1972) emphasized population as such as the main obstacle to development, whereas only three out of ten articles by Kenyans did so. One explanation to this racial difference in political standpoint could be the national awareness among the intellectual Kenyans that the NFPP is to 80–90% a foreign business, which obviously gives rise to suspiciousness about its objectives. Another factor might be the usually better knowledge about the realities of the country held by the Kenyans.

> There is little basic understanding and minimal social contact with the Kenya political milieu. Expatriates usually come with no language ability in Swahili, limited knowledge of the country, and no way to break out of European society. Friendship patterns tend to run in national groups, with infrequent contact with African counterparts. Part of this is due to the difficulty in establishing social contacts on a two-year visit, and part is due to the stratified nature of Nairobi society. Nevertheless, there is a tendency for these urbanized, isolated advisers to carry out programmes and draw up plans for rural peoples, usually working from a base of scant understanding or knowledge of local habits and life styles.[7]

With this in mind, the unfathomably unscientific misery of the foreign vindication of family planning as the saviour of Kenya's future is perhaps understandable, but hardly tolerable. The foreign influence and incompetence were also well manifested in the Five-Year Plan for the NFPP.[8] A pure office-work, with little or no attachment to realities, it mirrors all the foreign lack of understanding of human conditions in Kenya. The plan reviews the past in stating that, "To date no specific targets have been set in the FPP other than the rather vague one of reducing the excessive rate of natural increase", and the authors of the plan proudly specify their own target: "To reach a decrease in growth rate from 3·3% in 1972 to 3·05% in 1976, *227,447 births must be averted*" (emphasis added). No more, no less, but exactly 227 447 births, derived in the most dubious manner, as an arithmetical average of three entirely independent figures. Besides, "nowhere in the plan is there any inquiry as to whether this size of the programme is the best, or whether the programme should be larger or smaller. . . . The benefit's side of the analysis relate to 227 447 averted persons, the cost's side, in part, to the number of clinics. It is unclear as to how these are related".[9]

Table I shows a typical neo-Malthusian benefit analysis, as presented in the plan.

TABLE I. *Estimated GDP Per Capita in Kenya, 1970 and 2000.*

	1970	2000
GDP in £ million (increase of 8% yearly 1970–1980, and 7% yearly thereafter)	562	4 200
No family planning		
Population (thousands)	11 247	30 700
GDP per capita (K£)	49·8	136·8
Family planning		
Population (thousands)	11 247	23 200
GDP per capita (K£)	49·8	181·0

The authors of the plan seemed to be so impressed by their result, a difference of 44·2 pounds per capita in the year 2000, that they exclaimed that, "The sheer size of the economic gain would suffice to justify a family planning programme". This is the intellectual level of argumentation in favour of a programme that deals with personal relations of the Kenyan people.

The plan assumes that GDP grows independently of population growth. Whether the population is 30 or 23 million in the year 2000 has no effect whatsoever on the national product, according to the projectors. Does this mean that the difference of 7·5 million people are non-productive in the year 2000? Does it mean that there will be seven and a half million beggars roaming about Kenya after thirty years? Of course not. Even if we assumed that the "surplus" of 7·5 million people were not producers, they would at least be consumers in order to exist, and what they consume must be produced by somebody, i.e. must ultimately affect the GDP positively. It is now appropriate to consider some facts which were avoided in the above-mentioned reports.

Utilization of Land

First some basic demographic facts of Kenya:

—the growth of population increased continuously during the 1960s and was estimated around 3·4% in 1970. This comparatively high growth rate, if correct, is due to a high birth rate, 50–51 per thousand, and an exceptionally low death rate for African circumstances, 16–17 per thousand (partly explained by the young population—some 47% under 15 years of age).

—the total population was about 11·2 million (2·3 million households) in 1970, 13·2 million in 1975, and is expected to have passed the 25 million-mark by the year 2000.

—about 10% of the population were urban (agglomerations with more than 2000 inhabitants) in 1970, and close to 12% five years later. Presuming the present urban growth rate of about 7% will remain, about 30% will live in towns and cities around the turn of the century.

The land issue is widely discussed in Kenya. First, there is a fear that land will not suffice for a growing farm population and that agricultural production will not cope with the future total demand of food. On the other hand, the control over land is extremely biased in favour of the Kenyan bourgeoisie, and there is a continual process of land concentration in a few hands.

Out of Kenya's total land area of about 0·57 million sq. km,

68 000 sq. km, or 11·9%, have high agricultural potential,
32 000 sq. km, or 5·5%, have medium agricultural potential,
422 000 sq. km, or 74·1%, have low agricultural potential.[10]

On the land with high or medium potential, about 10 million hectares, there were about 1·5 million agricultural households around 1969 (the remaining rural households are pastoralists, to be found mainly in areas with low potential, and people engaged in other non-agricultural activities). Ideally, this would imply an average density of one household per 6–7 hectares, but the situation is, of course, much more complex than so.

First, only about half of the arable land is regularly cultivated. There are still vast areas that could be developed with known techniques, particularly irrigation, presuming more of the available resources of the country were allocated towards agriculture instead of satisfying the luxury needs of the urban bourgeoisie. Thus, large areas lie waste, while the new generation of peasants are forced to clear less fertile land or to split up already small plots.

Second, most of the cultivated land is underutilized or poorly farmed. If the choice lies between investments and consumption, the big landowners are not always interested in increasing production—even if this would lead to higher incomes in the long run. The small owner-cultivators do not produce a surplus sufficient to invest in improvements, and only a fraction of them are reached by agricultural credit institutions. Over half of the small-holders (Table II) make less than K£60 a year, including production for their own consumption. "It is obvious that at this low level of agricultural production and income these families must either exist in extreme poverty or must obtain income from sources other than their own farms by seeking work in the rural areas or in the towns". (ILO, p. 37). It is not uncommon that the male peasants seek seasonal work on large farms or in towns to earn extra money, which

> leaves a depleted family labour force who at peak work times may not be able to cultivate and tend all the family land properly, even if there is only a hectare or so. The results of neglect can be sizeable. In Vihiga, with an extremely high population density, small plot sizes and a very large number of adult males away in towns, it is estimated that 30% of the land on individual holdings remains uncultivated. If these seasonal peaks could be reduced or staggered, more land could be cultivated, or casual wage employment could be obtained on other farms. On a national scale this could substantially increase the amount of employment and income generation in the economy". (ILO, p. 41)

Third, as an element of the colonial heritage, the population is unevenly distributed over the country, even when comparing regions of the same agricultural potential. Thus,

> A large part of the rural population is concentrated in places which before the achievement of national independence formed the "African reserves". In most of these areas population density is very high in relation to the availability of good agricultural land. . . . In contrast, districts . . . which were once reserved almost exclusively for Europeans and formed the "Scheduled Areas", are still characterized by relatively lower population densities in relation to available land. Finally, there are districts . . . which contain large amounts of potentially good agricultural land but which were formerly reserved for certain of the pastoral tribes or were Crown lands on which settlement was not encouraged. These districts have the lowest population densities of all. Thus, while on average 0·8 hectares of good agricultural land (measured in high-potential land equivalents)

was available for each member of the rural population in 1969, there was over nine times this area available per person in Narok. On the other hand, in land shortage districts . . . the availability of good land was only about half of the national average. (ILO, p. 34)

Fourth, and directly related to the point above, land distribution within the respective districts is characterized by a high degree of inequality. As late as five years after independence, i.e. around 1969, only one-third of the area of the former larger European farms had been transferred to Africans. Due to incomplete land registration a full picture of land distribution cannot be obtained, but Table II may give an idea of this distribution.

TABLE II. *Size Distribution of Large Farms in 1970 and of Registered Small Holdings in 1969 (ILO, summary of Tables 2 and 3, p. 36).*

Size (hectares)	Number of farms/ holdings	% of farms/ holdings	Total area (thousand hectares)	% of area
Large farms				
less than 499	2 201	69·3	359	13·4
500–3999	848	26·7	1058	39·3
more than 4000	126*	4·0	1273	47·3
Total	3 175	100·0	2690	100·0
Small holdings (registered only)				
less than 0·99	212 000	27·2	117	4·5
1·0–1·9	192 000	24·7	274	10·3
2·0–4·9	232 000	29·8	707	26·5
more than 5·0	142 00	18·3	1522	58·7
Total	777 000	100·0	2646	100·0

* of which 15 with more than 20 000 hectares each.

Out of the 1·5 million agricultural households some 20% are landless, of whom most earn their living as permanent or seasonal labour on the farms. When taking the non-registered holdings into account, it is estimated that not more than some 60% of all cultivated land is held by Kenya's peasants. The rest is owned and controlled by Kenyan and foreign companies and by European and Kenyan landowners—not least the president himself, who had reached the position as the biggest landlord in the country (the popular politician

J. M. Kariuku, in opposition to the Kenyatta-rule, warned that the land question in Kenya will lead to bloodshed—in March 1975 he was murdered). To this unequal distribution of land should be added the fact that large farms are usually located in the most fertile areas.

The population pressure on land in Kenya has less to do with the crude birth rate and more with the uneven ownership of land and the lack of peasant control over their produce. If there is scarcity of land to feed the Kenyan population, how is it that the volume of exports of the three major agricultural export products—coffee, tea and sisal—could increase by 43% from 1969 to 1973?[11] It is obvious that those who benefit from this and other agricultural exports, and from the agricultural situation in general, would not recognize the capitalist pressure on the small peasants as the basic pressure problem in Kenya.

Needless to say, a division and redistribution of the area under large farms, or rather a collectivization of production, is a tremendous potential for the landless people, as well as for Kenya as a whole. Also organized livestock breeding and the utilization of the huge reserves of wildlife for meat production could engage a higher proportion of the rural population than at present. Scarcity of land is not a bottleneck in Kenya's development; even if it is politically opportune, it is hardly logical to define the population pressure on land as "too many people", when the wrong people control the best land and the needy majority survive on the wrong land.

The Urban Surplus

"The urbanization problem" is a misleading concept, as the drift to the cities is basically a rural stagnation and underdevelopment problem, accentuated by wide and increasing differentials between urban and rural real income. The urban-oriented economy is mirrored in availability of more and better social services, better sanitation and higher incomes in towns than in rural areas. About half of Kenya's doctors practice in urban areas, which accommodate only one-tenth of the country's population. The school-leavers' aspirations result from an urban-biased education, which does not fit the rural requirements. Students, therefore, have become a major rural–urban migratory group in Kenya. The concentration of purchasing power to the big towns is reflected in an average earning per employed town-dweller many times that of an average farm labourer. Earnings in Nairobi and Mombasa some years ago accounted for 83% of the total urban wages and probably a third of all personal income in the whole country—and yet, these towns cannot supply the people with sufficient jobs. The rural–urban imbalance is further aggravated by a decline in the terms of trade, to the disadvantage of the rural areas, by at least 13% from 1964 to 1970.

In one of its pamphlets IPPF relates unemployment, the growth of shanty towns, poverty, juvenile and adult crimes to the growth of Kenya's urban population, but this is at most a fraction of the truth.[12] Unemployment is due to the capital-intensive pattern of production, *inter alia*, with a very slow increase in job opportunities. When capital is valued higher than those who actually bring it into being, unemployment is a logical outcome. A person who lacks work is usually destitute of money and lives in poverty. He cannot afford a reasonable dwelling, but is bound to move into simple houses or hovels on cheap land. That is how shanty towns emerge. In urban areas of Kenya "the bulk of the houses completed so far have been for incomes in the middle range while almost 70% of the demand is by the lowest income group. Consequently, this shortage of housing has been met by houses built in a random and uncontrolled manner—usually by squatting on public and private land—resulting in a proliferation of mud, wattle, cardboard and tin shelters in all the major urban areas of Kenya".[13] Moreover, a person must survive, even if he belongs to the very lowest class. The fact that he steals for his daily living has nothing to do with the fertility of his mother or with an increasing number of neighbours, and the fact that crimes are registered more in towns than in rural areas is not due to the higher urban than rural density of population. Theft is not a demographic phenomenon but an economic reality.

Primarily the males join the queue of job-seekers, and it is no wonder that almost half a million of rural households are headed by women. The rural exodus, permanent and seasonal, becomes an urban surplus, manifested in a big reserve army of labour. The growth of the Kenyan economy has been impressive during the second half of the 1960s. From 1964 to 1970 production in enterprises (excluding agriculture, forestry and fishing), measured in constant prices, grew by 8% yearly,[14] on average. Employment in private industry and commerce grew by 3·5% yearly between 1964 and 1967 and then dropped to zero growth during the three following years.

In an agreement the first year after independence the labour unions accepted a wage-freeze for one year if private employers expanded employment by 10% and the Government by 15%. Over 200 000 workers soon registered for the new jobs and one-sixth were lucky enough to get them. In 1970 a similar agreement was reached to expand employment by 10%. In return, the employees agreed to a 12 months' wage standstill and to refrain from strikes. Some 45 000 jobs were provided under the scheme, of which two-thirds were in the private sector. Although both these attempts were more success-ful in attacking the unemployment problem than propagating birth control to the lumpen proletariate, they were bound to fail in the long run: "The effect was thus primarily to bring forward recruit-ment which would in any case have been undertaken within a year or so. . . . Most of those recruited under the agreement were later used to fill posts made vacant through turnover. Thus the second tripart-ite agreement, like the first, undoubtedly increased employment, but the direct effects had largely worked themselves out by the end of 1971". (ILO, pp. 91 and 95).

In 1971, only one out of every four applicants got a job. Despite a slowly increasing demand for labour the two following years, the absolute number of job-seekers, who failed to find a job, increased rapidly.

Why does a fast growing economy not create sufficient jobs? The import of advanced machinery serves to replace manpower by increasing labour productivity—by over 6% yearly from 1964 to 1970. According to one observer,

> Over the last thirty years, as many new industries have been introduced, they have tended to be import substituting indus-tries, dealing only with the final stage of a production process and being technologically capital intensive. The characteristic of these industries have been largely determined by overseas based giant international companies and are such as not even to have provided employment for the increase in population.[15]

The development in the modern agricultural sector shows a similar pattern:

> . . . while employment in the "modern" farming sector has been declining at the rate of 2·3% p.a. since 1964, total output has risen by about 1% p.a. What seems to have been happening in large farms is that rising costs coupled with stagnant or falling prices of agricultural products have forced farmers to economise on the use of labour by improved management and more mechanised production techniques.[16]

Despite higher wages and salaries (although much of it has been offset by a 39% increase in consumer prices between December 1968 and April 1974), the ratio of output to labour expenditure has constantly increased during the 1960s. This may explain "a likely *net export* of private capital 1964–1971 of some £80 million—roughly *double* the recorded private foreign investment in Kenya, including reinvested local profits, during the same period".[17] A profit-steered rapid technical progress and highly productive machinery have caused a substitution of capital and managerial input for unskilled labour. Thus, skilled employees increased by 12·5% yearly, on average, from 1968 to 1970, whereas unskilled labourers decreased by 2·9% yearly during the same period.[18] This structural change stands in sharp contrast against any rational solution to the unemployment problem of Kenya.

The owners of the means of production derive advantage from the existence of a reserve army from which workers can be selected when needed, not only by keeping the wages down, but also by forcing the employees to work longer hours. A random survey of 1600 Nairobi adults showed that only about 15% of the low-paid workers reported working less than 40 hours a week, while almost 30% reported working in excess of 60 hours.[19]

> The general view that Nairobi's labour force is made up, in addition to unemployed workers, of a large proportion of people who work irregularly and are involuntarily idle for much of the time is not correct. The working poor in general work long hours for low incomes. On the average, they work longer hours than persons who earn incomes of over 200 sh. a month. (ILO, pp. 62–3)

The effects of especially foreign investments on the employment situation in Kenya have been commented on in 1966 by the late minister, Tom Mboya:

Our incentives for stimulating the expansion of private industry may also have contributed to unemployment. They are patterned after intensive systems in advanced economies; economies in which there is a relative abundance of capital and shortage of labour. Except for the high and middle manpower of which there are some critical shortages, our position here is just the reverse".[20]

Tom Mboya, who had inspired the Sessional Paper No. 10, later repudiated the population growth control programme. This control of Kenya's population, he said, would not solve the food problem, "since large areas are uncultivated and the food that is produced is not properly distributed".[21] Like Kariuku, Mboya was also murdered by his opponents.

The views of Mboya have been expressed more frankly by members of the intellectual elite, who are not all tied up by government loyalties: "The present economic system cannot possibly absorb Kenya's potential labour force. This is why unemployment in Kenya is still high—25 to 30% of the labour force. There is very little chance of reducing this figure significantly in the future unless drastic measures are taken to transform the Kenyan economy".[22]

Reliable urban income statistics are lacking, but according to the ILO-report, "the top 10 and 20% of households (in Nairobi, Mombasa and Kisumu) account for 35 and 55% of the total urban household income respectively, while the bottom 25% receive a mere 6%. Correcting for the biases in the sample (both the proportion of those earning less than 200 sh. and of those earning more than 1000 sh. are underestimated) would almost certainly reduce the share received by the bottom 25% even further" (ILO, p. 76). Almost one-fourth of the adult males in Nairobi and much over half of the adult females lack the opportunity of earning a reasonable minimum income, that is they are unemployed or they earn less than 200 sh. per month (early 1970s). They are not poor because they are too many but because the few grab the bulk of Kenya's wealth.

Kenya is one of the most striking African examples of "growth without development": the economy is growing—at least so far (the "Brazilian backlash" may come)—and Kenyans are taking over jobs previously held by Europeans ("Kenyanization"). But all this has been achieved at the cost of marginalization and poverty. This waste of a ruthless capitalism is supposed to be cleaned up with a population growth control programme.

The Failure

We will here limit the discussion to a brief summary of the main findings of an evaluation made by the author in 1972:[23]
—The target, set by the Population Council, was to cut the birth rate from about 50 to 25 per thousand towards the end of this decade. In 1972 the birth rate was not below 49 per thousand. Almost ten years after the start, around 1977, the rate may have gone down to 48 per thousand. Nobody can tell how much of this small decline is attributed to the FPP as such.
—The number of acceptors, i.e. first visitors to FP-clinics who accepted contraception (about 92% of all first visitors), increased from about 11 000 in 1968 to almost 42 000 four years later. However, only about one-half of the acceptors remained in the programme after one year, and only about one-fifth after two years. With this in mind, the figure 42 000 should be compared with the Population Council-target of 200 000 for 1972. The number of new acceptors in 1972 was not more than half of the absolute increase in the female population, aged 15–49 years. Moreover, many of the new acceptors were women who were already practicing FP privately and took advantage of the new services provided free of charge.
—The IUD was hoped to be "successfully used in all but about a fourth to a fifth of the women who try it", or by some 150 000 women in 1972. Actually, in 1970 the IUD was used by 33% of the acceptors, in 1971 by 15·5% and in 1972 by 11%. This last figure corresponds to some 6500 women, or about 4% of the Population Council target.
—Whereas not more than one-third of all women in reproductive ages had any education in 1971, about two-thirds of all acceptors were educated (this bias is an interesting contradiction to the birth control in India, where the poorest people were the main target). Moreover, women with fewer children ever born were more frequent visitors to the FP-clinics than older women. Two-thirds of the acceptors were below 30 years of age and they had given birth to 2·8

children, on average. Hence, the programme is not forced upon the poor and upon those who have delivered many children (there are exceptional cases), but is rather a voluntary choice of the urban middle class. From the point of view of certain foreign agencies, the unceasing proliferation of the poor is probably the greatest failure of the programme.

—The FPP in Kenya is probably the most expensive programme of this kind in the world: in 1969/1970 the programme cost about £13 per acceptor and about £49 per prevented birth, which is, for instance, twice the cost in Malaysia and Tunisia, where the FPPs are known to be comparatively expensive.

Why has the programme failed? Local studies would undoubtedly reveal that the social and economic conditions in the villages do not motivate people to reduce the number of births. It is also a general prerequisite for a successful programme of family limitation that infant and child mortality must have declined to levels at which the survival of the family is no longer dependent on many deliveries. An average infant mortality rate of 120 per thousand is a relatively low figure for African circumstances, but it should be borne in mind that the rate is higher or much higher among the poorest half of the population. Among them, only about three out of five children born alive reach maturity. This may partially explain why so many studies have shown that the desired number of children is close to the actual number. Thus, there is no evidence to suggest that the pattern of reproduction in Kenya is random.

The Government was supposed to provide most of the NFPP-personnel, particularly in the field, but due to shortage of medical and paramedical personnel at all levels, and due to difficulties in releasing local skilled people for employment in the FPP, the amount of services given did not cope with the capacity of the existing clinics. In 1970, the Director of Medical Services in Kenya came out strongly against the programme: "Medical staff are already over-burdened with existing health work and do not consider the addition of family planning services a high priority".[24] The medical personnel either had to ignore the FP services or they had to steal time from activities more directly related to the health of people.

The Government financial contribution in the NFPP was only about 15% of total costs in 1970. Some of the foreign agencies involved in the programme were (in order according to financial contribution in 1970): IPPF, USAID, Netherlands (wisely withdrew its bilateral FP-aid in 1973), British Overseas Development Agency, Population Council, SIDA (Sweden), Ford Foundation, NORAD (Norway), Oxfam, Pathfinder Fund, US Peace Corps, World Neighbours, Population Services Inc. (University of North Carolina), World Assembly of Youth, World Education Council, FAO's Programme for Better Family Living, and lately the World Bank moved in.

British colonialism has indeed been replaced! With all those brokers, many being engaged for their own interest, the whole programme is characterized by a certain degree of disorder and confusion. In 1972 the Ministry of Economic Planning and Development was the policy-guiding institution in the programme, with an American in high position as an adviser. The assistant administrator in the Ministry of Health was a Swede, the head adviser in the same ministry an American paid by Population Council, and the evaluation of the programme was headed by a Dutchman. All above-mentioned foreigners in this ministry constituted the heaviest body in the Working Party, which outlined the plans for the FP activities.

> Although the Ministry of Health by government decree is the responsible agency for Kenya FP, many of the foreign donors fail to recognize this or to work closely with the ministry. Some observers feel the donor agencies do not particularly want closer co-ordination, but prefer to focus exclusively on their own small FP-activity. One such agency, a Health Ministry official noted, "believes it is running a private programme in Kenya. . . . It is hard to convince them they are working for the Ministry of Health". The attitude "We come, we see, we will conquer the difficulties" is characteristic of most donor agencies. There is little willingness to deal closely with the Ministry, to understand its problems, or to be involved in a wider bureaucracy than the donor's own.[25]

One would expect more emphasis on an evaluation of a programme with so many interests involved. Or perhaps not? In 1969 when there were complaints about the unsatisfactory evaluation, plans were underway for extension of the activities of the Evaluation Team, according to the foreign head adviser at the Ministry of Health. Five years later no significant progress had taken place. This negative attitude is understandable: continual studies of high quality would expose the lack of achievements of the programme, the causes of the failure and the limited possibilities of a successful continuation of the programme as it was run—a disclosure which would not meet the interest of those foreign agencies who were and still are so deeply involved in the reproduction of Kenya's population.

Notes

1. "Land and Population in East Africa" (1952). Colonial 290, HMSO p. 2. An excellent background picture of the Kenyan economy is given in R. van Zwanenberg L1072). "The Agricultural History of Kenya", East African Publishing House, Nairobi.
2. "East Africa Royal Commission 1953–55 Report", Cand. 9475, HMSO 1955, p. 34.
3. "Employment, Incomes and Equality, a Strategy for increasing Productive Employment in Kenya", ILO, Geneva, 1972. Henceforth we shall refer to this very important document as the "ILO-report".
4. "African Socialism and its Application to Planning in Kenya", Sessional Paper No. 10, 1963–65.
5. Ndeti, K. (1974). Kenyas befolkningspolitik. *In* "Mera folk" (Ed. by L. Bondestam), p. 15. Miljoforlaget, Stockholm.
6. "Family Planning in Kenya", Population Council of the USA, published by Ministry of Economic Planning and Development, Nairobi, 1967.
7. Miller, N. N. (1971). The politics of population, *Fieldstaff Reports*, East African Series, Vol. X, No. 2.
8. "The Kenya NFPP Five Year Plan" (draft), Family Planning Section, Ministry of Health, Nairobi, April 1972.
9. Fordyce, E. J. and Jones, A. P. (1972). "The Kenya FPP, A Research Proposal", Department of Sociology and Economics, University of Nairobi, p. 2.
10. "Statistical Abstract 1971", Table 73, Ministry of Finance and Planning, Nairobi.
11. "Economic Survey 1974", Table 3.9, Ministry of Finance and Planning, Nairobi.
12. "The People of Kenya", an IPPF Africa Handbook, Nairobi, June 1971, p. 9.
13. Kakuli, C. M. G. (1970). Tenant unionism, protection for tenants, *East Africa Journal*, April, p. 5.
14. "Statistical Abstract 1971", calculated from Table 44.
15. Zwanenberg, R. van (1972). History and theory of urban poverty in Nairobi, the problems of slum development, IDS, Discertation Paper No. 139, Nairobi.
16. Ghai, D. P. (1970). Employment performance, prospects and policies in Kenya, IDS, Discertation Paper No. 99, Nairobi, September, Table 2.

17. Lamb, G. (1975). In a review in *RAPE*, No. 3/75, of Colin Leys, "Underdevelopment in Kenya: The Political Economy of Neo-Colonialism 1964–71", London (unfortunately, when I wrote this article I had not had the opportunity of reading Leys' important book). See also "Who Controls Industry in Kenya?" (1968) by the National Christian Council of Kenya, East Africa Publishing House, Nairobi.
18. "Statistical Abstract 1971", calculated from Table 207.
19. Whitelaw, E. (1971). "Survey of Nairobi Households", IDS, Staff Paper No. 117, Nairobi 1971.
20. Mboya, T. J. (1967). Priorities in planning. *In* "Education, Employment and Rural Development" (Ed. by J. R. Sheffield), p. xix. East Africa Publishing House, Nairobi.
21. *Daily Nation*, September 6 and 14, 1968.
22. Ndeti, K. (1971). Differential deprivation and patterns of criminal behaviour in Kenya. *In* "Proceedings of the Conference on Psychology and Family Planning" (Ed. by H. P. David), p. 96. Nairobi.
23. Bondestam, L. (1972). "Population Growth Control in Kenya", Research Report No. 12, Scandinavian Institute of African Studies, Uppsala.
24. Likimani, J. C. (1973). "The Kenya NFPP", paper presented at an OECD-meeting in Paris, April, p. 3.
25. Miller, N., op. cit., p. 8.

Population Growth and Economic Growth in Tanzania—A Case Study of the Rungwe District[1]

J. J. Sterkenburg and H. A. Luning

Introduction

Most African countries show high rates of population growth, both when compared with previous rates in these countries and with the present rates outside Africa. In almost half of the countries the growth rate has surpassed 2·5% p.a. This highly complicates attempts of African governments to achieve improvements in the overall quality of the population, especially education and health. The governments' attempts to achieve their development objectives are further complicated by the low levels of domestic saving, which are again a direct result of the low income levels among large segments of the population. In turn, these low income levels are caused by the dependence of African countries on the industrialized world to sell their products. Due to this dependence the creation of sufficient investment capital locally poses often unsurmountable problems.[2] Consequently, African governments often have to rely on foreign public and private capital to implement their ambitious development programmes, which usually leads to reinforced and enlarged dependency.

It is sometimes stated that most African countries have no urgent "population problem". Admittedly, Africa is not heavily populated if compared to, e.g. South East Asia. However, it should be emphasized that it is not only the absolute number but also the rate of population growth which determines the magnitude of demographic investments. It is a widely held view by certain scholars that the high rate of population growth is primarily responsible for the low standard of living. Therefore, they say, measures first have to be taken on the demographic side, e.g. birth control, in order to achieve a higher standard of living. Two questions are of relevance in this respect. Firstly, are the conditions prevailing in the underdeveloped countries such that family planning programmes can be implemented successfully? Many studies show that in most cases they are not. More fundamental seems a second question: do measures in the demographic field have a larger impact on welfare conditions compared to those in the economic field? If the answer is in the negative, one may wonder whether the argument of those scholars is of any relevance at all.

Apart from the high rate of population growth, the population is very unevenly distributed over the African continent and the majority is concentrated in rather small areas. Tanzania is a clear example of this. The bulk of its population lives on a small number of fertile "islands", such as Bukoba, west of Lake Victoria, and Kilimanjaro, in the north near the border with Kenya. Also the Rungwe District, near Lake Nyasa in southern Tanzania, with a relatively high population density, is rather representative of many other parts of sub-Saharan Africa.

Evidently, the macro-economic apparatus by itself is insufficient for tackling the analytical problems connected with the population growth-economic growth relationship.[3] Therefore, more disaggregative analysis is required. The following case study analyses the growth of population and the increase of money income in one of the more densely populated and relatively developed—in the narrow sense of the degree of commercialization of agriculture and level of monetary income—parts of Tanzania. In order to find out the extent to which the population factor and the economic conditions contribute to the level of money income attained by the inhabitants of the district, a theoretical model was devised based on certain assumptions. The impact of economic factors, such as world market prices, on the per capita income will be compared to that of population growth.

The Rungwe District

The most striking feature of Rungwe District's physical environment is its heterogeneity. The district covers about 4700 sq. km. The eastern half has soils of volcanic origin and a high annual rainfall, while the western half is characterized by non-volcanic soils and a much lower precipitation. Within each of these two parts, there is a considerable variation in ecological conditions, mainly due to strong variations in altitude. Apart from the alluvial plain bordering Lake Nyasa, the whole district is very mountainous and dissected, with altitudes varying roughly between 500 m in the Lake plains and 3300 m in the north. The following areas may be distinguished within the district:

—*The Lakeshore*, a flat area with high rainfall and volcanic soils. The main cash crop is paddy, other crops being bananas, maize, cashew nuts and cocoa.

—*The intermediate zone*, a gently undulating area with, in some parts, rather stony soils and a drier climate than those areas to the north and south of it. The main crops are maize, beans, bananas, and, to a lesser extent, cocoa and mafura nuts.

—*Central and Northern Rungwe*, partly hilly, partly mountainous, especially in the north; soils are predominantly volcanic and towards the north there is a gradual decrease in rainfall. This is the district's most important agricultural area. The main cash crops are coffee, tea and pyrethrum, the main food crops bananas, maize, beans and cassava.

—*Bundali mountains*, a mountainous area with great variations in altitude, precipitation and soil conditions. The only cash crop is coffee whereas bananas, maize, beans and cassava are the main food crops.

—*Bulambia*, an area with much less favourable natural resources in terms of soils and rainfall. A distinct cash crop is lacking. The main food crops are maize, beans, millet and cassava.

The variations in natural resources within the district largely determine the possibilities to grow certain cash crops. This and other factors lead to strong differences in income between the areas. In addition, access to and the control of the various resources cause substantial income differences within the areas. Although income differences were not completely absent in times past, they considerably increased after the introduction of cash crops in the district. The differences between the areas can best be expressed in terms of money income per household, since all areas achieve to a large extent the aspired self-sufficiency in food production (Table I).

The table shows two important phenomena: the large fluctuations in money income per household from year to year, and the sizeable spatial variation in it. For the Lakeshore, these fluctuations are due to

TABLE I. *Average Money Income Per Household in the Rungwe District, 1967–1969 (in Tanzania shillings*).*

	Average money income per household					
Area	From agriculture only			Total money income including wage/salaries		
	1967	1968	1969	1967	1968	1969
1. Lakeshore	151	45	187	215	104	245
2. Intermediate zone	61	22	48	121	90	114
3. Central Rungwe	171	138	255	342	261	345
4. Northern Rungwe	355	119	64	372	135	80
5. Bundali	143	117	251	189	158	291
6. Bulambia	10	13	14	52	53	53

* The Tanzania shilling was valued 20 shillings to the £ prior to the 1967 devaluation of the £. In 1973 the exchange rate was 16·7 Tanzania shillings to the £, or 6·89 shillings per $.

the lack of water control in the paddy growing areas; for Northern Rungwe, the dramatic decrease of pyrethrum prices and subsequently lower supplies are responsible for the deterioration of the income situation; for Bundali and Central Rungwe the changes in the price of coffee and the resulting stagnation in total output are the main determinants for the fluctuations in money income. The income inequalities within the district are rather important in view of Tanzania's policy of *ujamaa*, which aims among other things to reduce such inequalities. For the rest of the argument we shall, however, simplify the actual situation and work with averages for the district as a whole.

Information on the Rungwe District is traceable to the beginning of the century. Although the data are scanty and of limited reliability, particularly concerning the population and its economic activities, there is no doubt that prior to 1948 there was very little noticeable development. Mission and government activities in the fields of education and health started at the beginning of the twentieth century, and the first cash crops, coffee and paddy, were introduced in the same period. Paddy was brought in by Arab traders, coffee by European missionaries. The few European settlers in the district successfully opposed the cultivation of coffee by African small holders for some time. Both for cash cropping and health/education activities only a small fraction of the population was involved. This situation changed around 1948. Because of the shortage of primary products in the industrialized countries after the Second World War, production had to be speeded up in the colonies. In Tanzania, an agricultural policy was formulated which aimed at improving small farms by introducing cash crops (improvement approach), resettling people in the uninhabited and sparsely populated parts of the country (transformation approach), and reorganizing the marketing system by establishing cooperatives.[4] In Rungwe District, the coffee production in particular was stimulated and a cooperative marketing system was set up for coffee and paddy. Moreover, in 1948 the first population census was carried out and reliable demographic data became available. That year, therefore, provides a good starting point for an analysis of the relation between population growth and economic growth in that part of Tanzania. Our analysis ends in 1967 when another census was held. Our economic data also refer to that year.

Population Growth, 1948–1967[5]

The 1948 census gives a population of 236 148 for the Rungwe District. In 1967 the population had increased to 359 976. This boils down to a growth of 52% over 19 years, or 2·5% p.a. The average density is 76·7 persons per sq. km, but the population is far from evenly distributed over the district. The majority of the population is concentrated in the most fertile and most developed parts, where cash crops are cultivated: 27% of the area contains 54% of the population.

Fertility, mortality and migration determine population growth. Lack of reliable vital statistics is a major constraint for an accurate calculation of fertility and mortality. However, it has been estimated that in 1967 the total fertility was around 6–7 (i.e. children ever born by women who have passed their reproductive age), the crude birth rate 52 per thousand, the infant mortality rate 160–170 per thousand (live born children who die before reaching one year of age), expectation of life at birth 37–39 years, and the crude death rate approximately 25 per thousand.

In the period 1948–1957 the mortality rate declined thanks to improvements in the medical facilities, including greater availability of vaccins and antibiotics, and a successful Government programme in the agricultural field (introduction of cassava as a "hunger crop" and expansion of local markets resulting in a more varied diet for large segments of the district's population). The changes in fertility for the same period are more difficult to assess. It may have increased as a result of better medical services, which also resulted in a decrease in infant mortality.

The inhabitants of the Rungwe District have a longstanding tradition of migration. Already in the early period of British rule they went to the Coast to earn a money income. Later, in the 1930s when the Lupa gold fields in Chunya—an area north-west of Rungwe—were being developed they readily seized the opportunity to find employment and sell their agricultural produce. During the Second World War the direction of labour migration changed completely and people started to go to the Copperbelt in Zambia and the Witwatersrand mining areas in South Africa. The number of migrants increased under the impact of various factors: ideas of higher standards of living were brought by returning soldiers which resulted in a greater demand for money and manufactured products. The demand for and price of cattle rose and good farming land started to become scarce. Finally, an increasing demand for mining labour coupled with higher wages and better transport facilities and means of recruitment were noticeable. On the other hand, the possibility of earning a money income by growing coffee reduced the magnitude of labour migration in the coffee-areas. In 1948 already some 12 500 men were employed abroad and in 1954–1955 this number was estimated at more than 14 000. This is equivalent to about 20% of all males of 15 years and over. The high percentage of migrants had only a limited effect on the fertility and mortality pattern and, therefore, did not cause any remarkable change in population growth. The death rate at the mines, as a result of dangerous work, neither affected the mortality significantly. A considerable number of men did not return to Rungwe after the migration came to a standstill in 1963 by order of the Tanganyika Government. This led to a decrease in the sex-ratio and allowed greater opportunities for polygamy. As is generally known, the number of children per woman is lower in polygamous households.

To summarize, over the period 1948–1967 the effect of labour migration on the population growth rate, which was 2·5% p.a., was rather limited. This means that Rungwe takes a middle position compared to other parts of tropical Africa in terms of the population growth rate.

Economic Growth, 1948–1967

The measurement of income is a complicated issue in an economy which is dominated by subsistence agriculture. In 1967, 97·6% of the working population was engaged in agriculture; in 1948 this percentage must have been even higher. As the district was still almost self-sufficient in 1967 and exports of food crops (except bananas) and imports were negligible, changes in the economic situation between 1948 and 1967 can to a large extent be measured by comparing the value of cash crop production and per capita money incomes in the two years. The non-agricultural sector will be omitted from the analysis, apart from labour migration, since the relevant data are lacking. This will hardly influence the figures in view of the negligible percentage of the working force employed outside agriculture. We fully recognize the limitations of per capita income as a measure of economic growth, and realize that alternative criteria (e.g. degree of labour absorption, degree of savings and consumption, income distribution) could have been selected. However, in view of the available data, we consider it the best yard-stick for this particular case-study.

Around 1930 Arabica coffee was introduced as a cash crop in peasant agriculture and coffee production increased slowly but steadily. In 1948 the total output amounted to 390 tons in Rungwe. This year compared favourably with previous ones, so the choice of this base year does not lead to an exaggerated growth rate. The only other crop, which was marketed in significant quantities in 1948 was paddy, which had been cultivated in the Lakeshore area by peasant farmers since the beginning of the century. A number of estates yielded a modest tea production in 1948. Of the total gross production value, about a quarter was paid out to hired labourers who were part-time farmers. The peasant population earned 3 million shillings in incomes from agriculture in 1948, to which should be added the cash and goods brought back by labour migrants from South Africa and the Copperbelt, valued at 3·3 million shillings.

The main changes in agricultural production over the period 1948–1967 are an expansion of the cash crops, including the introduction of tea on smallholder farms, and a further diversification of the agricultural economy (pyrethrum, mafura nut, cocoa, cashew nuts and bananas). This resulted in an increase in money income to 15·5 million shillings in 1967. The three main cash crops, coffee, paddy and tea, accounted for 84% of the total money income from agriculture.

A spectacular increase in coffee plantings and production occurred in the period 1952–1960. The main factors responsible for this increase were: a stimulating price level and the introduction of a price differential system (i.e. the produce was graded and better grades received higher prices); the expansion and improvements of the road system, particularly in the Bundali mountains;[6] and the establishment and improvement of şupporting services, such as agricultural extension and cooperatives. These organizations made available the necessary inputs, including expert advice, and organized the marketing of coffee.

The factors which influenced the growth in rice output in the period 1948–1958 were: the population growth in the Lakeshore area which resulted in an expansion of the area under this crop; an improvement of the marketing organization of paddy by establishing cooperatives; and the introduction of ploughs which were either bought by cash from incomes earned by labour migrants, or on credit from the newly established cooperatives. Of minor impact for the increase in paddy production was the occupation of land in the rice area by farmers from the northern coffee growing areas and the introduction of tractors during the 1960s. The larger quantity of consumer goods which became available in the area through the activities of private traders and cooperatives had a favourable impact on the willingness to produce cash crops. The increase in output of the major cash crops was chiefly the result of taking unused land into cultivation and of increasing the labour input of the farm population.

A strong increase in tea production in the period 1948–1967 chiefly took place on the big estates. Not only did they expand the area under cultivation, they also intensified the methods of crop husbandry by proper fertilizer application, improvements in plucking standards and pruning techniques, and even the application of sprinkling irrigation devices during the drier periods of the year. In 1962 the Tanzania Government embarked on a smallholder tea programme. Initially, expansion was slow but from 1965 onwards farmers applied in large numbers for the necessary assistance to grow this crop. Potential tea growers were carefully selected based on soil surveys and other factors. All inputs were made available to the grower, and a low number of growers per extension worker facilitated detailed expert guidance. The marketing was organized through the tea growers' association, while the manufacturing of green leaves initially took place in the factories of the estates and later in factories specially erected for the smallholders. Due to this package of inputs made available to the grower, a high standard of crop husbandry was attained, although some negative influence was exercised by absenteeism.[7] Summarizing, the following factors account for the changes in production between 1948 and 1967: (1) the comparatively favourable price level for coffee in the period 1948–1955, (2) the activities of the Tanzania Government in the field of road construction and in supplying agricultural inputs, particularly for coffee and tea production, (3) the improvement of the marketing organization, (4) initiative and additional labour input on the part of the local farmers and (5) better management on the tea estates.

Increased production does not necessarily go hand in hand with higher money income. And even if farmers attained a higher income, it does not have to mean increased purchasing power. A correction should therefore be made for inflation. With only scanty evidence available, we have estimated the annual rate of inflation at 1% p.a. during 1948–1960 and 2% thereafter.[8] Under these circumstances, the real money income increased from 6·3 to 12·0 million shillings (1948 prices), and the annual average growth in income during the 19 year period was 3·5%. Thus, the per capita income growth has outstripped the population growth by about 1% per year on average. A closer scrutiny of the time series discloses, however, a real income of 14·5 million shillings already in 1957, which implies an annual income increase of nearly 10% up to that year. The next ten years, a negative growth of real income of 2·0% p.a. is observed. Three factors are responsible for this retrogression:

(1) A decline in world market price of coffee. Coffee production had reached 1900 tons in 1963, but the total output more or less stagnated thereafter, with some fluctuations from year to year. The coffee price paid to farmers (before taxation) was around 3 shillings per lb in 1956–1957, but dropped to 2 shillings in 1958–1959 and reached a low ebb of 1·20 shillings in 1967–1968. The share of the coffee grower decreased from 53 % of the world market price in 1957 to 37 % in 1967. These lower prices paid to farmers strongly discouraged them from paying sufficient attention to their plots, which indirectly contributed to another serious problem—pests and diseases spread rapidly. Although both the number of growers and the area under crop increased, total output remained at the same level. Consequently, an increasing number of farmers with a larger area under cultivation produced a constant quantity of coffee of a deteriorating quality.

(2) A similar pattern is discernable for paddy; a steadily rising output until the late 1950s and thereafter a stagnation, albeit for different reasons. In this case, the main factor retarding the production increase is the lack of water control. Improved technology, i.e. better methods of cultivation and new inputs, cannot be introduced since it is not economic to use them as long as drainage facilities in particular are non-existent. At present, the main production constraint is that of labour in the peak period of weeding which limits the acreage cultivated per farmer. Farmers are not interested to increase their labour input in this period, as they are uncertain about the return. The fields may become flooded again, even shortly before the harvest.

(3) The Government's order to stop labour migration to the South African mines. South Africa's racial segregation and discrimination led in 1963 to the decision of the Tanganyika Government to boycott this country. This necessitated the import of certain goods from more expensive sources and may have meant the loss of markets for Tanganyika exports. For Rungwe District the most important consequence of the boycott was the halt of labour migration to the South African mines,[9] which meant a heavy loss of money income for Rungwe. While small numbers may still go to the Copperbelt, the demand for Tanzanian labour has also strongly decreased there. This can be explained by an increase in mechanization and a preference for Zambian citizens.

The small number of people migrating nowadays is in no way comparable to the many who left the district in the 1950s and the early 1960s.

The Relative Impact of Demographic and Economic Factors

The ability and willingness of producers to improve the use of production factors and increase the level of productivity are largely determined by the marketing possibilities for the products under consideration. Sometimes there is a tendency to underestimate the impact of this factor in favour of others such as the low level of education, the obstacles created by the community and/or the bureaucracy, and the lack of the necessary inputs. Without denying the relevance and the relative significance of such factors in various situations, they are often outweighed by the importance of good marketing opportunities. The study of the Rungwe coffee industry makes this abundantly clear.

To indicate the relative importance of the various demographic and economic factors on the level of cash income per capita, a simple model is constructed. The relative weight of the various factors is assessed by means of a forward projection of the indicators. We have only made a linear projection of the variables; unfortunately it was not possible to take account of the mutual dependence of the indicators, due to lack of data.

On the demographic side we assume on the one hand a considerably faster and on the other a considerably slower population growth rate between 1948 and 1967 than the one which actually occurred. Spectacular improvements in medical conditions could have led to a downward trend in the mortality rate and a concomitant increase in fertility, the latter also due to a decrease in sterility and lower mortality of women in the reproductive period. A higher fertility rate could also have been influenced by an increase in monogamous marriages and a higher marriage stability. In contrast, a considerably lower growth than the actual one could have materialized, although for this lower growth rate a traditional and a modern pattern should be distinguished. The traditional pattern is characterized by a high or even temporarily increasing mortality rate, and a constant or lower fertility under the conditions of a poor or even deteriorating level of medical care, the outbreaks of epidemics, an increasing sterility, and a deterioration of food production. A modern pattern of low population growth rate may materialize as a result of a decrease in mortality and a concomitant decrease in fertility, caused by good medical facilities, improved food conditions, i.e. a more varied and balanced diet, and a highly successful family planning programme. These considerations would imply the following hypothetical percentages of annual population increase: under high growth rate conditions 2·5% for 1948–1957 and 2·9% for 1957–1967; under low growth rate conditions 1·7 and 1·5% respectively for the two periods. One may argue that for African circumstances too low a growth rate was adopted. Experiences with family planning in Kenya have demonstrated that figures in the order of 2·1–2·3% are hard to attain. But the low rate adopted here is probably not unrealistic in view of Tanzania's pronounced development policy. Moreover, a more extreme rate may even more clearly reveal the relevance and impact of the demographic factors vis-a-vis the economic ones. If the lower growth rate alternative is too optimistic, then the impact of population growth control on income per capita is exaggerated.

The assumed population growth rates result in the following total populations (actual situation given for comparison):

	1957	1967
high rate	278 100	392 300
enumerated	271 300	360 000
low rate	254 700	319 600

The 1957 figure as given in the census report was adjusted for migration and undercount.

On the economic side, we assume a more favourable situation with regard to coffee prices on the world market and technological improvements in the paddy growing area. The average rate of increase of coffee production has been 15% p.a. for the period 1948–1957. During the early years, the growth rate was around 20%, tapering off to 10% towards the end of this period. Assuming that the 1957–1958 price of 2·50 shillings per lb paid to farmers could have been maintained during the period lasting up till 1967 and assuming an annual production growth of at least 6% after 1957 as a result of this favourable price level, total coffee output would have amounted to 2500 tons by 1967. The latter assumption is not unrealistic in view of a 1970–71 production level of 2400 tons which occurred after a price rise the previous year. Under these conditions the total income from cash crop production would have amounted to 18·3 million shillings in 1967 (1948 prices).

In the Lakeshore area the lack of drainage facilities strongly hampers an increase in paddy production. The flood problem is due to the small gradient of the land, the high rainfall in the area during a short period of the year and the fact that rivers crossing the plain frequently overspill their banks. Farming conditions in the area can be improved at relatively low costs by constructing dikes along the rivers and by changing the local drainage system. Construction costs of these works have been estimated to range between 33 and 85 shillings per acre.[10] If these structures had been built as from 1957 onwards, covering an area of 2000 ha out of the present rice area of 10 000 ha, estimated yields would have increased from 1000 to 2000 kg/ha on the improved area. Taking into account the increased costs of production, the total net money income would have risen by 1·2 million shillings by 1967.

Table II shows the total money income in the district in 1948, 1957 and 1967, on the basis of these assumptions: (1) the actual situation; (2) constant 1957 coffee prices and subsequent higher production; and (3) in addition to (2), investments in rice cultivation resulting in a higher paddy output.

TABLE II. *Total Money Income in Rungwe District Under Various Conditions (in Million Tanzanian Shillings at 1948 Prices—Corrected for Inflation).*

	1948	1957	1967
1. Actual situation	6·3	14·5	12·0
2. Stable coffee prices and higher production	6·3	14·5	18·3
3. Rice investments in addition to stable coffee prices and higher production	6·3	14·5	19·5

As we have seen earlier the actual annual growth of money income in constant prices has been on average 10% over the period 1948–1957, whereas a decrease of 2% p.a. occurred in the period 1957–1967. In the case of constant coffee prices at the 1957 level and higher production, the annual increase in total money income would have attained 2·5% p.a. With the addition of the rice investments, the percentage would further have risen to 3%.

We can now calculate the per capita money income for 1957 and 1967 at constant 1948 prices under the various demographic and economic conditions. Particulars are given in Table III.

TABLE III. *Per Capita Money Income in Rungwe District, 1948, 1957 and 1967 Under Various Conditions (in Tanzanian Shillings, at 1948 Constant Prices).*

Demographic conditions	1948	1957	1967		
			(1)	(2)	(3)
High population growth rate	27·1	52·1	30·6	46·6	49·7
Actual population growth rate	27·1	53·4	33·3	50·8	54·2
Low population growth rate	27·1	56·9	37·5	57·3	61·0

Under the actual economic conditions, the per capita money income would have decreased between 1957 and 1967 by 5·6% p.a. under high population growth conditions, and by over 4·0% under low population growth conditions. Under the coffee improvement assumption, the per capita money income would have decreased by 1·0% in the case of high population growth and increased by less than 0·1% in that of low population growth. If both coffee and paddy improvements had taken place, the per capita income would have decreased by 0·5% (high population growth) and increased by almost 1·0% (low population growth) respectively.

The relative importance of the economic and demographic factors are shown in Table IV, in which the per capita income figures for 1967 under the various conditions are expressed as indices of the actual population and the actual economic conditions of 1967.

TABLE IV. *Indices of the 1967 Per Capita Money Income Under Various Demographic and Economic Conditions.*

Demographic conditions	Economic conditions—1967		
	(1)	(2)	(3)
High growth rate	92	140	149
Actual growth rate	100	153	163
Low growth rate	113	172	183

The table clearly demonstrates the importance of stable commodity prices. Under the actual population growth rate a constant 1957 coffee price would have resulted in a 53% increase in per capita money income over the period 1957–1967, whereas technological improvements in paddy would add another 10%. The impact of the demographic factor lies in the same order of magnitude as that of the paddy improvement: a higher population growth rate would result in a decrease of 8%, a lower one in an increase of 13%. As the benefits of the "demographic investment" and the technical improvement in paddy cultivation lie in the same order of magnitude over the period under review, it is interesting to compare the cost aspect. If we assume that the family planning cost of a prevented birth in Tanzania amounts to half that of Kenya (i.e. £25 instead of £50), a decrease in fertility of 8 per thousand would boil down to 2000 prevented births p.a. in the Rungwe District, at a total cost of approximately 800 000 Tanzanian shillings. The cost of technical improvement in paddy on 2000 hectares would amount to only 400 000 Tanzanian shillings. In other words, in this case the cost of prevention of births in one years is twice that of the technical improvements in agriculture which last over a long period of time.

The limited impact of changes in the demographic factor *in the short run* (in our case 19 years) becomes abundantly clear. In addition, one may conclude that the relative impact of population growth and, consequently, of population planning programmes, is far outweighed by such structural measures as higher and stable prices of the main export products.

The question remains whether the conclusion arrived at here has a wider applicability. The expansion of agricultural production in the

Rungwe District occurred under the conditions of a "land surplus economy", i.e. the factor land was in abundance compared with other factors of production such as labour.[11] Under the agricultural system of the 1950s free labour was, however, also available. Thus, the expansion of agricultural production took place at zero opportunity costs of land and labour. Similar processes of growth of agricultural production have been recorded for many other parts of sub-Saharan Africa. Today, all the land of relatively good quality is occupied in Rungwe District and further production increases have to take place through higher productivity on the cultivated land. This implies the investment of capital which to a large extent has to be created through the export of agricultural products. Many African countries find themselves in similar circumstances: the land surplus economy is almost or wholly turned into a labour surplus economy and there is a heavy dependence on agricultural exports for capital formation.

It would be rather unrealistic to expect sudden and short-term changes in economic conditions in areas like Rungwe, where a labour surplus situation is emerging. It is unlikely that world market prices for most agricultural products will show drastic long-term improvements. This prospect has important consequences for planning. An overall increase in money income of 3–4% p.a. is extremely hard to achieve under the present political-economic conditions. In view of the prevailing low standard of living, any birth control programme would meet with very little success, if any. Moreover, experiences over the period 1948–1967 demonstrate that such a programme, even if highly successful, would have a smaller impact on the per capita income than stable world market prices for the main cash crops, and technological improvements in agriculture. Consequently, structural changes in the world economy are more relevant than birth control programmes in raising the living standard of the people of sub-Saharan Africa.

Notes

1. The authors wish to thank Klaas de Jonge and Lars Bondestam for their valuable remarks on an earlier draft of this paper.
2. The Tanzanian Minister of Finance stated in his 1973/1974 budget speech that during the first ten years of the country's independence an

estimated 2500 million shillings in purchasing power was lost as a result of unfavourable world price changes. Similarly, an estimated 2000 million was lost because of increases in import prices. See *Africa Research Bulletin*, Vol. 10, No. 6, July 1973, p. 2787.

3. See, for instance, Meilink, H. A. (1974). The population factor in economic growth theory. *In* "Population Growth and Economic Development in Africa" (Ed. by J. Sterkenburg and K. de Jonge), *Kroniek van Afriká* (special issue), Assen.

4. Ruthenberg, H. (1964). "Agricultural Development in Tanganyika", Berlin.

5. Data were chiefly taken from K. de Jonge and J. Sterkenburg, "Evaluation of the 1967 Tanzania Population Census in Rungwe (Tanzania)", Technical Paper No. 8, Leyden 1971. The main conclusions of this report have been included in the series of reports on the "Tanzania Population Census", Vol. VI, Government Printer, Dar es Salaam, 1973.

6. Luning, H. A. and Sterkenburg, J. (1973). A social cost–benefit analysis of road building for agricultural development: a case study from Tanzania. *J. Agric. Econom.* **XXIV**, 311–319.

7. See Sterkenburg, J. and Tempelman, A. (1969). "Occupation and Absenteeism of Tea Growers in Relation to the Quality of the Tea Plot, Rungwe Agro-Socio-Economic Research Project", Technical Paper No. 2, Leyden, October.

8. Based on "Survey of African Economics" (1969). Vol. 2, I.M.F., Washington, pp. 240–1 and Kimble, H. (1970). "Price Control in Tanzania", Nairobi, Dar es Salaam, Appendices.

9. Nyerere, J. K. (1966/1967). "Principles and Development", Mbioni, 3, 6, pp. 4–33. The text of this memorandum has also been published in Nyerere, J. K. (1968). "Freedom and Socialism", Ch. 21. Oxford University Press, Oxford.

10. Details are given in Luning, H. A. and Sterkenburg, J. (1971). "An Executive Plan for Agricultural Development in Rungwe District, 1971–1979", Leyden, Vol. I, pp. 39–44, and Vol. II, Annex G.

11. Helleiner, G. K. (1966). "Typology in Development Theory, The Land Surplus Economy", Stanford Food Research Studies, 6, pp. 181–194.

People and Underdevelopment—
The Example of Tanzania

Bertil Egerö

"Of all things in the world, people are the most precious"

(Chinese declaration, 1973)

"People and their hard work are the foundations of development"

(The Arusha Declaration, Tanzania 1967)

The Population Issue

"Population" and "population growth" have in recent decades been increasingly mentioned as key factors in the economic development of the poor parts of the world. Supported by a series of so-called objective studies of the effects of population growth on economic development, vast amounts of money and skilled manpower are being made available by the rich capitalist countries to promote programmes of population control, officially often named "family planning programmes". While in some cases providing poor birth control services for their own people, the rich countries go all out to sell these same services to the underdeveloped world. Contraceptive means regarded as unacceptable by the rich countries themselves, and even abortion and sterilization programmes with monetary incentives, are common features of the services offered.

This trend tends to obscure the valuable aspects of contraceptive services to the individual and their importance for the social emancipation of women. In fact, population control and provision of contraceptive services are two entirely independent questions. With birth control advice as part of a comprehensive health programme suited to the needs of the people, the effect could well be a higher rate of natural increase due to a reduction in mortality and fewer cases of involuntary infertility.

Despite the intensity of the population campaign over the last ten years, only a small number of independent African countries have responded to the call and established official family planning programmes. Among these are, not surprisingly, Kenya and Ghana with relatively high levels of capitalist economic growth and concomitant problems of unemployment and poverty. Tanzania's resistance to programmes of population control led the "populationists" to seek other ways of getting the message through. A non-governmental family planning association is working in close collaboration with the Ministry of Health in providing contraceptive advice through the maternity clinics; it seems to have been more successful in terms of acceptance rates than the official family planning programme in neighbouring Kenya. Meanwhile, at the University of Dar es Salaam, a demographic unit was created shortly after the 1967 population census and expanded its activities rapidly through generous inputs made by the Population Council. The unit spread for some years the neo-Malthusian message via teaching, internal "service papers" to the Government and expensive research on fertility differentials.

The international population campaign is run on many different levels and through both international and national bodies. Its relation to the problems of underdevelopment is real enough, but of a very different character from the one officially propagated. This paper aims at a brief outline to an analysis of the role of population in the dependent economies, which also will demonstrate the function of population campaigns in the retention of status quo in these countries. With Tanzania as an example, it will briefly approach the question of the role of population in a strategy for disengagement from international capitalism.

Tanzania's Population is Small but Growing Fast

The census in Tanzania in 1967 gave a population size more than a million above the official projection.[1] Under-enumeration in the 1957 census caused part of the discrepancy. But the difference also signifies a higher rate of population growth after independence, primarily as a result of reduced mortality. Fertility levels seem to have remained constant or even slightly increased.

Increasing rates of growth are common among countries in Africa

and in many parts of the Third World. Rural development programmes offering improved water supplies, malaria eradication, vaccin-
ation campaigns and the like reduce the mortality of the population
without basically changing their economic situation, thus fertility
levels remain high and rates of natural increase go up. In fact, high
fertility levels have been shown to be among the best indicators of
"developing" as distinguished from "developed" countries, to use
the current UN terminology.

Tanzania, with a birth rate of 47 per thousand,[2] undoubtedly
belongs to the former category. The death rate of 22 per thousand is
still high compared with that of the "developed" nations. This
mortality level means that, for instance, as much as one quarter of all
children born die before the age of 5 and only 60–65% reach the age
of 20. Life expectancy at birth, i.e. the average number of years a
newborn child is expected to live, is less than 45, far from the 70–75
years in the industrialized nations today.

But the death rate will certainly decline further, and the rate of natural
increase of 2·5% per year estimated for 1967 might soon reach perhaps
3% per year. This is not an unusual situation in Africa. Tanzania is near
the average for Tropical Africa in both levels and trends of population
increase. A growth rate of 3% was estimated for Kenya almost 15 years
ago, and more recent estimates are still a few points higher. This does
not seem to prevent Kenya's economy from growing at comparatively
high rates according to conventional standards of measurement.

Tanzania's population, 12·3 million in 1967, will have exceeded 18
million by 1980. Still, this is a small population for a country of the
size of Tanzania. A population density of 18 per sq.km is very low by
international comparison; although the average for Africa is 13, for
Asia it is 82 and for Europe 96! And these rates are still low in
comparison with, for instance, England and Wales's 326 or Holland's
334 persons per sq.km.[3] To replace the crude density rates with rates
based on, say, arable land, basically does not change this picture.

There is no Simple Relation Between Economic Growth and Either Density or Growth Rate of the Population

Thus, an international comparison immediately shows that there is
no direct relationship between the density of population and either

level or trend of economic growth. But in the neo-Malthusian ideology it is not so much the density as the rate of growth of the population that provides a brake on economic growth. Is there then any empirical evidence for such a relationship?

A well-known bourgeois economist, Simon Kuznets, has studied the correlation between population growth and per capita economic growth on an international scale.[4] He found that, for the capitalist world as a whole, there was a negative correlation so that high population growth tended to be accompanied by lower rates of economic growth. However, Kuznets proceeded to divide the countries into developed and developing, repeating his analysis for each such cluster. The correlations now dropped to zero, demonstrating that the overall correlation depended entirely on the large average differences between developed and developing countries.

A simple historical comparison would give the same picture. Improvements in agricultural technology in Europe provided the necessary surplus for the growth of an industrial sector and concomitant declines in mortality. Thus the industrial revolution took place in the midst of increasing rates of population growth. The decline of the growth rates appeared at very different stages in the process, however, and the idea of a uniform "demographic transition" from high to low growth rates does not hold at a closer look. In fact, a country like France never had much of a "demographic gap"; the decline in the birthrate started very soon after the mortality decline.

The lack of uniformity becomes even more pronounced for countries outside Europe. Japan initially repeated the average European experience of industrialization coupled with increasing rates of population growth. Fertility remained high until a much later stage in the process, when it was forced down through very liberal abortion legislation. In China the extreme poverty of the masses before the 1949 revolution kept population growth near zero. The gradual build-up of a socialist economy was reflected in improved living conditions and reduced mortality, and in a population increase which soon reached levels comparable to those in Africa today.

Kuznets studied the relationship between population growth and economic growth with nations as units. His results, like those of other later conducted studies, demonstrate the lack of any such relation either for the underdeveloped countries as a whole or for subgroups like the African countries. Kuznets' type of analysis can be applied also to subunits of a country, assuming a relatively close relationship between local resources and economic growth in a predominantly agricultural context.

For Tanzania, estimates of GDP provide an idea about local differences in average income. Comparing these with rates of population increase we find nothing to support the thesis of population growth as affecting levels of economic growth. If we use the 17 Mainland regions of 1967 as units the correlation turns out to be positive rather than negative. With the 60 districts the correlation is reduced to near zero.

These results are in no way surprising. Tanzania as a post-colony presents a pattern of internal structural underdevelopment which gradually crystallized through the creation of the colonial economy. Areas with European large-scale plantations, smallholder cashcrop areas and areas of labour recruitment were the three major types, with very different impact on the local peasant economy and standard of living.[5] Differential population growth could appear not as a cause but as a result of economic differentiation, through the effect of the economy on crucial factors such as mortality, infertility and migration.

The type of empirical evidence presented above is not in itself proof for or against any causal connection between population and economy. But it lends strong support to the thesis that the connection is complex, involving factors which can never be left out of the analysis. It would be misleading to present this relationship in a simple formula like the popular one of deducting population growth from economic growth. The impact of population is subordinated to and conditional on the economic system of society.

Population in the Periphery of the Capitalist System

Tanzania, like most former colonies, was by the time of independence well integrated into the international capitalist system. Colonial policies were aimed at maximizing the extraction of raw materials and foodstuffs required by the metropole. Thus the colonial economy was entirely geared to and dependent on the need of the colonial power.

The dependency structure remains largely intact even today. Sisal, cotton, coffee and tea provide the bulk of Tanzania's exports now as in the past. The products are exported for manufacturing overseas, in competition with other producers of the same goods and for prices determined by the rich countries. The unequal nature of this exchange is made possible through the continued access to cheap labour in an economy still largely controlled by alien interests.[6]

The small returns to peasants and workers in the peripheral economy effectively prevent the growth of a market for mass consumption. Instead, the economic "development" of countries like Tanzania is characterized by imports suited to the needs of the small ruling elite, a small industrial sector orientated in the same direction, and a rapidly expanding service sector. The periphery countries are first of all producers of cheap materials, and only to a minor degree receivers of manufactured goods from the centre.

The social aspects of this process is the increasing *marginalization* of the people of the dependent countries, the way they are becoming superfluous to the economy.[7] Unemployment and underemployment, the creation of urban proletariats and impoverished peasants are the characteristics of this process. Unemployment is an integral part of a capitalist economy, and has by its proponents even been called "a sign of a healthy economy". This is undoubtedly correct, as a certain level of unemployment increases the employer's control over labour market and wages. But the centre economies are based on mass consumption, and unemployment must be kept low so as to retain the purchasing power of the workers.

For a periphery economy the situation is quite different. Its importance for the international system lies in the low cost of production, not in the levels of consumption. The volume of production is adjusted to the needs of the centre economies, and the amount of capitalization is chosen to maximize profit extraction. If a capital-intensive production is more profitable, this is preferred irrespective of its effects on unemployment in the peripheral economy.

Examples of this policy abound in Tanzania. The Mwanza Textile Mill, built and run by a French contractor, employs less than a quarter of the number of workers in the Chinese-built Friendship Textile Mill, with the same production targets. The American contractor who a few years ago built the new road to Zambia chose to import an impressive park of gigantic road-machines to keep local employment down to a minimum. This policy should be compared with that of another Chinese contract, the Tazara railway from Dar es Salaam to Ndola in Zambia. Using labour-intensive methods, this project provided tens of thousands of workers not only with employment but with a vocational training badly needed by the two countries. The American-built road was completed at high cost in foreign currency, and no trained Tanzanians were available afterwards to build other roads in the country.

In Tanzania, the well-known "Ujamaa" policy of rural development has in fact meant very little to alleviate the problems of urban unemployment. Many Tanzanians were therefore some years ago surprised to learn that no less than Shs18 million would be spent on the construction of an automated bakery in Dar es Salaam, with which a few dozen employees could produce enough bread for the whole city.[8] The Canadian contractor did not seem to have given much thought to the fate of all those engaged in bread production, who would be left without work.

It can thus be demonstrated that unemployment and underemployment in no way are functions of population increase, and neither is the per capita growth of the monetary economy. They are, above all, the result of the position of the country within the capitalist system and of the dynamics of this system. But the marginalization of the masses in dependent economies represents a political threat to the system and its local representatives, the national ruling elite. It is here that population control or family planning comes in, to confuse issues for the worker and defend the interests of the class in power.

For the Peasant a Large Family is Often Economically Rational

In the dependent economy of a periphery country like Tanzania the peasant as a primary producer is at the mercy of the capitalist system, unable to plan or control his economic situation through his own efforts. The drastic layoffs in the Tanzanian sisal industry and the wild fluctuations of world prices for cotton and coffee are factors that hit directly at the Tanzanian peasant/labourer himself. His basic security will have to be found outside the money economy, in subsistence farming for himself and his family.[9]

To work outside the money economy means to be largely unable to employ labour. It means reliance on the resources available within the family itself, the more children the more labour power he will have at his disposal. The dependence on his smallholding is the same for the small cashcrop farmer and the wage labourer. Both are unable to control demands and prices for their products. Both have to plan for retirement without compensation for the labour put in during their active years. And old age security can only be provided by the next generation, their children.

Although mortality has dropped considerably since colonial times, levels of mortality still remain very high compared to those in the industrialized countries. In certain districts in Tanzania today, mortality is so high that a couple would have to give birth to four children to be reasonably sure that one son will survive to adult age and be able to take care of them when they grow old. Thus, until basic changes occur in the economic conditions of peasants and workers it is futile to expect any significant decline in fertility.

Population is an Important Factor in Socialist Planning

Within the capitalist system profit considerations dominate the planning; population enters the calculations only as "labour force" or—in the centre economies—as consumers of the products put out on the market. Questions of industrial location, choice of technique in production, levels of unemployment and wage levels are regarded primarily in terms of these two considerations. By contrast, in a planned economy investments and production plans can be adjusted to existing resources in manpower and capital. Full employment in meaningful production for the people is the goal that determines investments and choice of technology.

China started after the 1949 Revolution with many people and small capital reserves. Rather than planning for a production structure dependent on the import of capital, China decided to rely on the resources available within the country, the people. It is therefore in a very literal sense true that the people of China built their present wealth with their own hands, in the same way in which they have assisted Tanzania and Zambia with the construction of the important Tazara railway.

In the early stages of the transition to socialism the rate of population increase is a parameter to which planning will have to be adjusted. The more advanced socialist society is increasingly able to include the rate of increase among the parameters amenable to change. Such a situation only occurs where the interests of the nation coincide with those of the individual, i.e. in a society without antagonistic contradictions between ruler and ruled.

A policy of planned population increase is not necessarily identical to a policy of fertility reduction. The aims could vary according to local conditions, as illustrated in this quote from a Chinese statement:

> What we mean by planned childbirth is not only birth control, but adopting different measures according to different circumstances. In densely populated areas with high birth rates, we advocate late marriage and birth control, so that the age difference between the parents and their children will be about 30 years rather than 20 years. In ethnic minority areas and other sparsely populated areas, we adopt appropriate measures to help increase population and promote production; guidance and help are also given to those who desire to practice birth control.[10]

The Strategy of Transition

In Tanzania, only a few hesitant steps have been taken on the road to a nationally integrated economy. The nationalization of important sectors of the economy has not been accompanied by a long-term plan for economic and industrial development. The 1967 Ujamaa policy of collective agricultural production in communal villages has turned into a programme of forced villagization for increased cash crop cultivation. Worker's demands for collective management in accordance with the 1971 TANU Guidelines have all been turned down by the Government. The economy remains export-oriented and dependent on international trade relations, while the small industrial sector is unable to take care of domestic needs in either foodstuffs or material goods.

All experience points at the futility of expecting any better returns from international exchanges as long as this is not in the interests of capitalism. The UNCTAD conferences and the many efforts at establishing a New Economic World Order—all have given the same bitter lesson to the underdeveloped world. Only unity and economic strength among the dependent countries themselves will change the pattern of unequal exchange. For Tanzania as for the other countries, the valid domestic strategy appears to be disengagement from the international capitalist system, i.e. steps intended to give real meaning to Tanzania's goal of economic "self-reliance".

With its small and unintegrated industrial sector, Tanzania imports virtually all manufactured goods she needs, including spare parts for the maintenance of machines, etc. The disengagement strategy includes the establishment of an industrial sector capable of producing all these goods. The economic obstacles may seem unsurmountable, but various studies have convincingly shown that the material requirements of an industrial sector can all be met by a small number of basic industries.[11]

However, to build this set of basic industries requires surplus, for the maintenance of the workers who build the industry and for the material which at this stage has to be purchased from abroad. As with the agrarian revolution in Europe which gave the surplus to start industrialization and urbanization, so in the case of Tanzania or any other predominantly agricultural economy, the surplus must be produced by the countryside.

The Crucial Role of the Countryside

Thus, what the peasant produces on his smallholding must be sufficient not only for himself and his family, but also for his counterpart the urban worker who is to build the basis for economic self-reliance. The surplus generated and remaining in Tanzania is increasingly consumed by a growing state bureaucracy and service sector. If properly allocated, already this surplus would provide a good platform for an industrialization programme. Improved agricultural methods and more extensive use of arable land can also increase the surplus produced.

But is there room for an extension of cultivation—is there not in many parts of Tanzania a growing population pressure leading to land deterioration and impoverishment? Dodoma with its constant problems of drought and famine, or Sukumaland with overgrazing and large-scale migration in search of new land for cotton, are two apparent examples. So are the problems of land shortage in mountain areas like Kilimanjaro and Rungwe.

However, in every case subject to closer study these conclusions have had to be revized. Densely populated areas have enough land for everyone, but the monetary economy has turned land into a commodity and produced both big land holders and landless people. The result is a *relative* scarcity of land rather than an absolute.

For other areas the problem is one of agricultural technology. Cash cropping has often led to traditional methods of cultivation being abandoned without the introduction of other land-preserving measures. For pastoralists the growing dominance of cashcrop over foodcrop production have made cattle an important form of insurance against cashcropping hazards, and the herds have grown on the profits drawn from the cash crop.

There are certainly cases of high pressure on available land in parts of Tanzania, *with the existing system of land use and cultivation*. Still, a study done by John Moore revealed that, with the agricultural techniques and yields as they were in 1967, the country could accommodate 80% more people than recorded in the 1967 census and still provide everybody with a reasonable standard of living.[12] It is instructive to note (Fig. 1) that the areas with the highest potential for more people include a series of districts low on the scale of economic development. In Southern Tanzania, for instance, a band of poor districts from Lake Nyasa right across to the coast could carry three or more times the present number of people. The same seems true for a large underdeveloped area in the west, from the shores of Lake Victoria right down to the Southern Highlands.

Some of these areas were earlier regarded by the colonial administration as suitable for large-scale labour recruitment for the settler plantation agriculture. Others have been held back primarily through the withholding of assistance in cash crop cultivation and the lack of communications for marketing. Today they belong to the backward parts of the country, as a result of the uneven regional development resulting from forceful colonial intervention and disruption of the local economies.

From this it would seem clear that the extension of land under cultivation is both possible and desirable. Is there also room for

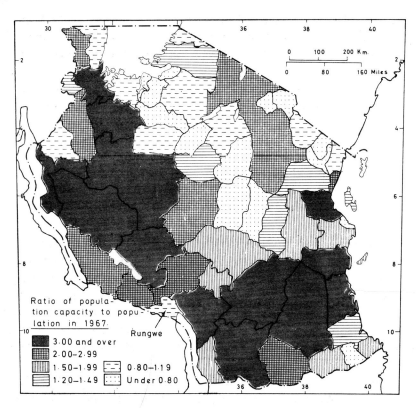

FIG. 1. *Relation between carrying capacity and population in 1967 according to Moore (1973).*

intensification, for higher yield per hectare under cultivation? Undoubtedly, because low returns are a characteristic feature for most agriculture in Tanzania, and comparatively small improvements in methods of cultivation could result in significantly higher yields. But intensification generally means higher labour input and therefore requires some impetus; before labour-demanding innovations are accepted there must be a felt need for them. Population pressure is one factor which can play an important role in improving agricultural systems:[13] two such diverse areas as Kilimanjaro and Ukerewe Island both have methods of intensive cultivation developed in response to shortage of land.

But for large areas of Tanzania the agricultural potential remains under-utilized, and overall only 10% of arable land is at present under cultivation. Different studies have over and over again pointed at the relative lack of people for local economic development. A study of the potential of the Rufiji river basin in the southern parts of Tanzania concluded that, with a fully developed irrigation system, this basin alone was capable of supporting many more than the total present population of the country. This indicates that planned rural development based on the efforts of now underemployed peasants can multiply the present surplus—without any large injections of foreign capital.

Structural Change is the Key Problem

There is no doubt that Tanzania has large untapped reserves in agriculture capable at generating the surplus required for industrialization. She also has a small but fast growing population. Large numbers of people are unemployed or producing far less than possible, as a result not of rapid population increase, but of the dependency structure of the economy. The main problem is, therefore, the structural changes required for the mobilization of available resources of people and land.[14]

High rates of population increase mean that the population is young, an important factor for a country attempting a radical departure from inherited forms of social and economic organization. But rapid population increase would seem to provide a serious obstacle in that it requires a fast expansion of, for instance, educational and health services just to keep pace with the growing numbers, let alone to make them universally available.

The basic fallacy of such a view is its implicit assumption that there exists only one system of social and medical services; that developed in the capitalist nations themselves. The examples of Cuba, Vietnam and China show that systems of education and medical care, like any other institution in society, are a product of the class in power. The former colonies inherited at independence a system of social services basically designed to serve the interests of the colonizer, not those subjected to colonization. For most of these countries, Tanzania not excluded, the system has been kept largely intact through the influence of foreign assistance and the vested interests of a growing local elite.

Yet systems of social services have been developed which do not require huge investments per student or patient and which are capable of reaching large numbers of people in a fairly short time. For these systems a rapid population increase constitutes no principal problem. But they are only applicable where people like the everpresent unemployed school leaver can be mobilized to work for the general interest, i.e. in a society geared towards basic transformation of social relations.

But socialist systems of education and medical care are based on the workings of small units of people sharing their resources in knowledge and production. Basic services are provided by members of the unit itself, and more specialized services by increasingly larger conglomerations of such units.

Likewise, rational organization of production, use of implements and tools, marketing and planning require a system of communally functioning units rather than individual scattered homesteads. Only a communal rural organization is capable of providing good services for the rural population as a whole. Only such an organization within a planned economy is capable of generating the surplus required for the industrialization of the country.

For a poor country in the periphery of the capitalist system, the marginalization of large numbers of the population must constitute a threat to the established order. To recommend population control as a remedy is no more than an attempt to preserve this order, retaining the country in a permanent state of dependency and underdevelopment.

Notes

1. Egerö, B. and Henin, R. (Eds) (1973). "The Population of Tanzania". BRALUP and Central Bureau of Statistics, Dar es Salaam.
2. Figures refer to estimates from the 1967 population census. More recent, nationwide estimates are as yet not available.
3. "UN Demographic Yearbook 1975". The figures for Africa etc. refer to 1975.
4. Kuznets, S. (1967). Population and economic growth, *Proc. Am. Phil. Soc.* **VIII**, 170–193.
5. Iliffe, J. (1971). "Agricultural Change in Modern Tanganyika", East African Publishing House, Nairobi.
6. Even if nationalization has been taken further in Tanzania than in many

other African countries, this method in itself does not guarantee a reduction in foreign control. See for instance Shivji, I. (1976). Capitalism unlimited: public corporations in partnerships with multinational corporations. *In* "Workers and Management" (Ed. by H. Mapulo). Dar es Salaam.

7. Amin, S. and Okediji, F. O. (1974). Introduction to chapter 7. *In* "Population in African Development" (Ed. by P. Cantrelle). Liège.

8. Raikes, P. (1973). Tanzania blazes its own trail. *African Development*, December.

9. Mamdani, M. (1976). The ideology of population control. *Econom. and Polit. Weekly* **XI**, 31–33, August, pp. 1141–1148.

10. Statement by China at the UNECAFE 29th Session, Tokyo, April 1973.

11. See, for instance, Thomas, C. (1974). "Dependence and Transformation". New York.

12. Moore, J., "Population Distribution and Density", in Egerö and Henin *op. cit.*

13. Boserup, E. (1968). "The Conditions of Agricultural Growth", London. Rothenberg, M. (Ed) (1968). "Smallholder Farming and Smallholder Development in Tanzania, Ten Case Studies", London. Kjekshus, H. (1977). "Ecology Control and Economic Development in East African History", London.

14. Obviously, the effect of structural changes will depend on the social division of power in the country. There is today for Tanzania over-whelming evidence that all the structural reforms carried out in the period since 1967 have not changed the basic class character of society. Through restrictions against private capital and increasing state control, a new ruling class—the "bureaucratic bourgeoisie"—has grown and consolidated its power in the economic and political spheres. See Shivji, I. (1976). "Class Struggles in Tanzania", London.

Bucharest and After

Erland Hofsten

Before Bucharest

When the UN appointed 1974 as the World Population Year, the background to this decision was of course the conviction that population problems are of great importance. But this conviction was not of long standing with the organization. To be sure, the UN had already in 1946 created a Population Commission and a corresponding division in the Secretariat, but for a couple of decades the activities of the UN in the field of population were of a purely technical and expert-like character. The semi-official World Population Conferences organized in Rome in 1954 and in Belgrade in 1965, in which many UN representatives participated, were primarily of a scientific character. However, gradually more and more people came to the conclusion that population was not only a technical topic but that population growth is intimately related to development and that "population problems" consequently have to be tackled also on a political level.

"Population problems" can imply a number of things, but to those who prior to the Bucharest Conference wanted to promote a greater interest by the UN in population, "the population problem" meant something quite specific, namely the rapid population growth of the developing countries and the necessity to take action in order to limit this growth through birth control. Population was thus looked upon in isolation from underdevelopment. In order to make the idea of birth control more easily digested the expression "family planning" was invented.

It took some time before this topic could be accepted in the UN. Already in the late 1950s some few and isolated members had tried to make the organization interested but they only found that the topic was considered more or less taboo. As late as 1965, on the occasion of the Belgrade Conference, it was only after strong opposition that it could be accepted that one out of a great number of sessions could be devoted to family planning. The final breakthrough occurred in December 1966, when the General Assembly of the UN unanimously adopted a resolution, which implied the acceptance of the involvement of the UN in all kinds of population activities, including those of an anti-natalist character.[1] Since 1966 the situation has changed rapidly.

Already in 1967 the UN Fund for Population Activities (UNFPA) was created and it soon grew to large proportions. The fund, as well as many other resources was used in order to start family planning programmes in developing countries. Furthermore, numerous conferences on population were held and the UN took the initiative to create five regional population institutes, in which demographers are trained and research is being carried out.

During this first phase numerous persons and organizations, primarily in developed countries, expressed the conviction that birth control in less developed countries was most important and that, consequently, family planning measures should be given top priority. Then president Lyndon B. Johnson's remark that $5 spent on family planning was worth more than $100 spent on development was often quoted. It was taken for granted that the people concerned would gladly accept birth control, once they were offered the means. The main problems were consequently considered to be the invention of new and better contraceptives, their efficient distribution, and to persuade reluctant governments of the expediency of family planning. The reluctance of the Catholic Church to accept contraception was often considered the main obstacle. This period now seems very distant.

The Bucharest Conference

The highlight of the World Population Year was the World Population Conference, which was held in Bucharest in August 1974. Whereas the two previous world population conferences had been of a scientific character, this conference would be of a political and policy-making character, i.e. the countries were to be represented by politically responsible delegations, and the conference was to take decisions of a political character.

Many of the initiators of the conference no doubt hoped that it would demonstrate a final breakthrough of family planning ideas in all countries of the world and would result in many new ideas about family planning and in vast resources being spent on such programmes. Nothing of that sort came out of the conference. Instead, it was admitted that family planning programmes do not work in isolation. No longer was Lyndon Johnson's remark quoted approvingly. A typical change of mind was that of John Rockefeller III, a man who for many years had shown strong interest in family planning, e.g. through his support of the Population Council. In a lecture at Bucharest he admitted that he had changed his mind and had come to the conclusion that population policy works only "within the context of general economic and social development". There were many similar statements from the discussions and documents.

Among the documents adopted by the conference, the Plan of Action is no doubt the most significant. As with other UN documents it is written to please everyone: it is vague, wordy and oblique. Moreover, it is full of contradictions. In its entirety—it contains 108 paragraphs, some of which are very long—it may not please anyone, yet everyone can selectively quote and use paragraphs in appropriate contexts.

In the documents distributed prior to the conference the impression was created that the main aim of the upcoming meeting was to express the opinion that the population of the world, as well as the population of most individual countries—particularly the developing countries— –was growing too rapidly and that measures were needed to check this growth. Nothing of this sort can be found in the final version of the Plan of Action. It contains only vacuous phrases of the type that countries which consider their present or expected rates of population growth to be hampering their goals of promoting human welfare are invited to consider adopting population policy. It is not even made clear whether "population policy" implies reduced or promoted population growth. And who can make anything out of a paragraph which states that in many parts of the world couples have more children than they want, while in others they have less than they want?

From the point of view of those who primarily considered the Bucharest Conference as a lever for promoting family planning ideas, the key clause of the Plan of Action was its paragraph 27. In the draft presented to the conference this paragraph contained the recommendation that "all countries . . . make available to all persons who so desire . . . not later than 1985, the necessary information and education about family planning and the means to practice family planning effectively and in accordance with their cultural values".

This paragraph was especially supported by the American delegation in Bucharest. At a press conference at an early stage of the conference, Russel W. Peterson, Vice-Chairman of the US delegation, said that a rejection of this paragraph would mean that "we'll either have to have another conference or find another way of getting the idea accepted without any amendment".[2] Paragraph 27 was rejected.

Why was the original draft of paragraph 27 rejected? A readily understandable answer is given by referring to the subsequent development in India. The Indian Government acted as if the above paragraph had been accepted and completely ignored the content of other paragraphs in the Plan of Action, such as the one in which it is stated that all countries should respect and ensure "the right of persons to determine, in a free, informed and responsible manner, the number and spacing of their children". As is well known, the Indian sterilization campaign defied this principle. Numerous persons were sterilized against their will, thus causing many personal tragedies. As a consequence of the anger of the people against this policy the Government of India had to resign in 1977.

The Non-Malthusian Group

Some months before the Bucharest Conference an "International Working Group of Population Growth and Social Development", later called the "Non-Malthusian Coalition Group", was formed on private initiative. In a statement signed by scientists and others in different parts of the world and released during the conference the group explained its viewpoints on the issues raised by the conference. In one of the key paragraphs it was said that "population growth must not be blamed for diseases of society. It is a deception to make people believe that it is possible to solve problems of society through birth control measures".

During the conference members of the Non-Malthusian Group were active in the sessions of the Population Tribune, an unofficial side-conference of the official conference. The group never had any other ambition than to act as an opposition group, but it found that the ideas put forward in its document and propagated during the Tribune sessions were received with much more interest than anticipated. Moreover, at the end of the conference the Non-Malthusian Group to its amazement and delight found that the same ideas had—independently—been accepted by the main conference. Family planning in isolation had been rejected, and the most important sections of the Plan of Action are those in which the necessity for action in order to promote rapid social and economic development in the less-developed countries is emphasized. The plan further states that neo-colonialism continues to be among the greatest obstacles to progress, and that women should have the right to a complete integration in the development process. Statements of this kind are important and deserve to be quoted and receive wide circulation.

Thus, the Bucharest Conference was transformed from an intended pro-family-planning manifestation to something quite different, namely a manifestation of the necessity to bridge the widening gap between developed and "developing" countries. In a concluding statement on the occasion of the World Population Tribune this was expressed in the following way by the author of this article, representing the Non-Malthusian Group:

> The Non-Malthusian Coalition Group considers that the World Population Conference and this Tribune have implied an important breakthrough and a considerable step forward to a correct understanding of what the main problems facing humanity today are. Only few people still maintain that family planning measures in isolation should be given top priority and that they imply any solution to development problems. Family planning policy is only meaningful within the framework of an all-round plan for the social and economic development of a country. Alas, only few countries have such plans, more than possibly on paper.[3]

After Bucharest

That the pro-family-planning Malthusian arguments were rejected in Bucharest does not imply that the conference was without significance with regard to the population issues. It has no doubt implied a widened interest in population. But this interest has primarily taken other forms than concentrating on fertility and family planning. There has, for instance, been an increased attention to migratory movement—both within and between countries—and to urbanization. The development of mortality has also been subject to an increased interest.

Those disappointed in the way the Bucharest Conference treated family planning have tried to cover their retreat by talking about the growing number of countries which have accepted family planning measures. Two years after Bucharest the UN made an inquiry among governments in order to find out to what extent they had implemented the statements made at the conference.[4] Among the findings is that nearly all countries now say that the availability and access to modern means of contraception is considered a human right. In so far as this implies a change of attitude, which it certainly does in many cases, this must be considered a step forward. Not only the Plan of Action but also the Statement of the Non-Malthusian Group were positive in this respect. Thus, the Statement said that "we are of the opinion that free access to efficient contraceptives and other means of birth control should be a human right and available to all, and we recognise the importance of effective family planning to health and well being".

The inquiry furthermore gave as a result that among the 156 countries who responded, 74 declared that they had a policy, related to modifying their levels of fertility. Among them, 40 would like to lower it, 20 to maintain it and 14 to raise it. Among the countries who have declared that they aim at a reduced fertility, nearly all Asian "developing countries" can be found. In other regions of the world, i.e. in Africa and Latin America, only few countries aim at a reduced fertility.

Data of this kind are sometimes taken to imply that the family planning ideas are after all gaining ground. However, there is a far cry from a government in a developing country accepting a principle to this policy being carried out in practice. The government may have no popular support at all and its power and methods for carrying out development policy may be quite limited and ineffective. When no real development takes place in a country there will normally be a high resistance against accepting new ideas, such as limitation of childbirths. However, a certain amount of fertility reduction may no doubt take place in countries with a high rate of growth. The present high rate of growth is primarily a consequence of a rapid reduction in mortality, especially among infants. In populations, which for hundreds of generations have experienced that a high rate of fertility is a necessity in order to compensate for the high mortality, it may take a generation or so before they react to the fact that many more children survive than in the past.

Population statistics for many less developed countries are far from satisfactory, but the data given in Table I for main regions of the world can nevertheless be considered reasonably accurate as regards the years 1950 and 1975, and the present growth rate (the data are quoted from the most recent UN projections).[5] Note that the data given for the year 2000 have a totally different character, as they are based on projections, which may not at all be confirmed by the actual course of events. These data are, according to the UN report, "the medium estimates (which) are intended to represent the most plausible future population trend". But do they really?

TABLE I. *World Population* 1950, 1975 *and* 2000.

	Inhabitants (billion)			Present yearly growth rate (%)
	1950	1975	2000	
More developed regions	0·86	1·13	1·36	0·86
China	0·56	0·84	1·15	1·66
Less developed regions	1·08	2·00	3·74	2·49
World total	2·50	3·97	6·25	1·89

Much publicity has been given to the fact that these recent estimates made by the UN are lower than previous estimates. Thus, five years earlier the UN gave as the most plausible estimate for the year 2000 a total world population of 6·49 billion, as against the present estimate of 6·25 billion. As regards the more developed regions and China the lower estimates are no doubt reasonable, taking into account the rapidly falling fertility in these regions. In view of the presently rapid fertility decline in most developed countries there is even reason to believe that the estimates for the year 2000 for more developed regions are still too high. An apparent fertility reduction is also taking place in countries such as Hong Kong, Korea, Malaysia, Singapore, Taiwan, Thailand and Vietnam. Furthermore, fertility is on the way down in Catholic countries, such as those in Latin America. There is no or only an insignificant fertility reduction in Moslem countries and in Africa south of the Sahara.[6]

As regards less developed regions in the table it would seem doubtful if a general decline in fertility will really come as soon and to the extent the UN believes. In the projection report it is stated that "fertility would decline as countries progressed in economic and social development in accordance with the theory of demographic transition", and that "in the long run, the fertility level is expected to decline continuously and to reach the replacement level in every country". This is most doubtful, unless a rapid economic and social development really takes place in all the countries concerned. Without development there is little reason to put faith in the UN statement that "the existing or anticipated family planning policies and efforts in a given country would expedite the process of fertility decline".

There are many countries which can without difficulty make room for a population considerably larger than the present one. But there are also countries which are already so densely populated that an immediate reduction in their rate of growth would imply a relief. In the long run no country can of course have an unlimited population growth. However, the main problem is nowhere the size of the population or its rate of growth. The real issue is that no development in the proper sense of the word takes place, a fact which is most often ignored. If real development occurs, all experience relates that a rapid reduction in fertility will follow. If no development takes place, on the other hand, a rapid reduction in fertility is much more remote.

Notes

1. Boserup, M. (1978). "Population as an International Social Science", UNESCO.
2. Franda, M. F. (1974). Reactions to America in Bucharest, *Southeast Europe Series* **XXI,** No. 3, Romania.

3. Hofsten, E. (1974). Statement at the concluding session of the World Population Tribune in Bucharest, *Concerned Demography* **4,** No. 2.
4. Measures undertaken at the national, regional and international levels to implement the world population plan of action. Report to the UN Population Commission 1976 (E/CN.9/325).
5. "World Population Prospects as Assessed in 1973", UN, New York 1977.
6. Mauldin, W. P. and Berelson, B., Cross cultural review of the effectiveness of family planning programs, IUSSP Conference, Mexico 1977.

Index

D/3   177.